Meaning in Linguistic Interac

Meaning in Linguistic Interaction

Semantics, Metasemantics,
Philosophy of Language

KASIA M. JASZCZOLT

OXFORD
UNIVERSITY PRESS

Great Clarendon Street, Oxford, OX2 6DP,
United Kingdom

Oxford University Press is a department of the University of Oxford.
It furthers the University's objective of excellence in research, scholarship,
and education by publishing worldwide. Oxford is a registered trade mark of
Oxford University Press in the UK and in certain other countries

© Kasia M. Jaszczolt 2016

The moral rights of the author have been asserted

First published 2016
First published in paperback 2018

Published in the United States of America by Oxford University Press
198 Madison Avenue, New York, NY 10016, United States of America

British Library Cataloguing in Publication Data
Data available

Library of Congress Cataloging in Publication Data
Data available

ISBN 978–0–19–960246–9 (Hbk.)
ISBN 978–0–19–883213–3 (Pbk.)

Contents

Preface

This book offers a semantic and metasemantic inquiry into the representation of meaning in linguistic interaction. Semantics is therefore understood broadly, as representing conceptual structures that rely not only on natural language expressions but also on other ways of conveying intended meanings. In all my monographs published so far I have assumed the utility of such tools and concepts as truth conditions, the metalanguage of predicate calculus, and post-Gricean intentions. I also argued that some form of the radical contextualists' take on the semantics/pragmatics boundary issue was the only promising stance as it allows one to select the cognitively plausible object of inquiry, namely the intended, primary meaning, and adopt it as a unit of semantic analysis in spite of the varying provenance of the contributing information— some of which is traceable to the lexicon and structure, but some of which has to be recovered through various pragmatic processes. These tools and assumptions are preserved in what follows but they are taken to the next level of defending a semantics that models the regularities over what agents intend to represent and what their interlocutors grasp as represented. Necessarily, such a semantics transcends the said/ implicated distinction and heavily relies on the dynamic construction of meaning in discourse, discussed on the levels of concepts associated with lexical items, structures understood here as mental structures corresponding to intended meanings externalized by all kinds of means, and speech acts conveyed through them.

A particular version of such a contextualist orientation that focused on such sources and processes of interpretation was offered in my *Default Semantics* (2005a) and in *Representing Time* (2009a). I focused on sources and processes rather than on maxims or heuristics because, in contrast to some post-Griceans, I consider the latter to be less worthy of attention as they are simply common-sense principles of rational human behaviour which Grice's intellectual descendants state in different ways, making a lot of unnecessary fuss about reclassifying his original maxims. Whether one presents them as four maxims à la Grice, three heuristics à la Levinson, two principles à la Horn, or finally one two-sided principle à la Sperber and Wilson makes little difference: all of these arrangements stress one and the same idea of the interplay between economy and informativeness, and as such a facet of rational conversational behaviour widely explored for various human activities and decision-making in social sciences. For this reason, I leave such debates aside.

The current project originated as a proposal to further develop my own take on semantics and pragmatics started in the first three chapters of my *Discourse, Beliefs and Intentions* (1999). However, it very soon became a more philosophical and often metasemantic journey through meaning in linguistic interaction, touching on some questions previously left out such as the status of semantic representation vis-à-vis conceptual structure, the philosophy of grammar, or the processing of meaning vis-à-vis the modularity-connectionism debate. Metasemantic inquiry also underlies the search for the proper understanding of compositionality, the object of truth-conditional analysis, metaphysics of reference, as well as, and most importantly, the scope of semantic theory itself. Some of these discussions grow out of my earlier expositions of the theory of Default Semantics, some develop ideas proposed by my colleagues in trade, mostly other post-Gricean pragmaticists and formal semanticists, and some are inspired by cognitive science. In short, the journey sums up to an inquiry into *meaning in linguistic interaction*.

Some of the sections contain further developments of ideas first introduced in my recent papers. The discussion of the lexicon/grammar/pragmatics trade-offs dates back at least to my *Default Semantics* (Jaszczolt 2005a) and is exemplified in temporal reference in my *Representing Time* (Jaszczolt 2009a) and 'Cross-linguistic differences in expressing time and universal principles of utterance interpretation' (Jaszczolt 2012a). I owe thanks to John Benjamins for allowing me to use some passages from the latter article. It is briefly referred to in Chapter 2 as a part of my précis of Default Semantics in order to show how the theory is able to handle the trade-offs. Introductions to Default Semantics have also appeared in various handbooks and manuals, for example in *The Oxford Handbook of Linguistic Analysis* (Jaszczolt 2010). The discussion of the types and roles of salience in Chapter 3 originated in my 'Default meanings, salient meanings, and automatic processing' (Jaszczolt 2011) and is now rethought in terms of Salience-Based Contextualism. Cancellation tests were first used for supporting the primary/secondary meaning distinction in my 'Cancellability and the primary/secondary meaning distinction' (Jaszczolt 2009b) but in a somewhat different way. Also in Chapter 3, the discussion of psychologism originated in my 'Psychological explanations in Gricean pragmatics: An argument from cultural *common ground*' (Jaszczolt 2008) but I have now reached rather different conclusions concerning the role of psychological considerations in formal semantics, for which I also employed the concept of metapsychologism. I am grateful to De Gruyter Mouton for allowing me to make use of these articles as a springboard for current discussions. The concept of fluid characters was first introduced in my ' "Pragmaticising" Kaplan: Flexible inferential bases and fluid characters' (Jaszczolt 2012c) and the discussion in Chapter 4 takes the discussion forward from there. Next, the case study of the first-person indexical in Chapter 5 pertains to an ongoing Cambridge project funded by The Leverhulme Trust *Expressing the Self: Cultural Diversity and Cognitive Universals* (Grant ID/Ref: RPG-2014-017). The chapter also draws on some ideas and examples from my 'First-person reference in discourse: Aims and strategies' (Jaszczolt 2013b) and, on more philosophical aspects, 'Contextualism and minimalism on *de se* belief ascription' (Jaszczolt 2013c), putting them to a somewhat different use. The overall discussion also benefits from a more in-depth study of different approaches to context that I conducted in 'Context: Gricean intentions vs. two-dimensional semantics'

(Jaszczolt 2012b). Pertinent sections in what follows offer further developments of the ideas presented there and, on some occasions, a change of direction in my analysis.

I owe thanks to many people who contributed to this project in one way or another. First of all, my gratitude goes to Keith Allan and Eros Corazza for their comments on the first draft. Next, I am grateful to John Davey of Oxford University Press for his encouragement and long-term interest in my ideas. I am also grateful to his successor, Julia Steer, for our successful and friendly collaboration on both fronts of my engagement with the Press: as the author of what follows and as managing editor of the book series *Oxford Studies of Time in Language and Thought*. To Caroline McLaughlin I owe thanks for careful and thoughtful copy-editing and to Kim Birchall for compiling the index. I wish to thank Yoseph Mengistu for his help with the Amharic data and Rodanthi Christofaki for the discussion of Japanese. The chapter on salient meanings owes some of its final touches to the comments by the participants of the workshop 'Salient meanings' which I co-organized with Keith Allan for the 11th *International Pragmatics Association Conference* in Melbourne 2009. In particular, I want to thank Keith Allan, Rachel Giora, Michael Haugh, Eleni Kapogianni, as well as other colleagues associated with this project in one way or another: Istvan Kecskes, Alyson Pitts, and Mikhail Kissine. Concerning my argument from cancellability, I am indebted to several colleagues who commented on my earlier work on this topic for their help to present the argument in the manner which is the least prone to misinterpretation. In particular, I would like to acknowledge the feedback from Keith Allan, Alessandro Capone, Michael Haugh, Eleni Kapogianni, and Alyson Pitts. I am also indebted to Jay Atlas for drawing the contentious issue of psychologism in pragmatic theory to my attention through his various papers. I am also grateful to the participants of the Pragmatics Reading Group in Cambridge (now called the Semantics, Pragmatics and Philosophy Group, or SPP) for our lively discussions of various pertinent topics. Here I wish to acknowledge the feedback from my recent and current PhD students: Minyao Huang, Chi-Hé Elder, Eleni Kapogianni, Eleni Savva, Michael Keane, Luca Sbordone, Roberto Sileo, and Rodanthi Christofaki. I also owe thanks to colleagues who have organized workshops and other events that helped with the development of what follows. Here I thank Keith Allan, Marcella Bertucelli, Tadeusz Ciecierski, Istvan Kecskes, Larry Horn, Barbara Lewandowska-Tomaszczyk, Jacob Mey, Maciej Witek, Louis de Saussure, Joanna Odrowąż-Sypniewska, Zhang Shaojie, Piotr Stalmaszczyk, Richmond Thomason, again, running the risk of forgetting some friends and colleagues. Also, thank you to the audiences of my talks and lecture series on Default Semantics and its various applications, in Cambridge, Oxford, Antwerp, Łódź, Warsaw, Szczecin, Changchun, Beijing, Shanghai, London, Brussels, Charlotte, Ann Arbor, Geneva, Bochum, St Andrews, Newcastle, Paris, Manchester, Leeds, Edinburgh, Melbourne, Neuchâtel, Belgrade, Kirchberg am Wechsel, Göteborg, Antwerp, among others. Charles and Lidia: thank you, as always, for making life fun.

Cambridge, 20 March 2015

Preface to the paperback edition

I owe thanks to Jay Atlas for sending me a list of suggested corrections to the paperback edition, but most of all for his commentary delivered at a book symposium devoted to *Meaning in Linguistic Interaction* at the American Philosophical Association meeting in San Francisco in spring 2016 when the book first appeared. My thanks also go to Prashant Parikh who contributed a commentary to the same book symposium, as well as to Eros Corazza for his review of the book in the *Journal of Pragmatics* and to Guocai Zeng for his review in *Interaction Studies*.

List of abbreviations and symbols

$\rightarrow_d$	default interpretation
$\rightarrow_E$	explicitly means
$\rightarrow_{GCI}$	conversationally implicates via a GCI
$\rightarrow_I$	conversationally implicates
$\rightarrow_m$	monotonic inference
$\rightarrow_{nm}$	nonmonotonic inference
$\rightarrow_{PM}$	(communicates as) primary meaning
$\rightarrow_{SM}$	(communicates as) secondary meaning
$>>$	semantic change
Δ	degree of acceptability (in ACC_Δ)
Σ	merger representation
1Sg	first-person singular number
Acc	accusative case
ACC	acceptability operator
att	attenuation (in ACC_Δ^{att})
CD	cognitive defaults
CM	Cognitive Minimalism
Contr	contrastive (conjunction)
CPI	conscious pragmatic inference
DemPart	demonstrative particle
Dist.Past.Inf	distant past inferential
DPL	Dynamic Predicate Logic
DRS	Discourse Representation Structure
DRT	Discourse Representation Theory
DS	Default Semantics
epf	epistemic possibility future (in ACC_Δ^{epf})
Erg	ergative
F	feminine gender
fp	futurate progressive (in ACC_Δ^{fp})
Fut	future tense

GCI	Generalized Conversational Implicature
Gen	genitive case
ICE-GB	International Corpus of English (British component)
IEM	immunity to error through misidentification
Inf	infinitive
Instr	instrumental case
IS	properties of human inferential system
KoS	conversation-oriented semantics
LF	logical form
M	masculine gender
Neg	negative particle
Nom	nominative case
NP	noun phrase
OLS	organizational lexical semantics
Past	past tense
PCI	Particularized Conversational Implicature
Perf	perfective aspect
Pl	plural number
pm	pertaining to primary meaning
Pres	present tense
PRO	empty category 'big pro'
PTQ	'The Proper Treatment of Quantification in Ordinary English' (Montague 1973)
QUD	question under discussion
Rec.Past.Exp	recent past experiential
Refl	reflexive particle
ReflPron	reflexive pronoun
rp	regular past (in $\text{ACC}_\Delta{}^{\text{rp}}$)
SC	stereotypes and presumptions about society and culture
SCWD	social, cultural, and world knowledge defaults
SD	situation of discourse
SDRT	Segmented Discourse Representation Theory
Sg	singular number
SM	semantic meaning
sm	pertaining to secondary meaning

Subj	subjunctive
TCL	type composition logic
TCP	truth-conditional pragmatics
TCS	truth-conditional semantics
tf	tenseless future (in ACC_Δ^{tf})
Top	topic marker
WK	world knowledge
WS	word meaning and sentence structure

LARGE CAPITALS used for words (not acronyms) stand for a concept as opposed to a word (e.g. SELF)

italics (when not used for emphasis or logical variables) stand for a word (e.g. *self*)

'single quotes' used for words stand for a form of the lexical item (e.g. 'self')

Introduction

'Wrong about meaning' is where we start in this project. There is to it a negative (or even destructive) as well as a positive (constructive) component. I start by assessing at some length what is wrong with the theories of meaning at large, focusing on the debates between (i) those who construe meaning rather 'minimally', as closely tied to the lexicon and the structure of the sentence; (ii) those who construe it 'maximally', as the message intended by the speaker and/or recovered by the addressee, helping themselves in the process in a liberal and rather unrestricted way to contextual, pragmatically recovered information (occasionalism, meaning eliminativism); as well as (iii) those whom I call here 'fixers', who propose different solutions in-between, such as (iii.a) rethinking the syntactic form in such a way that it provides an explanation for any unarticulated components that contribute to the semantic content (indexicalism) or (iii.b) pegging the semantic representation to the logical form of the sentence and to the speaker's intentions at the same time, allowing as a result for free pragmatic manipulations of the syntactic representation (moderate contextualism).

Risking oversimplification, one can say that what is wrong about meaning in these approaches across the board is their holding on to the assumption that minimalism and, at most, indexicalism go hand in hand with formalization of meaning, while moderate contextualism (that allows for syntactically uncontrolled enrichments of the proposition) and its radical counterpart, occasionalism, eschew it by definition. In the latter group of accounts, meaning has a cross-modular provenance, there are no formal counterparts in the sentence structure or word structure (if any) that can be made responsible for the output, and hence formalization is not an option. However, as I had begun to demonstrate in Default Semantics (e.g. 2005a, 2009a, 2010, and in what follows), this is not necessarily so. I have identified there a set of sources of information about meaning, a set of processes that interact to produce the required, psychologically real interpretation, as well as the mappings between these sources and processes. I have also suggested the overall principles on which meaning so construed can be formalized, employing a metalanguage modelled on that of Discourse Representation Theory (e.g. Kamp and Reyle 1993), but using it not on the level of linguistic structures, but rather on the level of the merger of information coming from these different sources through

Meaning in Linguistic Interaction. Kasia M. Jaszczolt.
© Kasia M. Jaszczolt 2016. Published 2016 by Oxford University Press.

these different and interacting processes (merger representations). Default Semantics did not subscribe to the solutions from the 'fixers' camp: not only was the meaning not dictated by the elements of the syntactic structure (as indexicalists have it), it was not even always guided by the logical form of the sentence at all. So, the contextualists' requirement that the semantic, truth-conditionally relevant content is the development, enrichment, modulation, and the like of the logical form of the sentence was also dropped (which I called the rejection of the syntactic constraint on the propositional representation).

Next, what is wrong with minimalism is that it is not 'minimalist enough': it necessitates some admixture of contextual information and it always relies on some minimal construct of a context. I call it in what follows Cognitive Minimalism. What is wrong with contextualism is that it is restricted by the logical form of the uttered sentence instead of representing the main intended meaning independently of whether it pertains to the logical form, an enriched logical form, or a different structure altogether. Instead of 'fixing' the logical form I propose here using context-driven salience as the main criterion for identifying the meaning to be represented in semantics. I call this view Salience-Based Contextualism.

Abandoning the syntactic constraint need not pose a problem for compositionality. There is no reason why compositionality should not be predicated of a representation that puts together information from various sources, arrived at through various processes, without giving a privileged role to the logical form. Instead of 'fixing' the logical form, what we arrive at in the semantics of linguistic interaction is a theory of acts of communication that pertains to the meaning intended by the speaker (and in normal circumstances modelled there, also recovered by the addressee), but at the same time a theory that is in principle formalizable. And this is the positive (constructive) part of the proposal mentioned above. We have a theory that accounts for speakers' intentions that are externalized through various means, and therefore adopts the 'maximalist' view of meaning, but at the same time adheres to the methodological principle of compositionality—compositionality predicated of the level of semantic representations that reflect the merger of information.

In the late 1990s and early 2000s it made sense to call such a theory 'Default Semantics'. It also made sense to portray it as a 'radical contextualist' stance. The debates surrounding the semantics/pragmatics interface that originated in the 1970s focused on the then novel idea of admitting the output of pragmatic processes into (truth-conditional) semantics. A theory that used truth conditions as its tool and admitted such pragmatic content was normally assigned to the contextualist camp, originally dubbed the 'radical pragmatics' camp, or advocates of semantic underdetermination, underspecification, or sense generality, among others.[1] So, 'semantics' and '(radical)

---

[1]   See Jaszczolt 1999, chapters 1–3 and Jaszczolt 2002a, chapter 11 for references.

contextualism' seemed the correct labels. 'Default' has a more modest origin. An important part of the debates among post-Gricean pragmaticists[2] was devoted to the status of the enrichments of meaning, such as the conditional perfection ('if' used in the sense of 'if and only if'), 'some' used in the sense of 'some but not all', 'or' used for 'one or the other but not both', and so on. On one side of the debate, we had strong, language-driven presumptive meanings (a kind of default) of Levinson's, on the other we had the relevance-theoretic view that all enrichment is context-driven, performed as and when it is needed (with no defaults of any kind). Subsequently, the debate focused on the presence or absence of unconscious, or 'automatic', interpretations.[3] My 'defaults' were supposed to constitute a voice in this debate. Among the types of process identified in Default Semantics there were cognitive defaults as well as defaults of a social and cultural, or general world-knowledge provenance. I meant by this that *in a specific context and for the specific interlocutors* (this is important!) some interpretations occur automatically, subconsciously, and effortlessly. Such 'defaults' are of course fundamentally different from Levinson's strong, language-system-driven presumptive meanings. They figured in the name of my theory in order to stress that 'maximalist' semantics is not all about syntax plus inferences; it is also about the cognitive architecture that triggers certain senses, and about society and culture to which the interlocutors belong, which, again, effortlessly and 'by default' make us understand what people say.

As it happened, the terms 'default' and 'semantics' caused a lot of uneasiness, with the side effect that some less careful readers identified all defaults with Levinson's presumptive meanings. As the scene in the semantics/pragmatics debate has changed, it now seems that there is a need to emphasize the interactive component of Default Semantics, and stress its affinities with late-Wittgensteinian occasion-meaning more than its commonalities with the 'fixers', i.e. with context-ualism of the type of Recanati's (e.g. 2004, 2010) Truth-Conditional Pragmatics or Sperber and Wilson's (e.g. 1995) Relevance Theory. This is the rationale for the current project that focuses on the principles of linguistic interaction, addressing such questions as the different sources of salience or the ways of representing inferential aspects of meaning, reopening in the process the question of the indexical/non-indexical distinction and the static vs. dynamic view on meaning components in a compositional analysis.

The book serves two purposes. First, it introduces the readers who are new to the subject to the issues in semantics mentioned above, allowing them to actively agree or disagree with different sides in the post-Gricean debates over the scope and proven-ance of the truth-conditional aspects of meaning. Second, it will interest a more specialized researcher who will be able to focus on the proposed new 'maximalist' vision of semantics offered here and on the concepts of Salience-Based

---

[2] E.g. Sperber and Wilson 1995; Levinson 2000.
[3] E.g. Recanati 2004, 2007; Carston 2007.

Contextualism, fluid character, and methodological psychologism, as well as on the proposals of interactive compositionality, primary/secondary meaning distinction that is orthogonal to the explicit/implicit, and finally on the attempt to relegate pure indexicality to the realm of philosophers' fiction—at least for the case study of first-person reference discussed in Chapter 5. The exposition in this book follows the method of teaching semantics and pragmatics I have been using at the University of Cambridge for the past twenty years, namely presenting a problem that appears attractive *because* both sides have good arguments to offer. This applies both to (i) the occasions where the stance is supported and the case for it is strengthened further through new arguments, as well as (ii) the occasions where the arguments against the stance make me reject it. In short, in my view, even a relative newcomer to semantics and pragmatics should aim at a level of interaction with the ideas presented here from which she can arrive at original, independent views, taking the problems or theories further.

All in all, although the semantics of linguistic interaction presented here offers a new 'maximalist' outlook on meaning, I cannot take all the credit for the solutions utilized. It is built upon the ideas that have been floating around in the past few decades, producing such approaches as Relevance Theory (Sperber and Wilson 1995), presumptive meanings (Levinson 2000), Default Semantics (Jaszczolt 2005a), Truth-Conditional Pragmatics (Recanati 2010), as well as the view on pragmatics expressed in Kaplan's (1989a) two-dimensional semantics or Perry's systematic emphasis on different kinds of content culminating (so far) in *Critical Pragmatics* (Korta and Perry 2011). The perspective on meaning presented in what follows owes a lot to this rich tradition and the lively debates of which the above constitute the avant-garde. But it also adds its own stamp, in exorcizing or reanalysing some of the well-entrenched distinctions such as the explicit/implicit content, what is said/what is implicated, indexical/non-indexical, character/content, and redefining some concepts that have gone astray through relentless misuse, such as default interpretations or compositionality of meaning.

The book is structured as follows. In the introductory chapter (Chapter 1), I present the debate surrounding the object of study of the theory of meaning, focusing on the differences, as well as points of agreement, between orientations within the camps of what I call the 'maximalists', the 'fixers', and the 'minimalists'. Making a case for what is 'wrong about meaning', I critically discuss the current state of the art of the debates and introduce some seminal questions and problems, such as those pertaining to the literal vs. non-literal distinction, context-free vs. context-driven meaning, language system vs. language use. I also introduce here the concepts of Salience-Based Contextualism and Cognitive Minimalism. Chapter 2 focuses on the interactive composition of meaning. Here I dispel some myths surrounding compositionality, truth conditions, and logical form and reinstate acts of communication as the main contender for the object of a truth-conditional analysis. The main part is devoted to a précis of Default Semantics and to examples of its applications that capture the lexicon/grammar/pragmatics trade-offs in conveying meaning. I also include a brief discussion of the metaphysics of grammar. Chapter 3 revisits the concept of default interpretations, addressing the questions of context-independent and context-driven salience and the role of salience in primary meanings, and presents some evidence from cancellability in favour of the primary/secondary vis-à-vis explicit/implicit meaning distinction. It concludes with remarks on the appropriate degree and form of psychologism that a semantic theory ought to subscribe to. Next, Chapter 4 focuses on the lexicon, emphasizing the dynamic nature of the units that enter into a compositional structure. These are analysed in terms of what I call 'fluid characters': context-driven but at the same time type- rather than token-individuated units whose delimitation is governed by equally flexible bases for inference and bases for default interpretation. I conclude with some remarks on the need for a conceptual-semantic approach to reference. Finally, Chapter 5 contains a case study of first-person reference from a cross-linguistic as well as philosophical perspective, concluding that pure indexicality is philosophers' fiction: markers of first-person reference convey more than the index and, in addition, the markers do not seem to be purpose-made for first-person reference but also perform some other functions. The solution is to 'pragmaticize' Kaplan's two-dimensional approach by relaxing the indexical/non-indexical distinction in terms of my fluid characters and a function-driven analysis of the conceptual structure, presented here in the form of merger representations of Default Semantics. The conclusion 'dispels semantic myths', summing up what is 'wrong about meaning', juxtaposed with the proposed stance on the role of truth conditions, compositionality, indexicality, and the relevant interfaces as adopted in the proposed semantics of linguistic interaction.

1

Wrong about meaning

'She wrote: "Of course ego, id and super-ego, indeed the libido itself, are metaphorical hypostasisations of what must be seen as".

She crossed out "seen" and wrote "could be felt as".

Both were metaphors. She wrote: "could be explained as events in an undifferentiated body of experience".

Body was a metaphor. (. . .) "Event" was possibly a metaphor, too.'

A. S. Byatt, *Possession* (1991, London, Vintage, p. 430)

1.1 Setting the scene

Meaning, and its theory in natural language semantics, used to be simple. Sentences have meaning: there is the lexicon, syntax, and likewise there is semantics that reads off these two. The principle of compositionality, attributed to Frege (1892), states that the meaning of the sentence is the meaning of its parts and the structure that combines them. The problem is that it simply does not work that way. If we want meaning to be read off the sentence alone, then all tokens of (1) or (2) would have to have the same meaning.

(1)   That is red.

(2)   I am here.

What use would a theory of meaning be if it did not have anything to say about relations sentences bear to the world, let alone concepts in the minds of language users? So, first, we bring in the world, reference, and referential semantics, and claim that there is a tiny bit more to meaning than what words and structures understood as elements of a *system* give us. This is still a minimalist approach to meaning. According to its advocates, minimalism is a '*predominantly* context-insensitive semantics' (Borg 2012: 216),[1] where any departure from this *reading the meaning off the lexicon and the structure* has to be externally motivated. Even if we make use of

---

[1]   My emphasis.

Meaning in Linguistic Interaction. Kasia M. Jaszczolt.
© Kasia M. Jaszczolt 2016. Published 2016 by Oxford University Press.

the context of utterance, this use has to be systematic and made on the level of types, not tokens: the presence of 'that', 'I', 'here', or even 'ready' as in (3) provides secure and systematic grounds for this resorting to context.

(3)   Lidia is ready.

This systematicity comes from the presence of a certain kind of a lexical item as in (1) and (2) or from the presence of a syntactic construction as in (3), where 'ready' enters into a logical form that requires an argument-like completion of the proposition, necessary for the truth-conditional evaluation. Minimalist solutions are discussed in more depth in Section 1.3.1. For now, we emphasize the methodological problem with the qualification 'predominantly' in the above quotation from Borg: the set of expressions that necessitates such a departure from a clear-cut 'reading semantics off the lexicon and syntax' seems to be fluctuating. In fact, the set seems to be growing as compared with the original proposal in Kaplan's (1989a) *Demonstratives*. In order to justify this new minimalist outlook, one has to adopt a theory of word meaning that would account for the missing bits of information and relax the morphosyntax/ semantics interface by adding reference—the relation of referring to an object external to language, be it in the natural world or some conceptual domain.[2] There is no doubt that one can arrive at an internally sound theory in the end, but the rationale for such an enterprise remains dubious. In order to defend it, we would have to believe that minimal propositions correspond to some cognitively real units in the brain, and that the theories of word meaning and grammar that save this minimalist outlook are the adequate ones in their own right, not just as allies to a view that is dubious in itself. Without such an assumption it would be difficult to justify any pragmatic admixture at all.

The next step up towards the recognition of contextual information is to maintain that meaning depends on the syntactic form of the sentence but to allow for the context-sensitivity of this syntactic form. This is supposed to kill two birds with one stone: intuitions about meaning are, at least to some extent, accounted for, and the proposition that is the object of the theory of meaning is read off the lexico-syntactic information. This group of approaches is dubbed *indexicalism* and is pursued among others in Stanley (2002) and Stanley and Szabó (2000) for whom context-sensitivity is accounted for by a covert variable: the logical form of the sentence contains variables that have to be filled in order to obtain the intuitively plausible truth conditions. There are also related views such as Larson and Ludlow's (1993) Inter- preted Logical Forms or the proposal that some generalized conversational implica- tures (such as, for example, 'some but not all' recovered from 'some', see Grice 1975) are generated by grammar when the semantic properties of the construction, such as

---

[2]   See Cappelen and Lepore 2005a, b; Borg 2004, and especially 2012.

its monotonicity, allow it (Chierchia 2004, 2013). A further step leads to contextualism: rejecting the sufficiency of the lexicon and syntax for providing meaning and
allowing for the so-called 'free enrichment' or 'modulation' that is not governed by
the grammatical form of the sentence (Sperber and Wilson 1995; Carston 1988, 2002;
Recanati 1989, 2004, 2010).

The use of the labels varies somewhat in the literature in that, on the one hand,
indexicalism exhibits some characteristics of minimalism (meaning is read off the
lexicon and syntax) as well as some characteristics of contextualism (meaning is
enriched with some invisible constituents in order to make it accord with speakers'
intentions). The labels notwithstanding, I subsume both of these approaches, of
indexical enrichment and free enrichment, under the category of 'fixers': they depart
from the minimalist view but attempt to *fix* the semantic content by proposing a
construct that is somewhere in-between the minimal content and the full, intuitively
most plausible, meaning as intended by language users on a particular occasion.[3] The
latter is, of course, inspired by the late-Wittgensteinian (1953) perspective of meaning as use, later developed into 'occasionalism' or 'meaning eliminativism'.[4] If we
want to use truth-value judgements in the semantics, then we must use them about
acts of communication, about the uses of sentences on particular occasions.

This list of orientations is far from exhaustive but it covers the seminal approaches
to meaning that have been principally engaged, in a more or less approbatory way,
with the proposition as object of study and with truth conditions as a methodological
tool that often, but not always, results from an ontological commitment to real
objects as semantic objects (in versions of referentialism). Now, wouldn't it be a
good idea to build a strong argument in support of one of these views and have a
good time spreading the word that this is the right way to go about meaning? Not
exactly. The problem is that there is something quite wrong with every one of them.
Radical minimalism (Bach 2001, 2004, 2005, 2006) falls out of the above assessment
in that it opts out of propositions and truth conditions and as a result it is unclear
what job it has left to do if it does not link sentences with the world in any practical
explanatory way: one would have to endow grammar with extraordinary powers.[5]
Minimalism of a propositionalist orientation (Borg 2004; Cappelen and Lepore
2005a) puts forward meanings that have little to do with intentions and intuitions,
and indeed with how sentences are used in discourse. As such, it struggles to find a
sense of purpose for itself, stuck in-between pure grammar-given meaning and

---

[3] For the present discussion I am leaving out the relativist position according to which truth, meaning,
and knowledge are to be analysed from the position from which they are *assessed* (see MacFarlane 2005,
2011, 2014; for a relativism/contextualism discussion see Cappelen and Hawthorne 2009).

[4] See e.g. Travis 1997, 2008, and Recanati 2005; Schneider 2009 for a discussion; Pulvermüller 2010 for
evidence from neuropragmatics.

[5] On this question see also Hinzen and Sheehan 2013.

intuitive meanings.[6] Indexicalists and free-enrichment contextualists are 'fixers': their meaning is closer to the intended and intuitively plausible content of utterances but it does not go far enough. It is restricted by the syntactic form of the uttered sentence, trying to find there the explanation for the unarticulated aspects (indexicalism), or allowing only relatively moderate alterations to the logical form of the sentence ('free-enrichment contextualism')—albeit, it has to be granted, 'free', 'top-down', truly 'pragmatic' ones. But it is still short of going the whole hog and acknowledging that the main communicated message is the proposition that they ought to be concerned with. And the logical form pertaining to this proposition often bears little or no resemblance to the logical form of the uttered sentence.[7]

Next, while occasionalism is by far the most intuitively plausible position that correlates with the layman's perception of what meaning in language use is, it is usually regarded as the end in itself: if meaning is use, we can study conversations, we can do some neuroimaging to see what neuronal structures and patterns of activation correspond to kinds of linguistic actions, but any abstraction along the lines of the mental lexicon and autonomous syntax is precluded by definition. Any formal semantic treatment that reads off syntax à la Montague (1974) is by necessity ruled out.[8]

Or is it? It seems that formal methods need not be ruled out, merely the material which they are used for. The problem with the extant approaches is their adhering to the assumption that we have a choice to make: we can have either a fairly minimal theory of meaning but a formalizable one, or a theory that reflects speakers' intentions and observers' intuitions that is messy, programmatic, confined pretty much to a slogan that 'meaning is use'. Although the past four or so decades witnessed some relaxation in formal semantics in the direction of accounting for dynamically developing discourses and therefore providing for cross-sentential anaphora and presupposition (notably Discourse Representation Theory (DRT), Kamp 1981, Kamp and Reyle 1993, van Eijck and Kamp 1997; its offshoots, e.g. Segmented Discourse Representation Theory (SDRT), Asher and Lascarides 2003; Dynamic Predicate Logic (DPL), Groenendijk and Stokhof 1991, 2000; see also Zeevat 2012), meaning is there read off the syntax, with the addition of various more, or less, representational solutions providing for binding: binding to lexico-syntactic units, or binding to conceptual units provided by the context or made up on the fly to make sense of the

---

[6] But see Borg's 2012 attempt to place the allowed contextual components of meaning in the 'organization of the lexicon'.

[7] In the case of the speech act of request, indirectness prevails in around 60–70 per cent of cases, as cross-linguistic evidence suggests. See Schneider's 2009 study of Russian and British English speakers' attitude to requests and her experimental data on Russian and British English, also discussed below in Section 1.3.2.

[8] See also Portner and Partee 2002.

sentence at hand.[9] Instead, if we were to spell out boldly what an ideal theory of meaning should be like, we would want it to (a) account for the main, intuitive, intentional meaning conveyed by the sentence at hand, and *at the same time* (b) offer a formal account of how a Model Speaker constructs meaning in his/her head, and how a Model Addressee recovers this intended message.[10] This option is signalled by a theory of Default Semantics (Jaszczolt, e.g. 2005a, 2009a, 2010). The theory is still in progress, developed and tested on new types of constructions and phenomena.[11] It attempts to put right what is wrong about meaning and marry the radical context-dependence of meaning—that is, modelling the primary message conveyed in the acts of communication—with the formalism of Truth-Conditional Semantics. It is a semantics of acts of communication; a semantics of a truth-conditional kind, where truth conditions are predicated of proposition-like units that are the outputs of various interacting processes. Hence, it is a *semantics of linguistic interaction*. The interacting processes obtain input from a variety of sources of information, without giving preference to any of them. In other words, there is no talk here of a logical form being 'enriched', 'developed', or 'modulated' as a result of contextual information. There is no attempt at 'fixing' mentioned above. The relevant semantic representation is the *merger representation* to which various identified sources contribute on an equal footing. Merger representations are then, so to speak, our radical equivalents of logical forms; they are truth-evaluable and are constructed through processes that yield to a formal treatment, using some tools of dynamic semantics. We have thereby an occasion-meaning, but an occasion-meaning for which we uncover regularities. However, these regularities pertain *not* to the lexicon and syntax of natural language, but instead to processing of all kinds of information that the interactants can lay their hands/minds on in the situation of discourse, be it linguistic or not linguistic in its provenance.

In short, 'wrong about meaning' is precisely being wrong about the relationship between full-blown context-dependence and intention-dependence of the object of semantic analysis on the one hand, and the availability of a formal, truth-conditional account on the other. The interactive approach of Default Semantics attempts to put this right.

[9] See e.g. van der Sandt 1992, 2012 on binding and accommodation.

[10] 'Model' because a theory of meaning would not be of much use, and, indeed, would not be a 'theory' at all, if it were to account for individual cases of meaning construction taking into account the idiosyncrasies such as temporary lack of attention, mental incapacitation, mismatch of background assumptions leading to misunderstandings, and the like. Meaning of acts of communication relativized to model interlocutors is the only way to arrive at a sufficient level of generalization to result in normativity and thereby predictive power, reflecting universal principles of rational human communication laid out in Grice 1989 and approved as pragmatic universals in e.g. von Fintel and Matthewson 2008; Evans and Levinson 2009; Jaszczolt 2012a and 2012e.

[11] Readers are referred to the monograph Default Semantics (Jaszczolt 2005a) or the summary of the revised version of the theory in Jaszczolt 2010, among other publications. A précis of Default Semantics is given below in Section 2.2.1 to facilitate the reading of semantic representations.

1.2 The point of departure: Language system or conversational interaction?

'What is meaning?' is the best question to start with. We now begin a more detailed assessment of some aspects of current disputes over the scope and content of semantic theory in order to spell out specific desiderata for the theory of meaning. The scope of semantic theory has differed substantially with time, undergoing periodic expansion and shrinking while oscillating between the two polar options presented above. To repeat, according to the first one, semantics accounts for the meaning of words and sentences as abstract units, where words belong to a language system considered at a stable, fixed synchronic state abstracted from its development. Words are arranged into sentences, considered in isolation, by fixed rules of syntactic composition of a provenance that differs between different ideologies. Pragmatics, the theory of language use, lies firmly outside the domain of semantics. According to the other polar view, semantics accounts for meaning as it is understood by the users of the language, and thereby as it is intended by the speakers and recovered in the inferential process by the addressees. Pragmatic processes of inference are subsumed under semantics. The cline in-between is occupied by 'fixers': different approaches that subscribe to different degrees of this incorporation of pragmatically attained information into semantic representation.

The options are not to be picked and chosen on a whim. The important preliminary question to ask is whether linguistic structure (that is, the structure built out of units of natural language) is to be regarded as being dissociated from the structure of thought (that is, the conceptual structure). If we follow the league of scholars who argue in favour of the dependence of thought on language, then we have to assume that when one comes up with a semantic representation of a natural language sentence, one thereby offers a semantic representation of the units of inner speech. A semanticist of this orientation is therefore much more inclined to 'look beneath the surface' of uttered sentences and represent even what is not strictly speaking physically uttered in them, in order to be true to the common-sense assessment of the speaker's actual thought. Otherwise, still adhering to the 'natural language = the language of thought' hypothesis, we would have to admit that there are natural language sentences that we *utter* and that there are natural language sentences that we *think in* and the question arises as to which sentences should be adopted as the object of study of semantic theory: the natural language sentences physically produced, or the natural language sentences used in thinking.

There is, of course, the possibility that from the point of view of the theory itself it does not really matter: once we have an adequate theory of meaning in place, we can use it to analyse conceptual structures as well as linguistic structures as they both use the same system. On the other hand, when we assume that language of thought and natural language are separate systems, we have less of an urgency to 'read into' natural language sentences what is not *physically* (in the sense of linguistic signs) there: natural language semantics can be regarded as a module and be responsible for the analysis of meaning of the strings formed out of the units of the system of a language such as English, Polish, Korean or Pirahã. But, of course, it does not have to be so conceived; on this construal of the relation, we can also assume that there are constituents of the syntactic representation of the natural language sentence that are not overtly articulated, or at least constituents of the syntactic representation that must be there because there just *has to be* some way for the sentence to relate to what it stands for in reality, even if the conceptual structure and the language faculty are teased apart. There also has to be some way in which the sentence interacts with the context (the latter understood in a way indicated by the adopted theory). The follow-up question as to whether the generative power lies with the conceptual structure or with the language structure (if indeed there is such a dichotomy) is still subject to heated debates to which I return in Section 1.5.4.[12]

In view of these 'big questions' concerning linguistic and conceptual representation, and also in view of the inevitable availability of potentially endless options when one settles for a view somewhere on the scale between the polar ends, it seems methodologically prudent to start with the basic problem, namely what *field of inquiry* has to be assumed in order to address the question 'What is meaning?' understood as meaning in linguistic interaction. Put simply, we just want to know what meaning is, bearing in mind that we want a (preferably normative) theory of it. More precisely, we want to know where to look for meaning: in the natural language that is abstracted in a form of a system, in language as a tool that is used for various purposes including communication, or in communicative interaction itself. Then, we have to address the question as to whether there is just this one 'meaning' that is to be found, or whether meaning in interaction is one kind of object of inquiry, to be sought in the domain of pragmatics, sociolinguistics, and linguistic anthropology, and meaning in the language system quite another, to be pursued in the domain of semantics (even better: formal semantics). The problem is that *language system* is an elusive and dubitable entity: in spite of many efforts, no one as yet has managed to describe and explain natural languages by appealing to some abstract system or systems. Deriving meaning from universal principles governing sentence structure as in Chomskyan generative linguistics or deriving meaning from the formalized links with actual and counterfactual situations (models) as in Montagovian Truth-Conditional Semantics are projects aiming at a high predictive power but each of them leaves a lot of types of constructions and a lot of phenomena without satisfactory explanations, to mention only anaphora, presupposition, propositional attitude reports, temporal reference, and semantic relevance of focus, among many others. In

---

[12] For some seminal contributions see Evans and Levinson 2009 on the generative power of conceptual structure; Jackendoff 2012 on the role of language in conceptual structure.

the course of the past two decades when I have battled with some of these problems,[13] the solutions I proposed have been characterized by the increasing reliance on the properties of conversational interaction as opposed to the properties of the conceptual system (such as intentionality of mental states) or properties of natural language as a formal system (such as the composition of the logical form). In what follows I take one further step towards a communicative-interaction-based theory of meaning and the answer to our question is that one has to investigate *not* the language system and its relation to context but principally the context of the interaction itself, with all its means of conveying information. 'Meaning' will now pertain to that meaning that is produced and recovered in discourse, in conversational interaction. The extent to which it draws on the systematic elements of language such as abstract word meaning and syntactic structure is a question, flagged in Section 1.1, that will be addressed in the process of this inquiry, in particular when we discuss the sources of information about meaning and the interacting processes that produce its representation (Sections 2.1.1, 4.1).

Having vaguely established the object of study, we have to move to the methods that are to be adopted. Here we have some freedom to adopt certain assumptions in preference to others if they seem more promising or plausible, and then follow them to their logical end. Since we are opting for the analysis of meaning as it is employed (and also understood, if the level of reflection about meaning is applicable) by conversational interactants, the methods will have to be suitable for this purpose. We can proceed here either through (i) an empirical inquiry, either experimental or corpus-based, or through (ii) constructing a hypothesis and supporting it through a theoretical argument, in the spirit of a rationalist inquiry normally practised in theoretical linguistics and philosophy of language. The latter can of course be illustrated with, and further supported by, empirical data. As I said, there is more freedom in following one's assumption about what counts as adequate methodology than there is in adopting the object of study. Systems are theoretical constructs while conversations are real, so the choice is not so free in the latter domain. Concerning the method, it seems that in the past more wrong turns have been taken in proceeding through ill-conceived experimental or other empirical inquiry than through logically sound theory construction. Theories may prove to be inadequate and they can be falsified, but the conceptual analysis itself, unless logically fallacious, is never a futile one. A rationalist, theoretical inquiry, testable at a later stage on corpus-based data, is what is needed first.

One good argument for this order of inquiry comes from the current state of experimental pragmatics where one of the most heated debates concerns default vis-à-vis inferred meanings. Some pragmaticists argue that when the speaker utters,

---

[13] See e.g. Jaszczolt 1999, 2005a on propositional attitudes, or Jaszczolt 2009a on temporal reference.

for example, (4), the 'stronger' meaning in (5) is the 'default' one, arrived at automatically. Others ascribe this enrichment to a pragmatic process of inference that is specific for the context at hand.

(4)   You can have beef or lamb.

(5)   You can have either beef or lamb but not both.

However, the debate seems to be so heated only because experimenters tend to focus on one particular 'defaultism' account that makes particularly strong claims about default meanings, namely that of presumptive meanings (Levinson 1995, 2000). This radical defaultism becomes a straw man, an easy target for falsification.[14] Defaults are ascribed there to expressions in isolation; they are strong, they come from the language system itself and from the general tendencies for how such constructions are used, and as such are *independent of the situations* in which they are identified. But when what we want is the distinction between meanings that are derived automatically as opposed to meanings that are derived through inference, there are other possible construals that are much less controversial. For example, we can peg automatic meanings on contexts and say that in this particular context of uttering (4), the 'one or the other but not both' meaning of the disjunctive connective *or* is produced automatically. This is the position taken in Default Semantics. This view is much less radical and much less controversial; unlike Levinson's language-system-based defaults, such automatic meanings come as no surprise and do not need to be subjected to such multiple attempts at falsification. Situation-based defaults of Default Semantics are just situation-based, automatically retrieved meanings. Falsifying this view would amount to falsifying individual prediction types and to an attempt to falsify the hypothesis that in meaning retrieval there is automaticity.[15]

The way to avoid such misdirected experimental endeavours is to put more effort into constructing a plausible theory of how different components of the overall 'meaning in interaction' are put together—a theory that would define these components, and at the same time a theory that would allocate aspects of meaning to these components and to the processes they are associated with. This answer to our question about the delimitation of the playing field provides the essential directive for Default Semantics—an ongoing enterprise in building a semantics of linguistic interaction that is further developed in what follows. Before I move to this task, the remainder of Chapter 1 sets the scene by providing a critical discussion of some debates concerning the scope and the role of semantics.

---

[14]   See especially contributions to Noveck and Sperber 2004.

[15]   See also Introduction. I say more about the kind of information such defaults provide in Chapters 2 and 3. See especially Section 3.1 on salience and defaults.

1.3 'Minimalists', 'maximalists', and 'fixers'

Let us begin by considering three simple and innocuous sentences (6)–(8).

(6)   Everyone admires Julia Roberts.

(7)   It is freezing cold.

(8)   I am late!

Semantically innocent as they may seem, these sentences exemplify a problem that gave rise to one of the most robust discussions in linguistics and philosophy in the past three decades, namely the delimitation of meaning. On the surface, the answer is simple: semantics piggy-backs on the meanings of the words and the structure of the sentences and throws up the meaning that comes from that composition of meaningful parts. This much we know from the principle of compositionality and from the standard semantics/pragmatics distinction where the first pertains to the meaning engendered by the language system with its lexicon and syntax, and the latter to the meaning understood as the message intentionally produced by an agent and, if all goes well, recovered by the addressee and other audience. The emphasis on the intention or, alternatively, on the recognition of the intention, differs from view to view and it is not essential to delve into it at this point. So, we seem to obtain the composed meanings represented by the words and structures in (6)–(8) as semantic content, and something to the effect of (6')–(8') as pragmatic content.

(6')   Everyone Kasia has ever talked to admires the actress Julia Roberts.

(7')   It is exceptionally cold in Cambridge on 7 October 2014.

(8')   Kasia is late for the concert.

Or, perhaps, one should be more generous about what kinds of meanings semantics equips us with and admit that the quantifier 'everyone' already signals a specific domain of quantification and therefore (6') is what the semantics yields. Similarly, a weather predicate already signals that there must be a location and time that the speaker talks about and therefore (7') is what the semantics yields. The first-person pronoun already signals that one, unique referent is intended, and perhaps also the predicate 'late' already signals that being late always means being 'late for something' and therefore (8') is what the semantics yields. Other solutions for semantic content are also possible.

     Next, assuming a 'rich' semantic content as in (6')–(8'), we are obliged to ask about the role and purpose of pragmatics. There are two: one is to contribute the 'bits', so to speak, that are not expressed and yet are included in such rich semantics. This results in a level of meaning that is called in the literature *what is said* (in the contextualist sense, e.g. Recanati 1989) or *explicature* (Sperber and Wilson 1995: 182), and is contrasted with *what is implicated*. The other is to take us from (6')–(8') to some other meanings that the speaker intended. On some occasions, such meanings may even be more salient and important than those in (6')–(8'); it is so when the speaker's main intended message is conveyed indirectly. For example, in using (6) I may intend to communicate, in the context of a particular conversation, something to the effect of (6"). By (7) I may intend to issue the main message as in (7"), and analogously (8") by uttering (8). Likewise, a myriad of other salient meanings can be derived in specific situations of discourse.

(6")   You won't regret seeing *Pretty Woman*.

(7")   I would like you to turn the heating up.

(8")   Please don't bother me with this story now, I don't have time.

The intuitive simplicity of such a tri-partite distinction notwithstanding, there are several problems. The first one I have already mentioned: Which aspects of meaning belong to semantics and which lie outside it? It is not the purpose of this discussion to give a historical exegesis of how meaning was muddied up following Grice's modest admission of some degree of pragmatics into semantics (in the form of reference assignment and disambiguation, see Grice 1978). Many post-Griceans have discussed this ongoing 'pragmatization' of meaning elsewhere (see Jaszczolt 1999, 2002a for an overview). Post-Gricean pragmatics emphasizes not only the need to provide referents for indexical expressions and disambiguation for lexical and grammatical ambiguities, but also the need to enrich propositions as for example in the case of precisification of sentential connectives in (9)–(11) or reference shift in (12), all of which are sometimes grouped under the label of the *modulation* of the uttered proposition (Recanati, e.g. 2010: 5; 2012a: 141). Modulation is a pragmatic process that is not governed by lexical items or grammatical structures but instead is, so to speak, *free*, *top-down*—where, in contrast, being constrained by the logical form of the sentence and triggered by the lexicon or structure would mean being *bottom-up*. In the examples below, the symbol '$\rightarrow_E$' stands for 'explicitly means'.

 (9)   Mary tripped Tom *and* ($\rightarrow_E$ *and as a result*) he fell.

(10)   You can have beef *or* chicken ($\rightarrow_E$ *but not both*).

(11)   I will tell you who did it *if* ($\rightarrow_E$ *if and only if*) you promise not to tell anyone.

(12)   *Number seven* ($\rightarrow_E$ *the holder of the ticket number seven*) is waiting for fish and chips.

The views in the literature are as diversified as they can possibly be, ranging from 'radical semantic minimalists' to 'radical contextualists'.[16] At the same time, it becomes increasingly evident that not all minimalists are sufficiently restrained

---

[16] Albeit not always 'semantic contextualists'; some are just, so to speak, 'contextualist as far as truth conditions are concerned', without subscribing to a rich scope of semantics.

about semantic content to justify the label, while, analogously, some contextualists are quite restrained about what pragmatic information they are prepared to include in the truth-conditional content. To repeat, calling it 'semantic content' won't do because the orthogonal complication is that while in the past semantics used to mean the truth-conditional content and pragmatics meant going 'beyond truth conditions', now we can either include some pragmatic content in the semantics and thereby in the truth-conditional content or, alternatively, dissociate truth conditions from semantics and apply them to pragmatic content instead. The way to look at it would be to think of truth conditions metaphorically as utensils—a fork and a knife, chopsticks, or what you like—for eating a food portion: you can use them to eat a little or you can use them to eat a lot—or even, arguably, you can use them to eat everything that is being served. These three 'size' options correspond to our (6)–(8), (6')–(8') and (6")–(8") above.

In Section 1.3.1 I assess some minimalist solutions and discuss points of divergence and convergence among minimalists and contextualists, revising some labels and introducing further seminal questions when such appear. The next sub-sections follow up with the assessment of 'fixers': free-enrichment contextualists and indexicalists, and with some proposed improvements.

1.3.1 *Options and prospects for 'minimalist' semantics*

To sum up the argument so far, an account of meaning in language can be founded on the ways the language system works or on the ways language is used by its speakers. If we confine it to the properties of the system alone, we thereby exclude any discussion of inference, intentions, goals, or plans. We include the decoding principles and principles of composition of complex expressions (sentence types). We are most likely, but not necessarily, to end up in the category of truth-conditionalists and minimalists where, as Emma Borg says, '[t]he truth-conditional semantic theory is governed, not by rich non-demonstrative inferential processes, but rather by formally triggered, deductive operations' (Borg 2004: 8; see also Borg 2012). Such semantics aims at a formal rigour and allegedly pertains to a specialized module in language processing: 'formal semantics and modularity about linguistic understanding seem to be a match made in heaven'—or so Borg (2004: 8) promises to convince us. Semantic processes are informationally encapsulated, while processing of speech acts is not.[17]

Formulated in these terms, minimalist semantics looks quite appealing, at least at first glance. After all, it spells out and precisifies the ideas that preceded the 'Gricean muddying of the waters' that he started with his 1978 'Further notes on logic and

---

[17] For a review see Jaszczolt 2005b.

conversation'. Semantics is about language system, deduction, and compositionality as traditionally understood. It is confined to a language module and utilizes the Tarskian/Davidsonian tool of truth conditions in a way that is close to standard in that no intentions or inferences are smuggled in.

Or is it? Indexical expressions, although they do not in themselves contain information about their referents but instead are equipped with what is sometimes called 'linguistic meaning' (such as 'the speaker' for the first-person singular pronoun *I*), would remain 'unfilled' on this semantics if some concession in the direction of what is not strictly speaking there in the sentence were not allowed. To repeat, were it not allowed, all tokens of (13) would have the same meaning.

(13)   That [demonstration] is red.

The content of (13) is by stipulation propositional, in that the assumption of propositionalism states that all well-formed sentences of natural language express propositions, are truth-evaluable. At the same time, the 'grasp of the semantic content of a token demonstrative does not entail that a hearer is able to non-linguistically identify the referent' (Borg 2012: 141).

And this is where the problems begin. For one, it makes little sense to make the semantics sensitive to the filling in of referents for indexicals but bar it from accounting for the way the user of that sentence fills this particular token of the indexical expression. To use our earlier metaphor, the fork and knife (the truth conditions) are used to eat a very modest meal: the content of the demonstrative 'that' is mysteriously filled in by latching onto a referent, but this referent is not the speaker's referent; it inhabits some mystical realm reserved for emergency treatment prescribed to keep propositional minimalism alive.

Next, and perhaps more importantly, one may argue that a 'true' minimalist, dedicated to the modular account of meaning, would keep the content of (13) stable, invariant, rather than help herself to a portion of the pragmaticky stuff to fill in the position of the demonstrative. Borg (2012) argues that, since minimalism assumes propositionalism, she has to admit a set of expressions that require such referential filling in. But the obvious question is, why merge propositionalism and minimalism? What are the explanatory benefits of such a hybrid?

Borg (2012) wants to restrict the 'pragmaticky stuff' to contextual resolutions that pertain to the type, rather than token, level. For example, for (13), it is the type of expression, the demonstrative pronoun, that is responsible for the pragmatic filling. In addition to standard indexicals, words such as 'right', 'left', 'local', or 'nearby' are examples of lexical expressions that belong to this stuffing-prone set. In (3), repeated as (14), it is the syntactic configuration, and thus the sentence type, that tells us that 'ready' requires another argument (ready for what?).

(14)   Lidia is ready.

In other words, there has to be some 'independent evidence' in the language itself (Borg 2012: 89) of this context-sensitivity.[18]

The problem is that, equally, one can flip the argument and use these examples for the defence of the view that there is no *true indexicality* in language, there are just *degrees* to which context has to be consulted. However, there is ample evidence, as well as theoretical arguments, attended to in detail in Chapter 5 below, showing that the first-person 'indexical' is a myth;[19] there is no indexical/non-indexical distinction as far as the markers of first-personhood are concerned, not even in English, although English gave rise to the bulk of theorizing about the special status of indexicals in semantics.[20] In the same vein, neither is there a clear boundary between constructions that provide 'independent evidence' for pragmatic stuffing (cf. 14) and constructions that do not; debates over the adicity of the predicate 'eat' and the status of the location for weather predicates as in (15) and (16) are good examples of this concern (see Recanati 2002).

(15)   Look, the baby is eating!

(16)   It is raining.

Facing the lack of support for the boundary between expressions requiring such pragmatic stuffing and expressions that do not, the case for propositionalist minimalists is dubious indeed.

For Borg (2004), truth conditions are 'liberal'; our fork and knife are flexible and potentially multifunctional. They are so flexible that one can eat with them what in fact is a 'virtual meal', such as (13), which differs from a 'real meal', such as (13').

(13')   The apple is red.

They are employed there to cater for virtual meals (pun unintended). Various contributors to the ensuing discussion (Recanati 2004, 2005; Atlas 2011, to mention some examples) pointed out that Borg's 'meal' is not even what we would call in our metaphorical language a 'minimal meal'. It is precisely a 'virtual meal'; a meal that is not a meal at all. In other words, meaning so construed is not meaning at all. Recanati (2004: 92–3) calls this an 'unacceptable weakening of the notion of truth-condition' in that the very *raison d'être* of truth in Truth-Conditional Semantics is to 'connect words and the world'. Allowing an analysis of the kind exemplified in (17') for the sentence in (17) throws away the conceptual elaborations that are necessary for recovering the intended proposition, at the same time throwing the meaning out of the picture.

---

[18]   On this topic, see also Ludlow's 2011 externalism about syntax.
[19]   See Jaszczolt 2013b, 2013c.
[20]   The literature is vast but see especially Kaplan 1989a.

(17)   He is not good enough.

(17′)   'He is not good enough' is true in the context *c* if and only if the male referent of 'he' in context *c* is not good enough for *something* in that context.

In Borg (2012), concessions to pragmatic 'stuffing', to continue with our metaphorical schema, seem to be painstakingly defended against all odds, with more enrichment being let into semantics and justified by rules of language.[21] This has the effect of pushing the theory in the direction of another (allegedly) minimalist account, namely Cappelen and Lepore's (2005a, b) *insensitive semantics*. Cappelen and Lepore construe semantics as being 'about how best to specify the semantic value of the lexical items and their contribution to the semantic values of complex expressions and sentences in which they occur' (2005a: 58). Semantics so construed is then supplemented with a pragmatics that recognizes the multiplicity of meanings that speakers can intend to convey by means of such structures, in accordance with their so-called *speech act pluralism*. Let us first focus on the semantics. They put forward two claims. First, semantic content is identical for all utterances of a particular sentence. At the same time, they recognize a set of what they call 'genuinely context-sensitive expressions' (p. 143), that is, expressions that 'interact with context' within, not outside, this semantic content. These include personal pronouns such as 'I' or 'he', demonstrative pronouns such as 'this' or 'that', deictic adverbs such as 'here', 'there', 'tomorrow' or 'now', adjectives 'actual' and 'present', and temporal expressions. This is how the contribution of context is always triggered by the lexicon and grammar and thereby maximally constrained—à la Kaplan's (1989a) list of indexical terms.

Now, once one concedes that context may have a role to play in the semantic content, one has redefined minimalism in such a way that it paradoxically seems to fit comfortably in the camp of the opposing orientation, namely contextualism. Resolution of reference requires consulting the speaker's intentions and once this is allowed into the theory, as Borg (2007), rightly observes, semantic content is no longer attainable via formal procedures. And it is the latter that has to remain the defining characteristic of minimalism if we want to be able to contrast it with contextualism. As further developments demonstrate, Cappelen and Lepore's more 'pragmaticky' minimalism was abandoned to the benefit of the defence of contextualism over relativism in Cappelen and Hawthorne (2009). Borg (2012) increases Cappelen and Lepore's 'basic set' of context-sensitive expressions, while Cappelen moves in the direction of contextualism proper. It appears that pragmatic stuffing increased for both minimalist accounts, executed in their respective ways.

Cappelen and Lepore's insensitive semantics has generated a level of interest in the literature that is clearly disproportionate to its utility and I will not add to

---

[21] See also Section 4.1 below.

the regurgitation of critical observations. Suffice it to repeat that minimalism so construed is in fact far from minimalism *sensu stricto*: it is an account that allows a fair amount of contextual information into the semantics proper. Neither does it come with a cognitively defensible pragmatic story: speech act pluralism proposes that there are multiple intended meanings associated with an uttered sentence. But, surely, what is of interest is that *one* of these meanings corresponds to the primary, main, strongly intended meaning. And there is no reason why we should focus on the fact that there may be *more than one* proposition intended in total by the speaker rather than on the fact that an utterance normally corresponds to some *one*, unique, intended message, and only contingently and less importantly may also carry some additional meanings. All in all, both semantics and pragmatics on Cappelen and Lepore's proposal are rather skewed away from the intuitive concept of meaning. It seems that what we have here is a rather parsimonious, constrained version of contextualism on which the semantic content does indeed depend on the speaker's intentions but only where there are overt indicators in the lexicon and grammar that intentions should be consulted. But, as I will argue in due course, equivalents of such a set of indicators simply do not exist in natural languages.

On the other hand, as far as Borg's argument from the formal route to meaning is concerned, the situation is not as simple as she presents it.[22] Contrary to her early claim, it now appears that allowing some dose of speaker intentions into the semantics does not shut off the formal route to meaning. There is no *a priori* reason why a language system understood as the lexicon and grammar should be the only vehicle of meaning that yields to formal methods. One can preserve a formal route to meaning in a variety of ways. For example, DPL provides a language of description for natural language semantics, at the same time adhering to the definition that the meaning of the sentence is the way this sentence changes the information state of the addressee (Groenendijk and Stokhof 1991, 2000). The *syntax* of this language is the same as that of ordinary predicate logic that was used in standard Montagovian formal semantic accounts (see e.g. Portner and Partee 2002). But the interpretation, the *semantics*, reflects a change in information states: it is dynamic but at the same time compositional. Discourse Representation Theory (Kamp and Reyle 1993) and Default Semantics advocate the same methodological approach to formalism vis-à-vis the dynamic nature of information in discourse, with different pragmatic aspects incorporated into the representations of meaning. I discuss the latter in more depth in Chapter 2.

[22] NB: minimalism so defined is a radical version of what is sometimes called 'literalism', according to which the truth conditions of a sentence are given by the rules of the language system as applied in a particular context (see the taxonomy of views in Recanati 2004). But in view of the difficulties with defining literal meaning discussed later in this chapter, the term 'literalism' appears vacuous and will not be used.

To conclude on propositional minimalism, it appears that construing semantics as 'predominantly context-insensitive' (Borg 2012: 216) does not give it clear enough foundations. 'Predominantly' is a vague term; the set of context-sensitive expressions ('that', 'I', 'left', 'tomorrow', 'actual')[23] and context-sensitive constructions ('x is ready', 'x is not good enough')[24] eschews convincing independent justification, even when one tries to use her organizational principles of the lexicon, loosely modelled on Carnap's (1952) meaning postulates, as an explanans.[25] Moreover, it takes a lot of loving care and unconditional trust to tease apart this version of minimalism and indexicalism; just as in indexicalism, there is a syntactic explanation for pragmatic stuffing. And once we enter the territory of indexicalism, indexicality tends to expand and the true debate becomes the one between indexicalists and the free-enrichment contextualists. This is a very different debate indeed, tangential to the issue of how minimal the semantic content ought to be taken to be.[26]

Before we proceed to a discussion of contextualist assumptions, there remains one big question to address that has been only hinted at so far. It concerns the role of truth conditions. I have employed here the culinary metaphor of a fork and a knife (truth conditions) used to eat a (minimal or pragmatically enhanced) meal. But it need not be assumed at all that if we want the 'meal' to be minimal, we have to use a fork and a knife to eat it. In other words, the question is whether we need truth conditions for semantic analysis, or even, more generally: Is the proposition the appropriate unit for semantic content? Asking precisely this question, Bach (2001, 2004, 2006) begins with an observation that sentences can be perfectly well formed and complete syntactically, and at the same time, from the semantic point of view, express incomplete content, like for example (14) above. Yet, as he suggests:

'[a]s long as it is not assumed that the job of semantics is to give truth conditions of (declarative) sentences, there is no reason to suppose that pragmatics needs to intrude on semantic.'

Bach (2004: 42)

Instead, semantics and pragmatics have a clear and uncomplicated boundary, where semantic properties resemble syntactic and phonological properties of expressions, and pragmatic properties belong to the entirely different domain of communicating, intending, and, in short, putting the language system into use. Put in this way, it is easy to argue that there is nothing particularly semantic about propositions;

---

[23] See Cappelen and Lepore (2005a: 144) for a list, called 'basic set'.

[24] See Borg 2012 for examples.

[25] I discuss this question in more detail in Section 4.1 while trying to delimit word meaning.

[26] For an excellent, comprehensive exposition of the problems with indexicalism see also Clapp 2012. Most importantly, expressions that do not seem to belong to the class of indexicals can *behave* like indexicals, and therefore a strict delimitation of indexicality is impossible. I attend to this problem in Chapter 5.

sentences can be semantically incomplete, require pragmatic filling in (and thereby consulting the speaker's intentions) to make up a proposition, and there is a long list of ways in which this 'propositionalization' of the sentence can be attained. The resulting proposition is thus more appropriately allocated a pragmatic rather than a semantic status.[27]

It would be difficult to disagree with a view that so obviously conforms to common sense and to intuitions. But what is difficult to agree with is its classification as a *minimalist* view. Bach calls it radical semantic minimalism in that it is arguably even more radical than the minimalisms that fall prey to propositionalism: on radical semantic minimalism, a proposition is not a unit of description. On the other hand, the view also fits in very well with the contextualist construal of meaning: there is some pre-propositional semantics that often has little in common with the speaker's intended meaning, and then there is the main proposition that is a hybrid of semantic and pragmatic content. If we remove the emphasis from this pre-propositional component, this is contextualism *tout court*: truth conditions and propositions are far from minimal, just the label 'semantics' is applied elsewhere.

So far we have seen that there is very little we can accumulate in defence of the various alleged minimalisms proposed in recent years. Perhaps, as Travis (2006a: 160) puts it, '[m]inimal propositions lead nowhere'. Perhaps, as he says in his seminal paper 'Pragmatics', 'Truth and falsity seem to correspond to understandings words may have, rather than to the words themselves' (Travis 1997: 126). Reverting to intuitions about meaning, it would seem that the onus of proof lies with those who attempt to cut out some theoretically sophisticated but cognitively dubious element of utterance meaning and call it the semantic foundation that is (i) more, or less, minimal, depending on the view; (ii) modular or not even modular, again depending on the view; and finally (iii) propositional or not propositional, depending on which minimalist we are engaging in a discussion with. So, it seems that searching for a candidate for meaning in the pragmatics-rich camp is what one should turn to next. In this camp I include both 'fixers' (indexicalists and free-enrichment contextualists) and meaning-occasionalists (Wittgenstein, Travis, and my Default Semantics—the latter *qua* a theory that allows for modelling indirect contents as primary meanings).[28]

---

[27] Bach (2001) makes a concession for those indexicals that come from narrowly understood context (pure indexicals) such as 'I' or 'here' as opposed to broadly understood context ('he', 'there'). See Chapter 5 for some problems with this distinction where I demonstrate that pure first-person indexical is a philosophers' fiction.

[28] See Introduction above, Jaszczolt 2005a, and the overview in Recanati 2005 for the wide scope assigned to the term 'contextualist'. On that classification, occasionalism/meaning eliminativism figures as a radical version of contextualism. Hence in the current discussion I sometimes qualify the term 'contextualism' by saying 'free-enrichment contextualism'.

1.3.2 *Options and prospects for 'maximalist' semantics*

Borg (2004: 261, also in 2012) argues that 'nothing which requires abductive reasoning (like mind-reading) can be treated as a proper part of the semantic theory'. The fact that there is also the intuitive content of an utterance, and intuitive truth conditions, does not invalidate the need for truly semantic content in addition. And neither do considerations of psychological reality; as she claims, when we want to, we exhibit a perfectly good capacity for grasping and even talking in terms of minimal meanings as in (18) below.

(18)   A: Everybody loves that dog.

B: Even the Pope?

But linguistic jokes cannot be a test for a utility of a level of representation. The fact that I am capable of responding to (18A) using (18B) does not in itself support minimal semantic content as a viable theoretical concept. It merely supports the intuition of what Travis (2008) calls *occasion-sensitivity*: different contexts lead to different meanings built upon the matrix of a certain sentence or sentence fragment uttered by the speaker. I emphasize 'sentence fragment' because it is important to note that sentences are by no means a condition *sine qua non* for expressing propositions. And neither are they, as can easily be tested, essential for expressing speech acts. Moreover, as Stainton (2006) convincingly argues, the preponderance of sentence fragments in discourse poses no problem for Truth-Conditional Semantics; propositions do not require underlying mental (complete) sentences.[29]

It seems that there is only one step from admitting this context-sensitivity *en masse* to the claim that the sentence as the backbone of propositions does not warrant endowing it with the privileged status of a separate level of linguistic analysis. This step is further facilitated by the fact that even the 'backbone' can be fragmentary, in the form of a sentence fragment, without a great loss to propositions and truth conditions. Throughout the following chapters I further develop this idea, pointing out that what looks like a 'backbone' is not necessarily a backbone at all. Instead, the meaning modelled in our semantics of linguistic interaction will be the main proposition intended by the speaker and normally also recovered by the addressee, where instead of the 'backbone and the dependent bones' or a 'skeleton and supported flesh' metaphor that is appropriate for minimalist accounts, we would be more justified in using a label of interacting components—all democratically admitted on an equal footing as equally privileged contributors to the representation of the overall intended meaning. This has always been the main preoccupation of Default Semantics.

---

[29] I discuss subsentential speech in Section 2.1.1.

One may wonder why Borg insists on the psychological reality of minimal meanings in the face of an overwhelming lack of evidence that language systems behave in a way her commitment to the semantic module would expect them to behave. She is ready to admit that those who construe content more sumptuously, namely the contextualists, are not in the wrong; their interests just differ from hers. But contextualism comes with a better supported metaphysics of language and a better supported theory of utterance interpretation; propositional minimalism hangs onto the role of deduction, the importance of modules, and the assumption that 'there are structures in the mind/brain which represent the basic elements of the minimalist theory' (Borg 2012: 63). In the light of evidence from neuropragmatics, these claims hardly hold water; it seems that speech-related actions are more likely to underpin patterns of neuronal activation than the lexico-syntactic vs. non-lexico-syntactic meaning divide.[30]

Let us now assess what the 'maximalist' stance has to offer in the semantics/pragmatics boundary disputes. I will take as the point of departure a discussion of some contextualist accounts that I had earlier included in 'fixers'. First, it has to be remembered that contextualism comes in different flavours which represent different stances on (i) what is semantics and what is pragmatics; (ii) what is literal and what is non-literal; or (iii) what is traceable to grammar and what is purely context-driven. For example, relevance theorists (Sperber and Wilson, e.g. 1995, 2012; Carston, e.g. 2002, 2007)[31] are committed to rich Truth-Conditional Semantics that includes pragmatic developments of the logical form of the uttered sentence.[32] What counts as such developments, and therefore what is included in the explicit content, has been evolving with time. While sentential connectives such as those in (9)–(11) above have always been regarded by relevance theorists as standard candidates for contextual enrichment, metaphorical meaning was added later, as a result of the reanalysis of concept formation vis-à-vis the explicit/implicit distinction.[33]

Literalness has never been regarded as a norm in constructing and recovering meaning by relevance theorists (Sperber and Wilson 1995: 233). More recently, the literal/non-literal distinction has been blurred further in the proposal that when we speak metaphorically, the uttered expressions give rise to a concept shift. In (19), the word 'fox' triggers an online concept construction that begins with the encoded concept FOX and ends with the context-specific FOX*—a so-called *ad hoc* concept,

---

[30] See e.g. Pulvermüller 2010.

[31] See also Clark 2013.

[32] Note that 'contextualism' in semantics and pragmatics has to be distinguished from 'contextualism' as it is used in epistemology. Contextualism in epistemology is a theory of sentences pertaining to knowledge, i.e. sentences of the form 'A knows that *p*' and it says that their truth conditions vary depending on the context in which they are employed. For an introduction and defence of epistemological context-ualism see DeRose 2009.

[33] See e.g. Carston 2002, chapter 5 on *ad hoc* concept construction.

specific for this context.[34] An analogous process takes place for the verb 'to sniff', according to what cognitive semanticists would call the same cognitive schema.[35]

(19)   Tom is a real fox ($\rightarrow_E$ FOX*), he always sniffs ($\rightarrow_E$ SNIFFS*) a bargain.

Such modifications of the encoded concepts contribute to the explicitly communicated proposition (Carston 2002: 334).

The move to incorporate concept shifts in the explicitly communicated content is an important one. It brings closer together the primary content of the message intended by the speaker and the primary object of semantic analysis for which, fairly standardly in post-Gricean tradition, truth conditions are employed. Relevance Theory captures this intentional and intuitive status of the object of analysis by using the truth-conditional 'fork and knife' to 'eat' the most psychologically adequate object of all possible ones, namely thoughts:

'…one might wonder what has become of the notion of the truth-conditional content of the utterance. In fact, it is not clear that we really want such a notion in our pragmatics at all, especially if, as relevance theorists argue, the proper domain of truth-conditional semantic theory is thoughts/assumptions (or, at least, their propositional forms), rather than sentences or utterances.'

Carston (2002: 337)

This, of course, has to be read in the context of the debate concerning the role of the conceptual system vis-à-vis the linguistic system discussed above, where relevance theorists recognize two different systems: the linguistic and the conceptual, at the same time also recognizing the existence of linguistic semantics as separate from the semantics proper.

But then, *pace* the quoted statement, perhaps there is a role for utterances to play as well. Since metaphorical uses are regarded as literal interpretations of speakers' thoughts in the sense that (19) *literally* means that Tom has a property of being cunning, swift and clever, just as (20) means that an animal of a certain species was spotted in the woodlands, the truth conditions become reinstated as an analytic tool for utterances as well. I return to the question of the literal/non-literal distinction in Section 1.4.

(20)   A silver fox was spotted in the woodlands last night.

The next noteworthy benefit of this 'psychologizing' of explicit content is that the apparent difference in which cognitive semantics and post-Gricean pragmatics approach metaphors has been gradually disappearing. In my *Semantics and*

---

[34] Relevance theorists assume Jerry Fodor's approach to concepts according to which concepts that correspond to simple words are atomic (non-decomposable); see e.g. Fodor 1998.

[35] See e.g. the seminal work by Lakoff and Johnson 1980 or Ungerer and Schmid 1996 for an introduction.

Pragmatics (Jaszczolt 2002a) I included a concluding section to the chapter on metaphor, entitling it 'Towards the reconciliation of truth-conditional and cognitive semantics',[36] in which I remarked on some clear points of convergence among truth-conditional contextualist accounts, Lakoff's cognitive-semantic account, and Searle's pragmatic account of metaphor. The main aspect of this convergence is the focusing on mental representations of reality. Although in subjectivist accounts such as that of Lakoff and Johnson (1980) or Johnson (1987) mental reality is all there is, while traditional Montagovian Truth-Conditional Semantics is an objectivist account that uses truth conditions for the purpose of answering the question as to *what the objective (and objectively construed as possible) world would have to be like for the sentence to be true*, both have to concede that mental representations, intensions, concepts, senses, or other labels that stand for the way the users of language think about objects and situations, have to be brought into the picture. It is the *degree* of this concession to the mental that is, in essence, what differentiates them, and this degree is significantly increasing.

Carston (2002: 354–5) approaches this compatibility somewhat differently. She points out that while her modified relevance-theoretic account of metaphor exposes the theoretical benefits of *ad hoc* concepts, cognitive semantics may provide an answer to the question as to how the shift from lexically encoded to *ad hoc* concepts is executed—via, for example, cognitivists' metaphorical schemas that facilitate metaphorical thought (see also Carston 2012: 488). Moreover, Relevance Theory claims that while some words encode concepts, others may encode something that falls short of a full concept, such as for instance an instruction (procedure, schema, and so forth) as to how to form a concept. Pronouns, for example, allegedly fall into this category. But there is only one step, albeit a significant and controversial one, from this view to claiming that a concept shift may in fact not occur at all but instead all there is, is a *concept construction* in context. This view, held famously by late Wittgenstein (1953), has now come back to the focus of attention under the label of 'meaning eliminativism' (e.g. Recanati 2005). Meaning eliminativism envisages that the contextually relevant sense of an expression is arrived at via a process that begins with information from past uses of the expression and yields this specific, context-dependent meaning. There is no intervening step of constructing linguistic meaning, be it lexical or pertaining to structured units, as it is understood in the language system (see Recanati 2005: 189–90). In other words, *abstraction* becomes conflated with *modulation*, producing one single step in processing. In this respect, (i) cognitivists' subjectivist construal of meaning and (ii) meaning eliminativism don't seem to be far apart. There are pragmatic processes that operate fairly independently of the constraints imposed by the structure of the sentence (Carston 2007; Recanati 2007)

---

[36] Section 17.7.

that are not unlike the exploitation of metaphorical schemas that are formed in response to physical (bodily), environmental and social factors; 'the categories we form are part of our experience' (Lakoff and Johnson 1999: 19).

Next, there remains the question as to whether the contextualist truth-conditional theory so construed is a theory of semantics or of pragmatics. Relevance theorists (e.g. Wilson and Carston 2007) choose to adopt Recanati's (2002, 2004, 2010) label of Truth-Conditional Pragmatics:

'... various contextual processes come into play in the determination of an utterance's truth conditions; not merely saturation – the contextual assignment of values to indexicals and free variables in the logical form of the sentence – but also free enrichment and other processes which are not linguistically triggered but are pragmatic through and through. That view I will henceforth refer to as "Truth-conditional pragmatics (TCP)".'

Recanati (2002: 302)

There are arguably good reasons for shifting from the 'Truth-Conditional Semantics' label to that of 'Truth-Conditional Pragmatics' (henceforth TCS and TCP, respectively). The main one has to do with the nature and description of the content. Truth conditions are now applied to that proposition which, allegedly, stands for what is intended by the speaker and/or recovered by the addressee. On the other hand, this proposition is not just any odd proposition that the speaker intends to get across. If, for example, the speaker conveys the message by means of an indirect speech act as in (21), (22) will *not*, alas, correspond to the proposition that is assumed there to be the object of the truth-conditional analysis.

(21)   The dog looks like he needs to go out.

(22)   The speaker is requesting that the addressee take the dog for a walk.

In order to qualify, in addition to serving as the intended proposition, such a proposition has to be, at the same time, *built upon* the matrix of the uttered sentence. It has to be recoverable from the uttered sentence by means of various forms of enrichment, embellishment, 'expansion and completion', 'fleshing out and filling in', or modulation, to name only a few of the pertinent labels.[37] In other words, the logical form of the uttered sentence undergoes certain modification ('fixing') that yields the intuitive proposition (and the intuitive truth-conditional content). Hence the epithet 'fixers'.

It is this latter characteristic, the reliance on the logical form of the sentence, that makes the TCP label rather questionable. Surely, when the main intended content is conveyed indirectly, as in (21), then pragmatics, be it truth-conditional or of

---

[37] See e.g. Carston 1988; Recanati 1989; Bach 1994 for these early discussions, and Recanati 2004 on modulation.

whatever other orientation, should opt for this main intended proposition as its object of study. Instead, TCP hovers between the minimal semantic content given in the logical form, which, by a general consensus, does not play any significant role in utterance interpretation, and the true pragmatic content that can, in situations such as that depicted in (21)–(22), be quite (or even completely) independent of the logical form of the uttered sentence. One wonders what is the use of clinging to the idea of a developed/modulated logical form of the sentence if the logical form itself is in no respect delimitable; word meanings are flexible, structures can be used idiomatically or metaphorically, and the most profitable, economical and reliable way of conveying a message may be indirect.

The answer seems to be: Tradition. The Gricean Tradition of distinguishing the explicit content (*what is said*) and the implicit content (an array of accompanying *implicata*, now known as *implicatures*, Grice 1975). Having given due recognition to the very important efforts of a number of eminent post-Griceans to redraw the boundary between what is said and what is implicated by noticing that not only disambiguation and reference assignment but also a number of other types of pragmatic processes are required to arrive at a *cognitively plausible what is said*, it is time to assess whether these efforts have gone far enough. In my view, they have not. Instead, they have preserved the explicit/implicit distinction, shifting the boundary between them to incorporate more 'former implicit' in the 'new explicit', but have not gone as far as acknowledging the fact that the boundary that is of crucial importance is a different one, namely the one between (i) the primary communicated content on the one hand and (ii) the array of additional communicated meanings on the other, *irrespective of their relation to the syntactic structure of the sentence.*

In this context, Recanati's (2004: 154) position is a puzzling one. On the one hand, he professes the following, broadly Strawsonian, view: 'By "Contextualism" I mean the view according to which it is speech acts, not sentences, which have a determinate content and are truth-evaluable.' This would suggest that when the speaker uses an indirect speech act, the indirect speech act should constitute the main object of our truth-conditional analysis in that the main content of this act is the main message intended by the speaker and therefore should rightly be called main or 'primary' meaning. But this is not the case. The complication arises in that next we have, according to Recanati (2007, 2010, 2012b), the process of pragmatic revision of the logical form, called modulation, that acts irrespective of the structure (top-down) but at the same time acts locally, that is, it contributes to the semantic representation incrementally. It is true that such pragmatic revision does not rely on annotations of the logical form as it does for indexicalists, but instead the burden for providing ammunition for this reinforcement is only shifted to the situation of evaluation which interacts with the semantic representation (called by him *lekton*) and produces an Austinian proposition.

This will not do. The main message communicated by the speaker will not conform to such restrictions. Recanati (2010: 134) attempts to spell out the advantages of his account over Relevance Theory, claiming that the latter is more 'syntactic' as 'it operates on representations and yields further representations' while his acknowledges the speech-act nature of the truth-conditional content and 'Gestaltist' compositionality predicated of them. But there is no such professed significant difference to be spotted between these two proposals. Both shun the final step to occasionalism that Common Sense and Respect for Speakers' Intuitions seem to necessitate but Traditionalism seems to prevent. To repeat, as I mentioned in the Introduction, the problem lies with his answer 'yes' in the view expressed below:

'Is semantic interpretation a matter of holistic guesswork (like the interpretation of kicks under the table), rather than an algorithmic, grammar-driven process as formal semanticists have claimed? Contextualism: Yes. Literalism: No.'

Recanati (2012a: 148)

The solution is, however, available and appealing. Recanati assumes that radical contextualism in which there is no local modulation but instead some form of still poorly understood interaction cannot be reconciled with the desideratum that semantic interpretation be grammar-driven. But, of course, it can, and it is.

There are two exceptions to this short-sightedness in assessing 'how far to go' in the direction of the speaker's primary intended message. One can be gleaned from Cappelen and Lepore's (2005a) version of minimalism, and the other is suggested in my Default Semantics and further spelled out in my proposed rejection of the explicit/implicit distinction (Jaszczolt 2009b and Chapters 2 and 3 below). To repeat, in keeping semantics relatively free from pragmatic 'contamination', Cappelen and Lepore recognize a fairly minimal content[38] and supplement it with the so-called *speech act pluralism*. On this account, there is no one, single 'what is said' that would deserve special attention as an interesting object of study. While this claim is very clearly contentious and goes against the intuitions and common sense that the speakers normally do mean one 'big thing' and in addition possibly some other 'smaller things', there is one positive outcome that emerges from this downplaying of what is said. Cappelen and Lepore (2005a: 204) claim that there is no theoretically interesting boundary between what is said and implicatures. As they say, 'sayings and implicatures are both on the pragmatic side of the divide' and '[t]he very same contextual features that determine the implicatures of an utterance influence what speakers say and assert by that utterance'. This is a very important observation. Strong resistance to it notwithstanding (see e.g. Korta and Perry 2007: 108–9, and the appeal to the authorities of Recanati, Searle, and Travis that they bring in), it is high

---

[38] See Section 1.3.1 above.

time to admit that the distinction between what is said and what is implicated *ought to be* blurred even further, only to place the boundary elsewhere.

Korta and Perry (p. 109) say that in making this claim the authors go 'against what everybody else accepts in pragmatics nowadays'. Considering the fact that in Default Semantics the primary meaning that is subjected to the truth-conditional analysis does not have to obey the constraints of the logical form of the uttered sentence, unlike the modulation or enrichment accounts of contextualist 'fixers', Korta and Perry's claim is plainly false. In Default Semantics, it is (22), not (21) or any of its 'fixed' versions that is the subject of truth-conditional analysis. A carefully worked out array of sources of information about meaning, and a carefully worked out system of processes of meaning construction, produce a representation that combines information provided by all those vehicles of meaning. Moreover, this representation is compositional, in the sense of pragmatic, Gestaltist compositionality proposed (albeit tentatively) by Recanati (2004) and further developed in Jaszczolt (2005a) and in Chapter 3 below. Default Semantics is precisely such a contextualist theory in which an *implicature can function as primary meaning and thereby as the object of the truth-conditional analysis*, while explicit meaning (that pertaining to the logical form of the uttered sentence, be it modulated or 'raw'), can on some occasions assume the status of secondary meaning. Instead of the explicit/implicit divide we have there the primary/secondary meaning divide that cuts across the explicit/implicit one, thereby giving due recognition to the facts that indirect method of conveying meaning is a common and natural one—and that it is so cross-culturally.

I give detailed support for this orthogonal division in Chapter 2. Evidence is not difficult to find. For example, Schneider (2009) demonstrated through a series of experiments that both in British English and in Russian, despite the different attitudes to indirectness prevailing in British and Russian linguistic communities, a substantial proportion of speech acts (over 60 per cent for English and over 70 per cent for Russian) that can (but need not) be understood as requests across a well-controlled array of scenarios trigger the response showing that the primary meaning, the intuitive what is said, is not affected by the similarity to the logical form of the uttered sentence.[39] As she says,

'[t]he results show that what matters for the type of proposition identified is the strength with which a certain interpretation is communicated by a particular requestive strategy rather than the fact that the speech act belongs to the broad category of direct, conventionally indirect, or non-conventionally indirect requests.'

Schneider (2009: iii)

---

[39] The instruction in the questionnaire read: 'Please read the dialogues given below. In the space provided after each dialogue, write your answer to the question: What is the main meaning communicated by the speaker in the underlined sentence?' In the Russian version of the questionnaire, 'main meaning' was rendered as 'osnovnoje značenje'. See Schneider 2009, Appendix B.

The question of the fundamental divide is an important one and it will dominate the presentation of Default Semantics in the remainder of this book. For now, we formulate it as: Is there a theoretically important distinction between what is said and implicatures? In view of the concerns flagged above, our answer, further developed in what follows, is a negative one.

Returning to the still unresolved question of the suitability of the label of TCP or TCS, this is what we have concluded so far. TCP is not an entirely inadequate label for the theory of the content delineated there in that this content includes a significant pragmatic component, viz. enrichments and other modulations of the logical form of the uttered sentence, dictated by the recognition of the speaker's intentions. At the same time, TCP is not the most suitable label in view of the fact that the content that is adopted for the purpose of the truth-conditional analysis, the *what is said* of Recanati's TCP and the *explicature* of Relevance Theory, fall short of recognizing the primary status of the contents that may radically depart from the uttered sentence, as in the example of an indirect speech act (21)–(22). They would relegate them to the status of a traditional implicature—a meaning that falls outside the truth-conditional content. It can be strongly communicated content, but an 'additional content' nevertheless. In this sense, the delineated content 'hovers' between semantics and pragmatics, justifying either label. On the other hand, I argued that adopting as the object of study a 'fixed' logical form is a problem for both TCS and TCP.

Bearing this in mind, we have the following two options:

Option 1
TCP ought to 'go the whole hog' and recognize indirect-speech-act content as the main proposition and the main object of study, while TCS should be minimal—as minimal as the principle of 'no contamination from pragmatics' allows.[40]

or

Option 2
TCP ought to be written off as a label, while TCS should 'go the whole hog' and adopt the primary intended content as its object of analysis, thereby taking the contextualist outlook to its methodological limits: the only meaning there is, and the only meaning that ought to be studied in semantic theory is the contextually immersed (and by assumption the contextually-generated) one. This is the meaning assigned to utterances in the course of linguistic interaction.

---

[40] See Sections 1.4.3 and mainly 4.2 below where I entertain the possibility that literal meaning is located in the concept of a Kaplanesque character.

It seems natural that if one adopts the contextualist outlook, one also buys into a certain ideology as far as the question 'What is meaning?' is concerned. Meaning, as understood by interactants in discourse, draws on many different sources and aspects of the situation: it is gleaned from the uttered sentence, but also from the physical surroundings, gestures, shared assumptions, shared general knowledge, and shared context-specific knowledge. Splitting the analysis of meaning according to sources does not result in any 'pure', more theoretically justifiable, conception of it and therefore it seems proper to reserve the label 'semantics', and thus, on our methodological assumption concerning the truth-conditional 'tool', also the label TCS, for a rich, multidimensional product. This is what Travis does in his 'occasion-sensitive' semantics. Travis's (1997, and other essays in his 2008) occasion-sensitivity of truth-conditional content is a good example of making the 'semantics' label compatible with the contextualist ideology. To repeat, according to Travis, truth values should be predicated of 'understandings' of words; semantics itself is occasion-sensitive. Imagine a maple tree whose naturally russet leaves are painted green. They are truthfully judged to be green by a photographer who is interested in the leaves' appearance, but equally they are also truthfully judged by a botanist to be russet. So, sentence (23) is true to the photographer but false to the botanist.

(23)   The leaves are green.
        (from Travis 1997: 111)

Travis (p. 113) concludes:

'...one *speaking* of [sentence (23)] may clearly state what is true, while another clearly states what is false. That can only be so if the semantics of [23] on some speakings of it is substantially richer than that fixed for it by the meanings of its constituents, and richer in different ways for different such speakings. So what [23] says on a speaking, of given leaves, etc., is not determined merely by what it, or its parts, mean.'

Travis adapts here the Strawsonian idea, also employed in Austin's (1962a) *Sense and Sensibilia*, according to which sentences cannot be true or false; instead, sentences as *uttered in certain specific circumstances* can be judged true or false. But again, this is not yet the logical limit to which contextualism can be pushed. Travis battles with the standard Fregean formulation of the principle of compositionality, according to which the meaning of the sentence is the meaning of its parts and the structure in which they are involved. That is why he is forced to claim that, to repeat, 'what [23] says on a speaking, of given leaves, etc., *is not determined merely by what it, or its parts, mean*'.[41] But all depends here on what understanding of 'parts' and 'mean' we adopt when we shift from the sentence to the utterance as the object of semantic analysis. The tension created in Frege's work by the compositionality principle on the

---

[41] My emphasis.

one hand and the context principle on the other seems thus to be alleviated by taking the context principle as the guiding directive.[42] Meaning has many sources and uses many different vehicles. Some of them pertain to linguistic units, some do not.

It is also important what ideology of words and concepts we adopt. One option is to say that 'words may have any of many semantics, compatibly with what they mean' (Travis 1997: 123) and rest with this claim, as Travis does, proposing that it does not make sense to think of 'a function from certain parameters of speaking to semantics, taking as value for each argument the semantics words would have where those values held'. He continues (p. 123):

'It thus also does not mean that there might be a precise theory, generating, for each semantics words might have, necessary and sufficient conditions for their having that. Still, we may describe how circumstances do their work.'

This conclusion may conform to our everyday experience with the use of language in discourse in that, indeed, the sources from which we grasp bits and pieces of the overall message are many and varied. But it is disappointing to see it proposed as the logical end of contextualism. Instead, it seems that it is worth trying to proceed from the very sources and vehicles that are active in meaning construction to developing an algorithm of how such discourse meaning is composed, starting with redefining the principle of semantic composition itself. Some of this work has already been done in formal dynamic approaches to meaning, some has been suggested by contextualists themselves—for example the 'Gestaltist', interactive compositionality in TCP (Recanati 2004) and the proposal of the *sources* of meaning information, and identification of *processes* that interact to compose such 'occasion-sensitive' meanings in my Default Semantics. The semantics of linguistic interaction presented in Chapter 2 is dedicated to developing and justifying TCS as proposed in Option 2 above, precisely by means of exploiting this multidimensionality of information about meaning in discourse.

At this point another pertinent question arises, namely to what extent it is justifiable to theorize in isolation about (a) the meaning that comes from the logical form as contrasted with the meaning that is affected by pragmatic processes of modulation; (b) the meaning that comes from the logical form as contrasted with the meaning pertaining to the main intended speech act, including indirect speech acts; and (c) the meaning that comes from the modulated proposition as contrasted with indirect but primary meaning such as that in (22). This question can only be fully answered on the basis of empirical data but there is already substantial evidence in the literature to suggest that interlocutors (at least those with fully developed pragmatic skills) don't seem to be aware of the minimal meaning but rather are aware of the main message intended by the speaker, irrespective of whether it corresponds to a bare logical form, a developed logical form of the uttered sentence, or to an

---

[42] See also Dummett 1973, 1981. Many thanks to Eros Corazza for his comments.

entirely different proposition altogether (see e.g. Nicolle and Clark 1999; Pitts 2005; Larson *et al.* 2009; Schneider 2009).[43]

Now, Recanati (2004, 2010) advocates a view of all-pervasive pragmatic enrichment (modulation). He claims that such contextual modulation is always present: 'there is no level of meaning which is both (i) propositional (truth-evaluable) and (ii) minimalist, that is, unaffected by top-down factors' (2004: 90). It has to be remembered that the defence of a non-minimalist level of meaning as the *only* level does not mean that the 'alterations' to the meaning as compared with that pertaining to the sentence alone cannot be absent on some occasions. Holding this view is perfectly compatible with admitting that, say, (24) is likely to have the intended meaning that matches the minimal one derived from the logical form of the sentence alone.

(24)   Fryderyk Chopin was born in 1810.

On the other hand, to repeat, it also has to be noted that contextualist accounts are not going far enough with the concept of what is said by confining it to 'fixing' the logical form (through enrichment or modulation). For example, (24), when used as an answer to (25A), produces very clearly primary meaning that amounts to something like (26). '→$_{PM}$' stands for 'communicates as primary meaning'.

(25)   A: Let us play some 18th century music, for example Fryderyk Chopin.
        B: Fryderyk Chopin was born in 1810!

(26)   →$_{PM}$ Chopin is not an 18th century composer.

Allowing primary speech acts such as (26) into the domain of a contextualist semantics is the final step that has to be taken to free theory of meaning from the artificial and insupportable constraints imposed by the emphasis on just one vehicle of meaning: the grammar of the sentence. This exorcizing of the syntactic constraint on the representation is the limit to which contextualism can, and ought to, be pushed.

Evasive solutions have also been suggested. One of the ways to avoid the question of the relevant content is to think up *many different kinds of content* and make each of them fit a different bill. This is what Perry (2001a) and Korta and Perry (2011) suggest. Sitting on the fence between minimalism and contextualism, Korta and Perry offer what they call a 'refined semantic content' which is founded on the utterance alone and which, for example for (27), amounts to (28).

(27)   I've invited everyone.

(28)   ∃X ∃y (the speaker of [27] is talking about X & the speaker of [27] is talking about y & the speaker of [27] has invited everyone in X to y).

(adapted from Korta and Perry 2011: 144–5)

---

[43] See also Noveck 2001, 2004; Papafragou and Musolino 2003; Chierchia *et al.* 2004 on developmental studies, the latter on a grammar-based explanation of some implicatures.

The *raison d'être* for this kind of content is, as they say, to have a proposition that is derived from the semantics of the words and the structure, and in this sense minimal, and at the same time true. The speaker could have chosen to utter (29) instead, which would also have been true.

(29)   I've invited everyone in our building to our holiday party.
         (from Korta and Perry 2011: 145)

The difference lies in the source of information: when the latter comes from the context, there is a significant difference between the *reflexive*, utterance-bound content, and the *referential*, contextually resolved content. The first one, however, is already 'refined' by adding certain aspects of the situation which come from the outlook they call 'critical pragmatics': there are aspects of the situation that make their way into the content of the first type. 'Fixing' galore.

This is, of course, an intelligently dressed version of Perry's early idea of inserting some constituents into the logical form for which we have only metaphysical (or, now also, presumably, cultural and epistemological) arguments in support: when it rains, it has to rain *somewhere* (*pace* some convoluted construals of 'raining in principle'); when we invite someone, we invite them *to something*. It suffers from the same old problem of circularity well pointed out by Recanati (1989): we have to know what to elaborate on in the sentence before the context is consulted. Since it is not only metaphysics that can be independently referred to (as in 'rain must take place at a location') but also cultural, social, and other standard practices, it is difficult to see how any confines can be placed on these elaborations to prevent circularity. Korta and Perry refer here to a rather murky concept of 'roles'. However, until the roles come with a principle and possibly a classification of what needs to be added to the logical form of the sentence and what need not, we are still in deep waters. It seems to me that such a classification is possible in principle, with the help of language structure, metaphysics, sociology, and other disciplinary insights. But no one has provided it as yet. On the other hand, putting all this information into *sources* of meaning rather than types of content that has been opted for in Default Semantics (see Section 2.2.1) seems to do the trick.

Our critical discussion of the state of the art and the future prospects of contextualism has been, by necessity, somewhat fragmentary. The ideology of pragmaticizing the truth-conditional content, be it in TCS or TCP, has engaged many great minds and has spanned many topics. Some of the views do not easily yield to classification as minimalist or contextualist but instead pave a way towards significant convergence and reconciliation. This is the topic to which I now turn.

1.3.3 *Some points of convergence*

The logical space between (i) extensive top-down modulation of contextualists (i.e. modulation that is not dictated by morphosyntax) and (ii) the minimal, sentence-based meaning of minimalists is not void. Different views fill the space and they differ not only with respect to the degree of pragmatic intrusion into the truth-conditional representation but also on the question of the provenance of this intrusion, and thereby on the proposed explanation of it. For example, Stanley proposes that the logical form contains variables that are to be filled in order to obtain the intuitively plausible truth conditions. There is such a slot for the location in (30) and for the domain of quantification in (31) (see Stanley 2000, 2002; Stanley and Szabó 2000, and other essays in Stanley 2007).

(30)   It is raining [in location l].

(31)   Every bottle [in the interlocutors' common perceptual space s] is empty.

The exact location of such a variable in the logical form is then carefully worked out in order to avoid the pitfalls of improbable interpretations or compromising compositionality. This view shares the features of contextualist and of minimalist outlooks. It is contextualist in that it admits more into the truth conditions than what the words and grammar produce; on the other hand, since the additions are attributable to the logical form, it is minimalist at the same time: there are no free, unrestricted, pragmatic rides within the truth-conditional domain. Like free-enrichment contextualists, indexicalists are, on my classification, 'fixers': logical form is tampered with in a way that produces the required results.

    This solution owes its origin to the concept of *hidden indices* (Schiffer 1977, 1992; Crimmins and Perry 1989) and *unarticulated constituents* proposed by Perry (1986). According to Perry, the meaning of the sentence (30), in virtue of sheer metaphysics, requires a specification of a location: it is a metaphysical fact that when it rains, it rains *somewhere*. This missing constituent is 'unarticulated', in the common sense of the term, but it is there. As decades passed by, the debate over unarticulated constituents has led to the distortion of the concept itself. According to Stanley, for example, this constituent, albeit physically not articulated by the speaker, is 'articulated', present on the level of the logical form. Recanati denies such presence, and, in fact, he is sceptical about the need for such constituents *tout court* in virtue of the fact that modulation is a local process, triggered not on the level of the entire sentence but rather on the level of its parts. As he now suggests (2007, 2010), the *what is said*, or *lekton*, is fully articulated; it is only the situation of evaluation with which it is paired that may be 'unarticulated' in some respects. As a result, unarticulated constituents belong to the lekton-situation pair, jointly equated with what is known as the Austinian proposition to which I return below.

    Now, it has to be remembered that unarticulated constituents are, as Perry suggests, those elements of the semantic representation that cannot be traced to the syntactic structure of the sentence. This definition, however, is of little help. Syntactic structure can be associated with sentences with a significant freedom and originality, depending on the theory and assumptions. Categories that are not visible on the surface but firmly present in the syntactic representation are no strangers to various generative syntactic accounts, and their number and diversity grows as counterexamples to the currently held view emerge. In order to 'save' one's favourite syntactic theory, one often has to be prepared to swallow an increasing number of invisible components of syntactic structure, and thereby (where applicable) tamper more and more with the metaphysics. Sennet (2011), for example, tentatively suggests that some form of a syntactic explanation of unarticulated constituents may be the least unpalatable option after all. In Chapters 3 and 4 we will see that his intuition is a well-supported one but for a very different reason, namely that the notion of the grammar has to be rethought in the context of the discussion of the linguistic vis-à-vis conceptual representation. In brief, since the sources from which the content intended by the speaker can be gleaned are so diverse and so intertwined in interaction, then, can we still justify the separation of the semantic and the conceptual? If not, then what is the syntactic representation a representation of? The issue of semantic and conceptual structure will occupy us considerably throughout the discussion and most immediately in Sections 1.5.4 and 2.1 below.

Next, the 'middle' position focuses on the additions to the meaning that can be gleaned from the sentence alone. It is occupied by those for whom interesting aspects of the 'pragmatics in the semantics' are the indexical ones. Kaplan (1989a) employs context to fix the referent of indexical expressions which, without such fixing, have a non-fixed *linguistic meaning* (character), such as the meaning 'third-person singular masculine pronoun' or 'contextually salient male' for 'he'. Next, he uses context to take a sentence with the now fixed determinants of its content through the standard Truth-Conditional Semantics: a mapping from circumstances of evaluation to extensions. Indexical expressions have the specific property that their content becomes fixed: once the reference of 'he', 'I', 'here', or 'now' is resolved for a particular act of communication, it does not vary with circumstances of evaluation. To put it crudely, for indexical expressions, unlike for non-indexicals, there is, in a sense, no need to apply the truth-conditional semantic tool of 'propositions being functions from possible words to truth values' in order to provide their meaning.

Kaplan's view has many various applications and yields itself to various extensions due to the open-ended nature of his notion of context, understood as an *index,* and a set of parameters. For Kaplan (1989a) context provides all the necessary parameters for semantics. The basic ones are those of the agent, time, location, and world, but new parameters can be added as required.[44] So, on the one hand it fits with propositional minimalists in that it advocates fairly minimal semantics on which the content of the indexicals has to become fixed. Cappelen and Lepore (on the 2005a version) and Borg offer a solution along the same lines, extending the set of context-

---

[44] See Section 4.2.

dependent expressions. But, on the other hand, the context-dependence is not strictly delimited. When we have to subject a difficult scenario to the theory, such as Travis's painted leaves scenario, Kaplan's theory can be made to deliver intuitively plausible truth conditions.[45] As such, it is not very minimalist about meaning after all, while remaining true to minimalism as far as the constituents of the propositional representation are concerned.

Stalnaker's two-dimensional semantics can be viewed as yet another such middle view. While Kaplan's two-dimensional semantics distinguishes linguistic meanings (characters, for example 'I' meaning the speaker) and contents (functions from circumstances of evaluation to extensions), Stalnaker's (1978, 2011) two-dimensional semantics focuses on intentions and intention recognition. For Stalnaker, an utterance (assertion) has the purpose of changing the set of presuppositions of the participants. His semantics explains the fact that an utterance with indexical terms can be regarded as true or as false by different interlocutors. For example, (32), uttered by Alf to the audience consisting of Beth and Caesar, can be understood by Beth as referring to Beth and by Caesar as referring to Caesar. In addition, Beth may 'agree' that she is wrong, while Alf may think that Beth is not wrong. In fact, Alf intended to refer to Caesar who, according to him, is indeed wrong.

(32)   You are wrong.

This scenario provides a dimension of *what is said* according to different participants. It also exhibits another dimension of what the participants *believe* (spelled out as different possible worlds). Putting the two dimensions together, we obtain a concept of, so to speak, *whatever is, according to various participants, said by the speaker, evaluated in the contexts of various participants' beliefs*. This is what Stalnaker calls a *propositional concept*. The matrix so construed produces a kind of proposition that can be placed between our contextualist and minimalist polar ends of the debate. Stalnaker calls it a *diagonal proposition*: with standard presuppositions and assumptions of cooperation in place, 'whatever is said by the speaker (is true)'.

These accounts of indexical expressions and indexical thoughts clearly demonstrate that there are several intertwined problems concerning the semantics/pragmatics boundary disputes that cannot be easily teased apart. One is the attempt to delimit semantics vis-à-vis pragmatics as a sub-discipline with its own object of study and research methods, and that is why, for example, in Borg's minimal semantics we have an emphasis on the semantic module. Another is to compare and contrast how pragmatic processes work when they are 'hooked onto', so to speak, some places or

---

[45]   See Predelli 2005a, b for an in-depth analysis of Travis's painted leaves puzzle in a neo-Kaplanesque framework, also discussed below in Section 1.4.3.

constituents in the structure of the sentence vis à-vis those that are not attached in this way. In other words, we can be interested in how far an indexical account of meaning can take us, or we can keep indexicality to the minimum, or even dispose of it in the semantics *tout court*. In what follows, in Default Semantics, we shall make a rather extensive use of indexicality, namely push it to its logical limits by extending and redefining the concept of Kaplan's linguistic meaning (the character) in such a way that what counts as an indexical expression will be dictated by the dynamic nature of discourse and as a result will emerge at the forefront of attention for a semantics of linguistic interaction. Suffice it to flag that the indexical/non-indexical distinction will prove to be much more difficult to justify for natural language systems than philosophers of language have led us to believe. I return to the idea briefly in Section 1.4 before developing it fully in Chapter 4.

1.4 Literal meaning: An orthogonal issue?

Redrawing of the boundaries between (i) semantics and pragmatics, (ii) truth-conditional and non-truth-conditional content, and (iii) explicit and implicit meaning is bound to affect the dispute concerning (iv) the literal/non-literal distinction. 'Literal' seems to be a conceptually clear-cut label when we juxtapose it with what has traditionally been regarded as figurative language use. But since 'figurative' use has long been revindicated as equally suitable for the purpose of directly expressing intended content as 'non-figurative' use (Sperber and Wilson 1995), there is a need to bring the term in line with the debates in (i)–(iii). This can proceed in either of the following two directions. Either (a) 'literal' is anchored to the primary, most suitable natural language counterpart of a speaker's thought and 'non-literal' collects the departures from such a fixed relationship, or (b) 'literal' remains close to the customary sense but does not allow for any context-driven additions, so it is akin to what we can call linguistic meaning. Needless to say, contextualists ought to opt for the first route, while true minimalists ought to opt for the latter. To sum up, the question can be formulated as follows: What is the role of the concept of literal meaning in the minimalism/contextualism debates? In what follows, I discuss the contextualists' muddying of the 'literal', concluding that what they are looking for is an altogether different concept that is in need of an altogether different label, and move on to spelling out the requirements for a simple, minimalist definition.

1.4.1 The 'literal' confounded

In contextualism, the object of study is the proposition intended by the speaker which, normally, when all goes well with the recovery of the speaker's intentions, is also the proposition that is recovered by the addressee. Alternatively, one could assume that the object of study is the proposition recovered by the addressee which, normally, when all goes well with the recovery of the speaker's intentions, is also the proposition that is intended by the speaker. Truth-conditional content is precisely such intentional content. Now, in order to make these theoretical assumptions compatible with the fact that word meaning is in itself flexible, perhaps even as flexible as Wittgenstein's (1953) meaning eliminativism suggests, one has to adjust the idea of literalness in language. A metaphorical expression is on some occasions the best way to capture the speaker's intended message. Then, arguably, it is the most 'literal', so to speak, externalization of the speaker's thought. This shift of the concept of literalness is evident in Relevance Theory research (see e.g. Carston 2002: 340). It reaches its surreal apex in Recanati's (2004, Chapter 5) *Literal Meaning* where the entire taxonomy of the senses of 'literal' is devised: we have *t*(ype)-literalness, *m* (inimal-departure)-literalness,[46] and *p*(rimary)-literalness.[47] For example, metaphorical expressions are *p*-literal in that their main, primary meaning is indeed the metaphorical one; there is no non-literalness in their use in this sense. Next, only a subset of metaphors counts as *figurative* language use. Within the subclass of *p*-literal we have meanings that are conscious or unconscious, deliberate or automatic, or noticeable or typical. The conscious, deliberate and noticeable alteration of the standard sense is necessary for a meaning to be called figurative. So, the latter three distinctions pertain to a different classificatory dimension within the *p*-literal category.

Clearly, something has gone awry if one feels compelled to split the intuitively simple concept of literalness into such a mind-boggling taxonomy, and, to make things worse, also subsume 'customary non-literal' under a sub-type of 'literal'. Surely, the search for the cognitive reality of the unit of the truth-conditional analysis which is the leading directive for contextualists cannot require such conceptual contortions and sacrifices of common sense. Where the reasoning that leads to the distinctions in the typology is faultless while the resulting theoretical labels end up out of kilter, one has to address the issue of the source of the trouble.

---

[46] The criterion for an *m*-non-literal meaning seems to be that the meaning cannot be recovered through the conventions of the language. For example, the referent of an indexical such as 'I' is recoverable through a convention of the English language and therefore the meaning 'Kasia' for 'I' constitutes only a minimal departure and is *m*-literal (but *t*-non-literal as it involves context). An indirect, context-triggered speech act constitutes a non-minimal departure.

[47] A meaning is *p*-literal when it is not secondary, that is, when it is not an implicature recovered from some other proposition. For example, (9)–(11) repeated below represent *p*-literal (but *m*-non-literal) meanings:

(9) Mary tripped Tom *and* ($\rightarrow_E$ *and as a result*) he fell.

(10) You can have beef *or* chicken ($\rightarrow_E$ *but not both*).

(11) I will tell you who did it *if* ($\rightarrow_E$ *if and only if*) you promise not to tell anyone.

1.4.2 Why 'literal' can't be restored

It seems that the problem is this. Recanati's taxonomy is in itself perfectly fine; it follows the carefully worked out and widely accepted distinctions such as that between grammar-driven and free enrichment, or automatic and conscious enrichment. The problem lies in superimposing the distinctions onto the concept of literalness itself. Let us first take the relevance-theoretic proposal of fixing literalness to thoughts. Carston (2002: 340) discusses what she calls an 'apparent paradox' whereby 'metaphorical (and other loose) uses are no less *literal* interpretations of speakers' thoughts than standard literal uses are'. This is of course fine on the proviso that we define literalness as she does, and underwrite it using thoughts as she does. But let us see how this, let us call it *r*(elevance)-literalness, fares with *c*(ommon-sense) literalness. In example (19), adapted below as (33a) and (33b), the qualifier 'literally' has been added as a test.

(33a)   Tom is a real fox ($\rightarrow_E$ FOX*), literally. He always sniffs ($\rightarrow_E$ SNIFFS*) a bargain.

(33b)   Tom is a real fox ($\rightarrow_E$ FOX*), he always sniffs ($\rightarrow_E$ SNIFFS*) a bargain, literally.

The result is not discouraging at all. What is happening here seems to be the shift in the sense of 'literally' itself—or, as meaning eliminativists would have it, not a shift, because there is nothing to 'shift from' on that account, but contextual endowment of meaning that makes 'literally' itself, so to speak, non-literal. But while this is indeed how language is used in conversation (although a sound empirical study using a good corpus, such as for example the GB component of the International Corpus of English (ICE-GB), would be very useful here), there is no methodologically justified reason to proceed from such uses to redefining 'literal' itself. One option would be in fact to dump it as a theoretical label, in view of the fact that it is so context-dependent itself and, in principle, triggers an infinite regress when used as a theoretical term. This would be a solution that is in line with meaning eliminativism.

1.4.3   ...or can it?

Other solutions involve rescuing literalness in some form or other. For example, a methodologically justified option would be to say that thoughts are indeed pegged on some primary contents, expressed propositions, main meanings, intuitively truth-conditional representations, and the like, but literalness is a label that has nothing in common with the theoretical decision to adopt 'rich', contextualist truth-conditional content and thereby to reject lexical concepts and logical forms of uttered sentences as primary indicators of truth-conditional content. The claim is that literalness is truly orthogonal to the debate. 'Fox' is literally an animal belonging to the biological family *canidae*, no matter whether this literal meaning is activated in the process of utterance interpretation or not. This is the minimalist option for literalness that is further pursued below.

Another possibility is offered by the so-called *salient meanings.*[48] There is strong experimental evidence that lexical meanings that are incompatible with the intended content but nevertheless are salient to the interlocutors are indeed activated. These salient meanings can themselves be 'literal' in the standard sense or 'non-literal' (Giora, e.g. 2003, 2012; Peleg and Giora 2011). For this purpose we have to examine two observations by Giora:

'Though literal meanings tend to be highly salient, their literality is not a component of salience. The criterion or threshold a meaning has to reach to be considered salient is related only to its accessibility in memory due to such factors as frequency of use or experiential familiarity.'

Giora (2003: 33)

and

'...the evidence (...) shows that familiar instances of metaphor and irony activated their salient (figurative and literal) meanings initially, regardless of contextual information.'

Giora (2003: 140)

Granting that the evidence accumulated in support of these claims is sufficiently robust, it seems that the concept of salience that largely (but not completely) overlaps with that of literalness as far as the sets of selected meanings are concerned, is of much more use for a theory of utterance meaning than the concept of literalness itself. One interesting option would be to use this empirical evidence and redefine 'literal' in terms of 'salient': a speaker means something 'literally', the speaker's meaning is 'literal' *not* because it is fixed to the speaker's thought, and neither is it literal because it is fixed by the systems of the language's lexicon and grammar. Instead, it is literal because it is salient, automatically activated (albeit activated to a greater or lesser degree, in accordance with Giora's (2003) Graded Salience Hypothesis), and thereby on the level of language description it *appears literal in the natural sense of the term.*

It seems that redefining salience in terms of literalness (and vice versa) has significant methodological advantages. Salience is a matter of degree—a matter of activation of a certain context-free meaning in certain contexts. Literalness, on the other hand, is a non-gradable, one-or-nothing label that can capture the standard, salient, default meaning, where 'default' is understood as the most obvious, automatically attained meaning for the speaker and for the context, as defined in my Default Semantics (Jaszczolt 2005a, 2010, and especially 2011). Salient meanings are,

---

[48] Salient meanings are the topic of Section 3.1 below.

or at least should be, of fundamental importance for contextualist approaches and I return to this topic at length in Chapter 3.

To conclude, it seems that the label that contextualists have been looking for may not be the label 'literal' after all. The objective has been to capture the idea that abstracted meaning, meaning as defined with relation to language system and in isolation from its use in discourse, has little (or no) role to play in language processing and thereby in a theory of language use. But manipulating the term 'literal' may not be the best way to capture this idea. What contextualists have been looking for is an altogether different concept that is in need of an altogether different label. 'Salient' may be able to fulfil this role, and so may 'primary', 'automatic', 'default' (after a careful removal of the patina of system-based, Levinson-style defaults). This remains to be decided as experimenting and theorizing progress. The conclusion so far has been a reductive one: 'literal' has to be either exorcized (replaced with salience) or reinstated in its traditional sense. The latter option is the one to which we now turn.

The outcome of the above reasoning is that literalness should be tied either to (i) salience or, if such exists, to (ii) some minimal meaning that is context-independent and triggered by the language system alone. The best locus for such minimal literalness in option (ii) seems to be Kaplan's character discussed in earlier sections. To repeat, according to Kaplan, indexicals have 'linguistic meanings' ('characters') that have to undergo contextual specification before a truth-conditional semantic analysis (a function from circumstances of evaluation to truth values) endows them with content. On the other hand, non-indexicals undergo no such contextual fixing. In (34), 'he' has a context-independent aspect of the meaning, which is that of the third-person singular masculine pronoun. This meaning is its character—a function from possible contexts to contents.

(34)   He is the greatest novelist who has ever lived.

In the first dimension, the pronoun 'he' has to be assigned a contextually appropriate, actual referent. The second, counterfactual, dimension, is for assigning content, in the standard way, as a function from circumstances of evaluation to truth values.[49] Non-indexicals, on the other hand, such as 'novelist', have a 'fixed' character; all contexts produce the same content. This means that if 'novelist' can adopt different referents, this is so not because of the context understood as a filler for an indexical expression as above but because of *different ways the world might have been*, or different *circumstances of evaluation* leading to different *extensions*. Content (*intension*) is a function from such circumstances of evaluation (akin to possible worlds, possible scenarios) to extensions.

---

[49] On the two dimensions see also Chalmers 2006; Brogaard 2012 and Jaszczolt 2012c.

Now, the concept of a character is a possible locus for our literalness in that character is a 'clean-cut', 'language-only' dimension of meaning that, on its standard, original version, does not allow for any contextual admixture. Context contributes to two-dimensional semantics in two different ways but neither of these ways blurs the definition of the character.[50] First, characters of indexicals require contextual resolution but this resolution is not part of the concept of the character itself; characters of non-indexicals are allegedly fixed and contexts do not figure in them at all; other expressions such as proper names require a disambiguation by context but this disambiguation is (most likely) pre-semantic, so the context used in this way does not blur the character either. Second, context is also understood as the circumstances of evaluation (in the second, counterfactual dimension) but it is obvious that this role of context has no effect on the clear-cut concept of a character either.

It remains to explain what exactly it would mean for literalness to be located in characters. An indexical expression 'he' *literally* means something to the effect 'a contextually salient male'; 'bank' corresponds to two characters, so it has two *literal* meanings, and which of the two is relevant in the context at hand is resolved pre-semantically (Kaplan 1989a); 'novelist', a non-indexical term, has a fixed character and a literal meaning.

But we are moving too fast: we have ring-fenced 'literal' from contextual contamination but we have not defined it. If we were to follow Kaplan's thread all the way through, we would now move to the second dimension of his semantics and say that literal meaning equals the content: the function from circumstances of evaluation to extensions. This, however, opens up another option. We have just rejected the possibility that 'literal' means 'most suitable for representing the thought' but now we have a not dissimilar possibility elsewhere, namely that the circumstances of evaluation can include scenarios on which the word or the complex expression is used in a non-standard way. And there is a very good reason why it would not be prudent to reject this possibility; this reason is provided by the empirical fact that in discourse there is no boundary between literal and non-literal when we try to find it in the remits of the boundaries between circumstances of evaluation. Let us take the example of Travis's (1997) 'painted leaves' scenarios discussed earlier. For example, let us assess a point of evaluation or perspective from which a sentence is to be judged as true or false. Russet leaves of a maple tree that are painted green are judged to be green by a photographer (producing a true statement), but they are also truthfully judged by a botanist to be russet. This produces an apparent problem with a mismatch between possible worlds and truth values: in one and the same possible world the sentence can be judged to be true or false by different agents. Predelli (2005a, b) offers an explanation in terms of so-called *applications*, functions that add

---

[50] See Kaplan 1989b on context as a set of parameters and Jaszczolt 2012b, c for a discussion.

points of evaluation to the standard conditions the world would have to fulfil for the sentence/utterance to be true. But this is not the end of the difficulty. For example, one and the same sentence can be judged true by one and the same speaker when taken ironically, and false when taken non-ironically, viz. (35).

(35)   Tom is a real genius.

Analogously, and importantly for the issue at hand, one and the same sentence can be judged true when taken metaphorically and false when taken non-metaphorically, viz. (36).

(36)   Tom's heart is made of pure gold.

It appears that we would have to tweak the circumstances of evaluation *ad libitum* in order to account for such contributions to content. This would account for the intuition that there are salient uses that are context-dependent and not 'literal' in the sense of being language-system-dependent. But if we want to be true to our earlier methodological option of uncontaminated, context-free meanings, that is if we do not want to be smuggling in context through the back door, we would have to resort to a data-based, empirical account; we would have to base the account on an adequate database of language use and form the definition of the content on the basis of (i) the fixed characters of non-indexicals, supplemented with (ii) circumstances of evaluation that allow for points of view, points of evaluation, or perspectives à la Predelli.

Points of evaluation constitute the essential component that adds information on how the situation is to be looked at. Predelli formalizes it as follows:

'... given a representation of z by means of the clause-index pair $<s,i>$ and the application a, z is true with respect to worldly conditions w iff $j(a(w)) = $ truth, where j is the intension associated by [an interpretive system] S with $<s,i>$.'

Predelli (2005a: 366)

This solution avoids the pitfalls of the relatively unrestricted 'ad-hocness' of concept formation of Relevance Theory and the radical unrestricted 'ad-hocness' of concept formation of meaning eliminativism à la late Wittgenstein. Literalness could still be located in the character, with the outcome that 'literal' will in effect mean 'salient for the context' because circumstances of evaluation are relaxed in such a way as to accommodate points of view of the evaluators.[51]

---

[51]   For a very different application of Kaplan's theory to metaphor see Stern 2000:

'Just as Kaplan invented "Dthat [Φ]" to lexically represent the demonstrative interpretation of an arbitrary definite description Φ, I shall now create an analogue "Mthat [Φ]" to lexically represent the metaphorical interpretation of an arbitrary (literal) expression Φ.'

Stern (2000: 106)

An alternative option of relaxing literal meaning while locating it in the character is offered in my so-called 'fluid characters' (Jaszczolt 2012c and Section 4.2 below). I suggest there that Kaplan's two-dimensional approach be 'pragmaticized' so as to acknowledge the fact that in utterance processing agents have relative freedom in 'forming' characters. As the process of interpretation progresses incrementally, the addressee makes inferences using as the so-called 'inferential base' units that are not necessarily words or phrases but can correspond to constructions of very different lengths, depending on a multitude of factors that sum up to the relevant background information. For example, using a notorious case of scalar inference, (37) can trigger inferences (or automatic meaning assignment) immediately after hearing 'some', or after 'some people' has been heard, or 'some people say', or sometimes on the basis of the entire sentence.

(37)   Some people say that you are arrogant.

Analogously, different expressions can correspond to the character, depending on the length and constitution of such an inferential base. Such fluid characters are also a potential locus for literalness.

The fact is, of course, that when we pragmaticize the character in a way that makes it context-dependent, and possibly even, somewhat contrary to Kaplan's initial idea, intention-recovery-dependent,[52] we, so to speak, begin with context-dependence and only ban it within the two-dimensional approach when the context has already had its say. All in all, be that as it may, contextualism will have to get in through a back door, window, or otherwise.

1.5 Rethinking the contextualist outlook

There is no doubt that contextualism, possibly even in its most radical form of occasionalism, offers the most language-user-friendly and the most intuitively plausible construal of meaning. It is the most appropriate orientation for the search for the semantics of linguistic interaction. The question is, when we assume that this psychological plausibility is what a theory of meaning should follow as its guiding star, how far can we take it in the direction of reflecting the conceptual representation, at the same time not losing sight of what we would like to delimit as 'natural language meaning'? This is a difficult and multi-faceted question, some of the aspects of which are attended to in what follows.

---

[52] But see Kaplan 1989b and a discussion in Jaszczolt 2012c on the role of directing intentions of demonstratives. The scope of application of Kaplan's directing intentions is, however, open to informed speculations.

1.5.1 *The systematicity issue*

The question of the logical limits of contextualism, to which my answer was to part company with the idea that grammar dictates the pragmatic modulations of the main proposition under investigation (and thereby with the *what is said* or *explicature* as understood by Recanati and relevance theorists respectively), can legitimately be said to be at the forefront of current discussions. Recanati explicitly disagrees that the limits can be pushed so far as to establish the indirectly communicated proposition as the main object of study. He appeals here to the criterion of systematicity. I repeat the quotation of the offending passage again:

'Is semantic interpretation a matter of holistic guesswork (like the interpretation of kicks under the table), rather than an algorithmic, grammar-driven process as formal semanticists have claimed? Contextualism: Yes. Literalism: No.

On that issue I am happy to part company with the most radical contextualists—the 'sceptics' who would go for the holistic guesswork answer (assuming they exist, which I doubt). Like Stanley and the formal semanticists, I maintain that semantic interpretation is grammar-driven.'

Recanati (2012a: 148)

However, he only disagrees with the putative 'most radical contextualists' because he assumes that pushing the limits that far would indeed amount to a 'holistic guess-work'. We have found this assumption somewhat short-sighted. Instead of assuming that one of the dimensions of meaning, namely the grammar of the uttered sentence, has a privileged role to play in order to provide the backbone for a systematic composition, we assume that all dimensions of meaning, that is, all dimensions that contribute to the truth-conditional content on this radical version of context-ualism, should be treated on an equal footing. Indeed, the onus of proof seems to lie with those who, like the 'fixers', try to impose the privileged status on one of the aspects of meaning or one of the sources of information. Instead, the lexicon, grammar, recognition of intentions, recognition of goals and situation types, social and cultural conventions, general (including scientific) knowledge, and other sources of contributing information are all equally important in communication and thus are equally important for representing meaning in communication. The next step is an important one: *assuming this equality of dimensions does not entail the need to give up systematicity*. It simply entails that the algorithmic process has to be sought else-where, on the level of the *interaction* of these dimensions. This is how systematicity and pushing the boundaries of contextualism can both be maintained, and this is what has been attempted in Default Semantics and further justified throughout this more philosophical discussion of the foundations of a semantics of linguistic inter-action in what follows.

Surprisingly, Recanati was in fact not far off such an interactive account. He says (2012a: 148):

'Even though free pragmatic processes, i.e. pragmatic processes that are not mandated by the standing meaning of any expression in the sentence, are allowed to enter into the determination of truth-conditional content, still, in the framework I have sketched, they *come into the picture as part of the compositional machinery.* Semantic interpretation remains *grammar-driven* even if, in the course of semantic interpretation, semantics is appealed to not only to assign contextual values to indexicals and free variables but also to freely modulate the senses of the constituents in a top-down manner.'

These claims, unlike the previous quotation, are in fact neutral on the issue of the type and location for compositionality. They could possibly be reconciled with the view on which compositionality of meaning has to be, like on Default Semantics, 'kicked up' to the level of the merger of information about meaning that comes from different sources. The view on grammar, however, has to be adjusted. We seem to be one step here from admitting that grammar is not sentence grammar; it is not the grammar of linguistic strings, but instead, in a more cognitivist fashion, a conceptual grammar, a grammar of mental representations. Various degrees of convergence between post-Griceans and cognitive semanticists notwithstanding, no one so far in the contextualist camp has gone as far as to exorcize the clearly inadequate view of sentence grammar in favour of the cognitively adequate, albeit admittedly more challenging to harness, grammar of mental representations. It is, however, high time to concede to the 'opposition'[53] and take from the proponents of conceptual structures what seems useful, at the same time reserving the right to search for formalisms and algorithms at the level *not* of the language, but of the interaction of the linguistic and non-linguistic dimensions of meaning of acts of communication. This is how late Wittgenstein, Montague, Grice, and their intellectual descendants are *all* partly right after all.

1.5.2 Salience-Based Contextualism

The choices concerning the truth-conditional semantic content begin with morphemes and words—the smallest units, atoms of meaning, and the way they are described and explained. If words had clear, satisfactory definitions, or if they corresponded to clearly delineable concepts, or else if they had clear, satisfactory metaphysical correlates in the real world, the choices concerning the truth-conditional semantic content would begin with larger units because there would be little to debate as regards word meaning (See Section 4.1). The mental lexicon would be clear-cut: when the speaker utters the word *fox*, the entry for the concept FOX and for the class of objects called 'fox' would be activated. But the word-concept-referent relations are not that clear. Moreover, there is all-pervasive evidence that literal meaning is not always the salient one, as was discussed in Section 1.4.3. It is not

---

[53] See Section 2.1.2.

always activated prior to and in preference to some culturally well-entrenched figurative meaning, on the common-sense definition of 'literal' and 'figurative'.

The full extent of this phenomenon is still to be investigated but extant evidence is compelling. In view of this indubitable fact about literalness, the rational option seems to be to admit that the extent to which word meaning is shaped in the context of use is significant for the description and explanation in lexical semantics. In other words, a theory of word meaning has to acknowledge the fact of the gross contextual variation and instead of the search for what may prove to be the Holy Grail, namely the Word Meaning in Abstraction, it should make the most of the fact that language users are guided by past experiences of discourse they were engaged in; they have the memory of the use of a word and this memory guides them in the word selection for the situation at hand. Also, they co-construct the meaning as conversation unfolds.[54] The question is, do we have to resort to meaning eliminativism to account for this dynamism and flexibility of the lexicon? While the onus of proof lies with those who search for the abstraction and systematic meaning, theoretical and methodological considerations are on the side of those who abandon such a search and settle for language as a socio-cultural phenomenon, formed and reformed in use. But 'eliminativism' is too strong a label, bearing in mind that words and structures come with salient, automatically retrieved, albeit sometimes irrelevant, meanings.[55] This is therefore the theoretical choice we are going to make in our semantics of linguistic interaction as pursued in Default Semantics: the form of contextualism adopted can be called *Salience-Based Contextualism*.

Salience-Based Contextualism:

Words and structures come with salient, automatically retrieved, albeit sometimes irrelevant, meanings. This is guaranteed by the facts that language is (i) a socio-cultural phenomenon, formed and reformed in use, as well as (ii) a cognitive phenomenon that is governed by, and restricted by, the structure and operations of the brain.

I return to a detailed discussion of salience and defaults in Chapter 3, while the consequences for lexical semantics are further explored throughout Chapter 4.

1.5.3 Whose meaning?

Another dimension of these debates is that of production vis-à-vis comprehension. Paul Grice was interested in *implicature*, by which he meant the *process* by which speakers convey more than what is said; they convey the *implicata*. During the four decades that followed the publication of the seminal 'Logic and conversation' (Grice

---

[54] See Clark 1996.
[55] See also Gärdenfors 2014a, b on the social aspects of the construction of meaning and their conceptual representation.

1975), 'implicature' seems to have undergone a tacit reanalysis from denoting the process to denoting its product, while the term 'implicatum' (plural: 'implicata') has largely gone out of pragmatic parlance.[56] This slight semantic shift notwithstanding, the fact remains that Grice was interested in intentions and intended meaning: the meaning as it is intended by an average speaker who is governed by rational principles of cooperative language use. On the other hand, relevance theorists (Sperber and Wilson 1995, 2012) focus on the product of utterance interpretation: a communicative intention and an informative intention embedded in it are fulfilled when they lead to communicating something. It is this message, notably the interpretation of the utterance, that is arrived at by the addressee with the help of the tacitly operating principle of effectiveness and economy, that is the object of study.

Does it mean that we are facing a choice here as to *whose meaning* the theory is to model: the speaker's or the addressee's? Not exactly. Grice's interests were philosophical ones; he was not engaged with the psychological issues to do with utterance processing, with all the concomitant problems of miscommunication, communication breakdown, and so forth. He saw human conversational agents as rational beings who normally succeed in communicating their intentions without pitfalls, and it is precisely the general mechanisms that allow them to do so that were of interest to him and constitute the foundation of his normative theory. So, it would be misrepresenting his views and his interests to say that he opted for the speaker's perspective while some 'post-Griceans' opted for the hearer's perspective. Like Frege before him, who was famous for his ban on psychologism from mathematics and by extension from scientific inquiry, Grice focused on general principles.[57] In his case, these were principles governing cooperative discourse. On this construal, the question 'whose meaning' does not arise and, as Saul (2002) rightly observes, the inquiries conducted by those interested in discourse processing and those interested in universal pragmatic principles can co-exist, differences in the perspective notwithstanding.

On the other hand, within the research on the psychology of discourse processing itself, there are clear differences in methodological preferences. For example, Clark (1996) and Haugh (2010) adopt an interactive stance, arguing that pragmatics should present both the speaker's and the addressee's perspective. This methodological choice is probably the most difficult one to implement but at the same time it is the one that is most influenced by the Gricean philosophical ('neutral') stance. Interactants project their intentions but also make assumptions about the interlocutor's intentions. It goes without saying that an approach to processing that has a well worked out theory of both components has a greater explanatory power than an approach that opts for perspective-taking.

---

[56] See also Horn 2012 on implying vs. inferring.

[57] But see my defence of modest psychologism in pragmatic theory in Jaszczolt 2008 and Chapter 3 below.

In this respect, Default Semantics can be classified as somewhat of a hybrid. On the one hand, it follows the goals of a philosophical-semantic orientation and aims at developing a formal paradigm of how discourse meaning is composed from linguistic and non-linguistic components. On the other, it supplements this search for a formal, compositional theory of meaning (called there Model Speaker's/Model Addressee's meaning, in view of the fact that the search for universal pragmatic principles is not concerned with misfires and misinterpretations) with a search for a set of clearly delineated processes that interact in producing this meaning. So, philosophical semantics of conversational interaction is supported with the psychology of processing—in the form of a hypothesized and partially supported set of types of mental activities, differentiated largely on the basis of the source of information and the type of information they make use of. I return to the principles of Default Semantics in Section 2.2.1.

When presenting these views to various audiences, I have sometimes been confronted with the objection that when one focuses on general principles and normativity and downplays the question 'whose meaning', one's theory runs the risk of avoiding one of the most important questions, namely that of conversational errors and miscommunication. The problem is allegedly the methodological one, and it has to do with predictive power: arguably, if a theory does not explain miscommunication, it is not to be preferred to a theory that does. I don't think this objection stands up to scrutiny though. A theory that lays down principles of composition of discourse meaning does not keep a blind eye on miscommunication; it acknowledges it as an empirical fact and leaves it to empirical research to find out which of the factors involved in the composition of meaning (on the production or comprehension side) was misused. 'Misuse' is not to be confused here with the 'abuse' or 'violation'; the latter, as is well known from Grice, results in communicating implicatures. 'Misuse' on the other hand is a general concept that falls in the category of speech-act terms such as Austin's (1962b) 'infelicitous' or Searle and Vanderveken's (1985) 'unsuccessful' and 'defective'[58] but differs in remaining non-committal as to the ownership and source of the miscommunication problem. Such occasional misuses of the general principles are not the theory's business; they are of interest to conversation analysts or discourse analysts (to be differentiated in what follows) who analyse transcripts of particular conversational interactions and try to find out what went wrong. Conversation analysis confines its aims to description, or, at best, conflates explanation with description: it is guided by the ethnomethodological principle which says that what a researcher does on the level of description has to follow closely what the interactants themselves do in conversation; no ideology is to be implanted. But discourse analysts of a more psychological or anthropological

---

[58] See also Searle 1969.

orientation may in addition want to find out *why* things went wrong. Trying to answer such questions, as well as devise a compositional theory of discourse meaning, would result in a medley where no part of it is given sufficient attention and sufficiently goal-specific methods. A 'theory of everything' may be the Holy Grail of natural scientists because they are in the business of understanding one, single object of study: the physical world, in its macro- and micro- dimensions. But it will not work for linguistics, anthropology, sociology, and psychology with their specific interests and foci.[59] Even though they may all have to be consulted while addressing meaning in linguistic interaction, the methods and objectives must remain those specific to the theory of meaning alone. These are founded on a tool of the truth-conditional analysis and the assumption of interactive compositionality.

1.5.4 *In search of the adequate content*

The question *What is meaning the meaning of?* is a crucial one before we proceed any further. We have effectively answered it in the most radical contextualist spirit, by opting for the meaning as the principal content of a message that is intended by the speaker and recovered by the addressee, under normal conditions where rules of rational cooperation apply in discourse. Now, semantic theory is about providing representations of discourse units. The theory achieves cognitive plausibility when these representations have at the same time the status of mental representations. For example, in DRT, the representations called Discourse Representation Structures (DRSs) were assumed (hypothesized) to be suitable models for mental representations. Merger representations of Default Semantics follow the same principle.[60] Likewise, in what follows, we will be opting for a search for mental, conceptual representations. We are also adopting here the terminological assumption that by *semantic representations* we will mean conceptual representations. The semantics of linguistic interaction rests on conceptual, compositional representations.

At this point we have to reopen the question of the status of *linguistic representations* vis-à-vis *conceptual representations*, where by the first we mean, to repeat, the representation of expressions of natural language. Are they the same thing? Carruthers, for example (e.g. 1996), argues persuasively in defence of this position and against the thesis, well-established nowadays, that thought is independent of language. The latter is best exemplified in Fodor's (1975, 2008) hypothesis of the language of thought.

The way to look at this issue is this. What speakers say can be interpreted in different ways. A sentence with a disjunction 'or' could have been used to mean that

[59] I developed this argument in my criticism of Bara's cognitive pragmatics in Jaszczolt 2012d.

[60] Readers who are not familiar with the theory will find examples of merger representations in Chapter 2.

both disjuncts are possible or to mean 'one or the other but not both', as in (4)–(5), repeated below as (38)–(39).

(38)   You can have beef or lamb.

(39)   You can have either beef or lamb but not both.

Similarly, an observation that a dog looks frisky could have been made by the speaker in order to request that the addressee takes it for a walk. Here the difference between the uttered sentence and the primary intended meaning is more 'qualitative' than 'quantitative': we don't just enrich what was physically uttered in order to arrive at what was primarily intended but adjust it in a more substantial way as in (21)–(22), adapted below as (40)–(41).

(40)   The dog looks like he needs to go out.

(41) $\rightarrow_{PM}$ The speaker is requesting that the addressee takes the dog for a walk.

The overall objective, as was stipulated earlier, is to represent the meaning of (38) and (40). But (39) and (41) are in fact sentences of some language in which we *think* them. The question is whether, when we opt for these as the object to be represented by our semantics, we are still representing the meaning of the *sentences of the English language*, namely (38) and (40). First of all, for a truly radical contextualist (like late Wittgenstein, other ordinary language philosophers, and representatives of the ensuing ideology of speech act theory), the meaning of the sentence *is* the meaning of its utterance in its context. So far so good: (39) and (41) are justified on these grounds to provide the meanings of (38) and (40). The question of the language of thought need not arise.

Whether this rich, contextually-construed meaning is still the meaning of natural language expressions is a separate question. But, in a sense, asking for an upfront commitment at this point is not necessary. What we have to do instead is acknowledge that expressions of natural language constitute one of the sources of information about utterance meaning; they are its most obvious vehicle. For linguists, this vehicle is a vehicle of meaning *sine qua non*: DRT or Default Semantics revolve around linguistic units in context. For philosophers like Paul Grice, this is just one of the vehicles 'utterances' (in his wide, philosophical sense of the term) can make use of: showing a photograph or drawing a picture can be accomplished with equally clear intentions as articulating words of a natural language. But even if we depart from Grice and confine the object of analysis to linguistic expressions, we have to acknowledge that expressions of natural language *contribute* somehow or other to the overall conceptual representation. They either (i) correspond to some units of the language of thought or (ii) are constituted of the same material as the language of thought.

In addressing (ii), we can also go one step further and exclude the theoretical possibility that the sentences that are actually uttered *are identical with* the sentences of the language of thought.[61] Sentences of the language of thought may prove to be sentences of natural language but they cannot be the same as the uttered sentences. This option seems available to contextualists of a less radical, 'free enrichment' orientation who claim that the logical form of the sentence undergoes some filling in, fleshing out, enrichment, modulation, and so forth before it represents the intuitively plausible and 'intuitively truth-evaluable' content. But when we want to go the whole hog, as we do in the Salience-Based Contextualism, and admit that it is (41) that our theory should represent as the primary meaning, this option is no longer viable: (40) cannot 'transform itself', so to speak, into (41) by any reasonable principles of modification analogous to quantifier domain restriction, conditional perfection, temporal reading of conjunction, and so forth. It would be nonsensical to claim that in producing (40), what was *actually uttered* was (41). Note that at the same time, it would not seem so nonsensical to claim that in uttering (38) what was *actually uttered* was (39). But in this case the difference between the physical utterance and the intended primary content is less radical and therefore this case is of no use in our argument; we would still have to account for a radical difference such as that between (40) and (41). To clarify, we would have to account for it because there is substantial experimental evidence, and strong intuitive support, for the view that the addressee need not go through the conscious process of inference from literal to non-literal content in the cases such as that from (40) to (41). That is, the speaker may not have to assign the meaning to the syntactic string that corresponds to the uttered sentence before inferring the primary intended content whose representation does not preserve this syntactic form, like (41).

To wrap up, first we summarized two options:

(i)   Semantic representation is the conceptual representation;

and

(ii)   Semantic representation is not the conceptual representation.

We selected (i) in preference to (ii) because this is the natural concomitant of adopting Salience-Based Contextualism, justified on independent grounds. Next, we presented two sub-alternatives within (i):

---

[61] See Recanati (2010: 137–41) for a discussion of this controversial position. He differentiates between the view according to which the sentence of the inner speech is what is actually uttered and the view on which the uttered sentence stands in some fairly clearly delineated relation to the sentence that represents the thought, listing eminent supporters for each view. But this discussion has a distinct whiff of a terminological war and borders on splitting hairs. There is no reason for muddying the perfectly simple term 'uttered'; the existence of various sources and vehicles of meaning, and of their interaction in discourse, cannot be denied, and the rationale behind adopting this outcome of the interaction as the semantic *qua* conceptual object of inquiry is pretty robust without hijacking the term 'uttered'. In other words, there is no need to dub 'uttered' the sentence pertaining to the speaker's thought.

(i.a)   Conceptual representation is a natural language representation;

and

(i.b)   Conceptual representation is not a natural language representation.

Here we observed that the answer to this challenging question can wait; it will only be relevant when we reach the point of discussing the details of the interaction of the processes that produce utterance meaning. Until then, nothing depends on the answer—which we do not have anyway, and will not have by the end of this book, apart from a bow in the direction of neo-Whorfianism in the way merger representations are constructed. This procrastination, however, is not a drawback, since, having adopted (i), we also subscribe to the view that the generative power belongs in principle with the conceptual system. As Evans and Levinson (2009: 443) aptly put it on the basis of a large-scale cross-linguistic investigation, '... the generative power would seem to lie in the semantics/pragmatics or the conceptual structure in all languages, but only in some it is also a property of the syntax'. Whether 'in all languages' should be better formulated as 'for all languages' is of course the controversy between (i.a) and (i.b) above. Levinson's (2003: 301–7) neo-Whorfianism may constitute a middle solution: conceptual representations use atomic building blocks from which words are built. While 'atoms' are universal, 'molecules' are language-specific.

1.6 Semantics, pragmatics, and their boundary: Beyond the state of the art

Having set the scene for Salience-Based Contextualism, it remains to return briefly to the labels 'semantics' and 'pragmatics' in order to reflect on the purpose they are now left with. It appears that processes of meaning production and comprehension are for our purposes pragmatic processes, the ideology of a theory of meaning so construed with the help of intentions and inferences is also pragmatic, but the theory of meaning of utterances as intended by Model Speakers and recovered by Model Addressees is best labelled a semantic theory. To repeat, this is the semantics of conceptual, mental representations, but the semantics that is at the same time the only theory of meaning that can account for utterance meaning as well as sentence meaning and word meaning. It is the semantics of linguistic interaction. Salience-Based Contextualism, and in particular the lack of convincing arguments for abstraction, contrasted with ample evidence of context-specific meaning (but not of meaning shifts), point in this direction. Does it indicate the demise of semantic minimalism? The consequences for a minimalist construal are explored in the following section.

1.6.1 The role of the language system and Cognitive Minimalism

The radical attempts to focus on the real, rich, intended content at the expense of the abstract, the minimal, or the literal need not result in 'border wars' (Horn 2006) between semantics and pragmatics. They can simply be viewed for what they are: attempts to focus on intentions, language processing, intentional meaning, and the applicability of the formal apparatus, and most notably truth conditions, to this kind of object of inquiry. Radical contextualism promoted by Travis among others, adopts as its manifesto the thesis that sentences (albeit perhaps not those pertaining to mathematical statements) have context-dependent truth conditions. But what if we were to admit that one can vary one's object of inquiry *ad libitum*? To trivialize, after breakfast, a philosopher of language may find herself interested in the powers of the language system and therefore in the questions of the structure and meaning of abstract units (sentences), while in the afternoon she can inquire into meaning as intentions, inferences, and the dynamic nature of meaning in discourse. Is there anything that would prevent her from doing so without falling into contradictions and inconsistencies?

Yes and no. Borg (2004) claims that contextualists are free to pursue their goals in parallel to those of minimal semanticists. But the answer in its entirety is not so simple, in that these goals require adopting some assumptions about the language system. If we take Wittgenstein's radical, use-based approach to its logical limits, we have the position on which word meanings do not exist in abstraction from the situation in which the proposition composed out of them is evaluated. Travis and Austin have adopted that view; others have not gone quite that far. Montminy (2010: 322), for example, argues that 'the fact that different utterances of the same sentence may bear different understandings does not entail that this sentence lacks context-independent truth conditions'. He discusses the well-mulled-over examples of (42) and (43), attributable to Travis and Searle respectively, pointing out that the potential difficulties with evaluating them in the respective situations (where, for (42), a decoy duck is pointed to, and, for (43), Bill took a knife to the turf) do not yet lead to the conclusion that some more general, context-independent meaning cannot be extracted.

(42)   That's a duck.

(43)   Bill cut the grass.

It seems to me that neither party in this debate is entirely right. Let us take a simple sentence presented to the recipient in isolation from any immediate context, for example (44).

(44)   The computer is infernally slow.

What does it mean to maintain that this sentence has truth conditions independently of the context? It can mean that there is something we understand when we hear this sentence in isolation, such as that the speaker's (or someone's) computer is working uncommonly slowly. It can also mean that a semanticist would be able to assign some abstract, core meanings to the lexical items and compose the equally abstract meaning of the sentence by the scrutiny of the structure, interpreting the resulting logical form with respect to possible worlds. But it can also mean that it is not so difficult to *make up a default context* for sentences like this one and assess its meaning with respect to this virtual context, maintaining that this is what it means to assess the meaning of the sentence 'in isolation'. It seems to me that it is the latter that we tend to mean: different sentences produce different intuitions concerning the truth-evaluability outside context; mathematical sentences are at the context-free end of these intuitions, and sentences such as (45) at the heavily context-dependent end.

(45)   The boy is not old enough.

One can, of course, follow the radical minimalists and maintain that there is a proposition there that corresponds to a great many possible situations of evaluation, or one can follow even more radical minimalists and claim that semantics is not about propositions or truth conditions in the first place. But these are just theoretical options open to us to pursue and play with. The psychology-of-processing-driven minimalism would be something altogether different. It would, no doubt, produce a conclusion that the context-free evaluation is a matter of degree. This psychology-of-processing-driven, or cognition-driven, minimalism can be presented as follows. Let us call it *Cognitive Minimalism*.

Cognitive Minimalism:

Sentences issued out of context come with different degrees of plausibility and these degrees correlate with different intuitions concerning context-free evaluability with respect to truth and falsity. The plausibility and the intuitions all depend on the accessibility of a default, 'made-up' context that can be used as a tool for such a 'neutral', apparently context-free, evaluation.

The advantage of Cognitive Minimalism is that it unmasks the fact about gradation of acceptability of context-free truth conditions and employs this fact in theory construction. In other words, it takes us from the reality of context-free sentences to the view on semantics according to which it is the availability of a plausible circumstance of evaluation, or a set of plausible circumstances of evaluation, that directs the investigator's path in the direction of radical contextualism or a version of minimalism. To put it simply, some are convinced by easy examples that are akin to mathematical laws and stress the need for minimal semantics, while others are attracted to the difficult ones that such semantics would leave out and they opt for radical contextualism. Our putative cognitive minimalist sits in the middle, recognizing the fact that minimalist meaning sometimes plays a role in communication, either because it equals intended (contextualists') meaning, as it is normally the case with sentences expressing mathematical laws, or because it can be utilized in some other way, for example for the purpose of irony, sarcasm, or in a pun. Cognitive Minimalism is therefore not apparently compatible with that version of radical contextualism according to which contextual effects are always present, or at least are always potentially present. It is, however, compatible with Default Semantics further discussed in the next chapters in that 'no context' is a form of 'context within a context': even when the speaker says 'I am ready' and the completion to, say, 'Kasia is ready to start her plenary talk' is readily available, one can easily imagine someone listening to the recording of this sentence and trying to map it with a situation of evaluation. As such, 'I am ready' appears significantly more difficult to map than, say, (46), but significantly easier than, say, (47). Q.E.D.

(46)   The area of a rectangle equals the length of its base times its height.

(47)   Peter liquidized the cat.

The conclusion that stems out of this discussion is that instead of asking the question as to who is right, minimalists or contextualists, or even whether the two orientations are compatible, one should be asking an altogether different question, namely the question as to whether these terms make sense as labels for opposing orientations. But there is one caveat if one wants to proceed in this way: one has to concede that, paired with the default, 'virtual' context of evaluation, a sentence has its 'context-free' truth conditions because it is some standard meaning of the words and the structure that lead the addressee to a pairing with a situation. This is what our Salience-Based Contextualism captures. 'Standard' need not mean 'literal' though; to repeat, as Giora (2003, 2012) demonstrated experimentally, and convincingly argued in theoretical discussions, salient meaning need not necessarily be the literal one. So, when the recipient is faced with (48) out of context, the default situation can be the one that picks out the metaphorical sense, with reference to a sudden demise of a movie star, rather than the reference to an astronomical phenomenon.

(48)   A star has died.

It seems much more plausible to rank sentences on such a scale of 'difficulty of context-provision' than expend energy in futile discussions as to who is right in the minimalism/contextualism wars.

But it has to be noticed that our Cognitive Minimalism is in fact a contextualist stance in disguise. To qualify as a minimalist stance, minimal meaning would have to be distinguishable in isolation from *any* context, real or virtual, as I argued earlier in my criticism of Cappelen and Lepore. Instead, we arrived at cognitive representations. Needless to say, in the light of my discussion of (48), the other dichotomy that is in the forefront of attention, notably that between literalism and contextualism, does not even begin to stand up to scrutiny: the terms are orthogonal and, as I have argued, the first one has a rather limited (if any) role to play.

1.6.2 The role of a formal metalanguage in 'meaning as use'

Now, while natural language is one of several vehicles that are used by the speaker in communicating the intended content, we also need a language of description of utterance meaning that can cater for the output of other contributing vehicles. This is not an easy task but it obtains help from elsewhere. In Section 1.5.4, I argued that a representation of utterance meaning has to perform the function of modelling a mental representation in that any respectable semantic theory wants to achieve this level of explanatory adequacy. So, the formal metalanguage is at the same time to be the formal metalanguage for representing mental states. To date, the most successful formalized theories of discourse, such as DRT and its offshoots, or DPL and other post-Montagovian truth-conditional approaches, have opted for a metalanguage that is more or less closely based on predicate logic, with some amendments in the syntax or the interpretation. This practice is also followed in Default Semantics, with the proviso that the role the latter assigns to the structure of the uttered sentence is much less prominent; semantic representations do not obey the 'syntactic constraint'. To repeat, (41), not (40), ends up being modelled: the primary meaning that is modelled in the semantics pertains to the main (intended and recovered) speech act, whatever its relation to the syntactic form of what has been physically uttered. In this sense we are merging here the insights of speech-act based theories with the tool of truth-conditional analysis. Finally, since in Section 1.5.4 we have left the question of the relation of the language of thought to natural language unresolved, we follow suit with leaving the question of the relation of the metalanguage to natural language equally unresolved, with an analogous justification.

1.7 Concluding remarks and 'post-border-wars' reflections

An adequate account of the composition of meaning in human communication cannot be merely a descriptive story. If we were to leave it at that, it would be no more than a fairly arbitrary speculation, necessarily based on limited empirical evidence. Instead, to stand a chance of success, a theory of meaning has to gather together scraps of information which different means used by humans for communication provide. One has to gather together information about the properties and functions of different vehicles of meaning. A 'vehicle' is a rather enigmatic term that is reminiscent of the 19th/early 20th-century phenomenological tradition whereby meaning was discussed in terms of meaning-giving acts[62] and it will not suffice as an explanatorily adequate theoretical construct. In what follows we will separate this quest into a search for answers to the questions as to (i) where information comes from (sources of meaning) and (ii) how it is processed. Next, (ii) will be further

---

[62] Husserl 1900–1901; see Jaszczolt 1999 for a discussion.

subdivided into (ii.a) types of processes and (ii.b) the process of integrating the outputs of these processes. In this respect, the current pursuit within Default Semantics builds upon the earlier findings presented in the original (Jaszczolt 2005a) and revised (Jaszczolt 2009a, 2010) versions of the theory but it takes them further especially as regards (ii.b) by pursuing the role of the lexicon. It also tests (i) and (ii.a) on a new phenomenon, namely a canonical type of indexicality (Chapter 5). The purpose of this introductory chapter has been to discuss and justify certain theoretical choices that have been made, such as the radical, speech-act based (and thereby salience-based) version of contextualism; the application of the truth-conditional apparatus to utterance meaning; labelling the theory of utterance meaning a semantic theory; or the immersion of the preferred stance in, and the consequences for, the minimalism/contextualism, semantics/pragmatics, literal/non-literal meaning debates.

One important background belief that will underlie what follows is that when discussing meaning in language we always have to pay attention to what we do as humans to foster the links that form societies, families, or linguistic communities. The overview presented in this chapter allows us to reflect on the past three decades or so of the semantics/pragmatics 'border wars' with more detachment than is usually permitted and tolerated. In the past, discussions focused largely on the logical form of the uttered sentence and the search for the best way to bring this logical form in line with the intuitively intended, meant proposition. This has, in a gross approximation, been the focus of the post-Gricean debates. 'Post-late-Wittgensteinians', on the other hand, have gradually slid into the periphery of public attention[63] in that speech act theory has lost its momentum, having no satisfactory formal account to offer.[64] As often, the route to success is in the middle, in recognizing the importance of both the multidimensional nature of meaning (that is, its many different sources and ways) and the formal methods of representation. This is what I attempted to establish in Section 1.1, addressing the problem of what is 'wrong about meaning'.

Concerning the first issue, the multidimensional nature of meaning, it is also important to acknowledge the extent of language diversity. Montagovian semantics is founded on the *semantic universal* understood as the principle of compositionality; Gricean pragmatics is founded on the *pragmatic universal* understood as maxims, principles or heuristics of rational conversational cooperation.[65] Such accounts are committed to what is common in natural languages but are not necessarily committed

---

[63] On an original analysis of this phenomenon see Kissine 2013.

[64] Albeit attempts have been made to reconcile the formalization of propositional content with the formalization of illocutionary force, see Searle and Vanderveken 1985.

[65] See von Fintel and Matthewson 2008 for an in-depth analysis of candidates for semantic and pragmatic universals.

to syntactic universals, to a universal, invariable, innate language system. Perhaps universals are to be found on the level of the conceptual structure—the semantics as it is understood in our Salience-Based Contextualism, that is, on the level where vehicles of meaning all meet, rather than on any of the subordinate levels.[66] In the face of growing evidence that languages differ more significantly than alleged syntactic universals could cater for, it is prudent to keep an open mind in discussing the sources of information about meaning without making a hasty commitment to universalism or relativity. In his article 'The social instinct', Everett (2012: 32) observes:

'For the past 50 years or so, the dominant theory followed Plato, asserting that language is an innate capacity of the human brain – and culture is at best peripheral to understanding the faculty of language. Throughout the 20th century, theorists such as Roman Jakobson and Noam Chomsky developed the hypothesis in extremely interesting ways. In Chomsky's version, individual languages are elaborations on a computational system (grammar) provided by the human genome. Culture is irrelevant for the core aspects of this system.

I must admit I am puzzled by the continued popularity of nativism. For decades, research supported the idea that language is formed by a number of independent factors, leaving little, if any, work for a "universal grammar" or "language instinct" to do. Some researchers go as far as to argue that universal grammar is nothing more than tautology: humans have language because humans have language.'

Everett's somewhat tongue-in-cheek and inequitable précis of the debate may be going a little too far but it certainly exposes the biases that pervade approaches to meaning on each end of the nativism/cultural relativism debate. Default Semantics features constituents in the semantic representation for both linguistic and non-linguistic information as well as templates for processes that, depending on where cross-linguistic evidence takes us on the question of universals, can be filled in different ways. Therefore, to repeat, it adopts the most neutral stance: there are universals on the level of conceptual (here: semantic) structure, but this is as far as we can legitimately go with making informed assumptions.

---

[66] See Section 1.5.4 and Evans and Levinson 2009 on the generative power of semantics and pragmatics as a potential conceptual universal.

2

Interactive composition of meaning

'And what were the concerns of the day? In the leaders, grand subordinate clauses orbited elliptically about their starry main verbs, but in the letters pages no one was in any doubt. The planets were out of kilter and the letter writers knew in their anxious hearts that the country was sinking into despair and rage and desperate self-harm.'

Ian McEwan, *Sweet Tooth* (2013, London, Vintage, p. 27)

In his inspiring *Meaning: A Slim Guide to Semantics*, Paul Elbourne (2011) aptly points out why it is that we can clearly feel an 'intellectual excitement' that runs through the study of meaning. This excitement arises mostly from 'the extraordinarily wide range of subjects that the study of meaning either touches on or crucially involves' (p. 157). What I suggest in this chapter is that this spanning of various disciplines pertains not only to finding answers to semantic questions but also to identifying the questions themselves. In other words, when we talk about meaning, we talk about a wide variety of vehicles of meaning and restricting this talk to the linguistic vehicle is as good as pouring the baby out with the bath water.

In brief, the adequate account of the composition of meaning requires a radical rethinking of compositionality. It has already been pointed out in the literature that a contextualist account of meaning requires a pragmatic stance on compositionality (Recanati 2004, 2005; Jaszczolt 2005a, 2010). But the far-reaching implications of this pragmatic compositionality on the understanding of the role of grammar, the role of truth conditions, and the properties of the lexicon have not as yet acquired an in-depth discussion. At the same time, these topics are of fundamental importance not only to the proper understanding of compositionality on the pragmatics-rich, dynamic and interactive picture of meaning but also for the proper understanding of the ongoing debates on the metaphysics of grammar and the epistemological implications of the employment of truth in a theory of meaning.

2.1 Compositionality and its myths

Compositionality as it is understood in formal semantics requires that there be a formal procedure for obtaining meanings of complex expressions from the meanings

Meaning in Linguistic Interaction. Kasia M. Jaszczolt.

of the component parts. It is the foundation of various Montagovian approaches to meaning (Montague Grammar as well as, for example, more recent dynamic semantics). It is standardly traced back to the *Grundlagen der Arithmetik* (Frege 1884a) and Frege's emphasis on contextuality on the one hand, namely the observation that words have meaning only in the context of a sentence rather than in isolation, and on the other on compositionality as a function from meanings of words and structures to meanings of sentences.[1]

Arguably, any theory of natural language meaning has to be founded on compositionality: there has to be a formal procedure for composing meaning from the constituent parts in order to theorize about propositions or some other linguistic-semantic representation of thoughts. But as is well known, there are types of constructions (intensional contexts) that require quite sophisticated manipulations of lexical meanings or structures before the requirement of substitutivity can be fulfilled: belief reports, for example, require the contribution of some conceptual information that is context- or speaker-specific so that their meaning is faithfully represented.

Another option is, of course, to preserve strict compositionality but dissociate truth conditions, and truth values on an interpretation, from speakers' judgements of truth and falsity. The latter option steers semantics into the domain of an enterprise that focuses on the formal system of lexical and syntactic devices to express meanings but far away from meaning that is conveyed by speakers in the use of the sentences. For the latter reason we opt out of system-driven approaches and assume that semantic theory *qua* a theory of natural language meaning principally has to account for meanings that are intended by the speakers and, unless background assumptions are misjudged, are also recovered by the audience.

Next, we leave the situations where the background assumptions are misjudged as falling outside the domain of a theory of meaning and in the domain of psychology and psycholinguistics. This leaves us with a more promising project of an inquiry into discourse meaning, expressed either in the form of full sentences or as sentence fragments, but uniformly conceived of as propositions intended by the speakers and recovered by the addressees.

Sentence fragments are not often discussed in this context but it has to be remembered that there are prevalent discourse strategies, attested cross-linguistically, that rely on incomplete sentences. For example, incomplete disjunctive questions can use the final 'or' as a discourse marker in order to express politeness. In example (1), politeness is expressed through hedging the illocutionary force of request.

(1)   Would you mind moving your car a bit or . . . [perhaps it is an imposition to ask].
                                            (adapted from Jaszczolt *et al.* 2016: 256)

---

[1] See e.g. Janssen 1997.

A similar phenomenon is attested in the case of conditionals with missing consequents as in (2).

(2)   If you keep smoking twenty cigarettes a day... [you are risking lung cancer].[2]

There is no question that sentence fragments are widespread in discourse and have given rise to heated discussions concerning their analysis.[3] In delimiting the object of study that is appropriate for natural language semantics it seems proper to include subsentential speech that communicates full propositions. With this proviso, (1) and (2) merit semantic (contextualist) representation, whereas example (3) does not in that it does not pertain to a complete thought.

(3)   Speaking about Scottish independence, I think...

It has been well acknowledged in contextualist circles that non-sentential speech does not pose a threat to Truth-Conditional Semantics. As Stainton (2006: 186) aptly puts it, 'we can make and understand arguments without having to deploy sentences'. These arguments can proceed in the form of propositions that are easily recovered from sentence fragments. This means that speech acts can be performed using sentence fragments. These 'subsentences' are not short forms of full sentences, in that they can rarely be unpacked by appealing to ellipsis. What we need on the one hand is a pragmatic, rather than syntactic, strategy for this 'unpacking', and on the other, an approach to fragments that foregrounds the fact that the proper unit of a conversation is a speech act.[4]

2.1.1 Misplaced truth conditions

The reasons for so construing the playing field, including sentence fragments but only those that pertain to full propositions, are twofold. First, a theory of meaning has to rely on a unit of meaning that reflects thoughts. The second reason is methodological: it is the wish to retain truth conditions as a methodological tool in theorizing about meaning. While a truth-conditional, formal semantics of sentences as abstract objects encounters problems with compositionality as well as problems with practical utility in not capturing the kind of meaning we normally want to capture, truth conditions as such arguably remain the most adequate tool for the analysis of meaning. But the tools have to be applied to cognitively real objects such as *conceptual representations of utterances*—be it complete or incomplete, intended to convey a message directly or indirectly. It is only in the context of a conceptual representation of meaning that draws

---

[2] See Elder 2014 for an analysis of incomplete conditionals in terms of Default Semantics.

[3] See e.g. Merchant 2004 and Predelli 2011a in the traditionalists' camp and Stainton 2006, Corazza 2011 and Jaszczolt *et al.* 2016 in the contextualists' (albeit not uniform) flanks.

[4] See here Harnish 2009.

on diversified (linguistic and non-linguistic) resources for its expression that truth conditions do the job that they are supposed to do.

Discussing truth conditions cannot be done without also discussing model theory in that truth conditions are normally supposed to deliver a truth value relativized to a model. But suffice it to say that the association of a truth-conditional method of analysis with the employment of models is not mandatory. Model-theoretic semantics, and in particular PTQ (see 'The proper treatment of quantification in ordinary English', Montague 1973), relativizes truth to the world. Now, Lepore (1983) attempts to assess model theory *qua* a theory of understanding. Understanding a sentence such as 'All children like cats' means, on some high level of abstraction, being able to sift the worlds in which it is true from those in which it is not by assessing the extensions of the predicate 'like'. The actual world will be among the selected ones or among the ones left out. As a member of one set or the other, it will provide the sentence with a truth value—in the actual world, assuming that the actual world is conceivable in terms of a model, the value is probably 'false'. Lepore then follows Montague in saying that being able to single out the actual world and the actual interpretation would dispose of the model-theoretic analysis. And this is the task that one cannot possibly accomplish in that neither model theory nor any empirical methods of description offer us the means to do so. Moreover, as has often been pointed out, models, as they are understood in Montagovian semantics, are indeed superfluous for an account of language learning and understanding in that they do not capture what speakers of a language actually *know* in knowing a word.[5] It appears that the relation between meaning and truth, while contentious in itself, need not be discussed in conjunction with the relativization of truth to models. We are not able to single out the actual model because there isn't any: words alter their extensions almost *ad libitum*, with the only constraints coming from past uses and the context and purpose of talk. Sentences assume truth values depending on the context and purpose of their uttering.[6]

What follows is a need to rethink the role of truth and truth conditions in this radical contextualist but nevertheless compositional outlook on meaning. What needs to be retained is the condition itself: 'a proposition is true if and only if...' The truth condition gives us the foundation for a compositional account. But next, in Default Semantics, we invoke the conceptual representation in the form of merger representation to appeal to the composition of the intended proposition. Actual world appears as the essential empirical counterpart at precisely this stage. In a slogan:

Truth as explanans needs truth conditions to be functional but does not require relative truth conditions.

---

[5] For an excellent argument see Higginbotham 1988.
[6] I discuss word meaning in more depth in Chapter 4.

The question remains as to how far this account generalizes to the diversity of speech acts. First, does it generalize to assertives expressing moral statements? Here one can follow expressivism and argue that moral sentences are true or false on a par with descriptive sentences in that they express beliefs, or, as Schroeder (2008) puts it, they express 'desire-like states of mind' or states of 'being for'. For example, (4) expresses a belief and it is compositional just as descriptive sentences are.

(4)   Murder is wrong.

Truth conditions rely there on assertability. As Schroeder (2008: 141–2) puts it:

'...truth-conditions are the product of the assertability conditions on sentences given by their expressivist semantics, with independent mistake conditions on the state of mind that is required by those assertability conditions. If you make either kind of mistake, being in that state when it is a mistake to, or asserting the sentence when you are not licensed to, you violate the truth-conditions for the sentence. That is just what truth-conditions *are*, on this picture.'

Expressivist semantics for moral statements can easily be incorporated into the contextualist account proposed here on which, just like in its mother theory DRT, semantic representation is mental representation. We can also extend it to some other semantic problems currently in vogue, such as predicates of personal taste as in (5), without invoking a logical form indexed for attitudes *de se*.[7]

(5)   Risotto is disgusting.

This issue is part of a more general question as to what kind of meaning we ought to, as theorists of meaning, apply a truth-conditional analysis to. Here it appears that one could offer a simple answer: we apply a truth-conditional analysis to what is said, and therefore we should strive to agree upon the most suitable notion of it. To repeat, if we proceed along the dimension adopted in post-Gricean pragmatics, we become embroiled in the debate concerning the scope of the pragmatic contribution to what is said: Grice's (1978) proposal of including reference assignment and disambigu-ation opened up a flood gate to other types of enrichment in contextualist literature that we can either embrace without asking for the linguistic provenance of these aspects of what is said or curtail by admitting only those that stem from the logical form. Or, as Bach (2001: 28) puts it, 'cognitive and intuitive considerations do not undermine a purely semantic notion of what is said'; communicative intentions inform the intuitive truth conditions, not the truth conditions pertaining to what is said. Assuming that we are interested in the kind of meaning that is intended and recovered in discourse, this minimalist stance opens up two possibilities. Either we accept the minimal what is said but say nevertheless that our object of study is to

---

[7] The literature on this topic is vast. For an excellent recent account see Pearson 2013.

provide intuitive truth conditions and we model, *pace* minimalists, discourse meaning, or we reject the minimalist what is said and make it intuitive instead. For
example, Corazza (2012) opts to keep what is said minimal, á la Grice and Kaplan,
but the expressed content is construed as pluri-propositional, á la Bach, or as a
proposition with different kinds of content, á la Perry. The problem is that, put this
way, the debate becomes merely terminological. There is a much more pertinent
question to address, namely whether it is only the *scope* of the contextual contribution that we should debate, or perhaps something else: the purpose at hand, the
ethical, political, and other constraints that make the speaker produce a particular
speech act, the contrast between the high stakes and low stakes scenarios,[8] and so
forth. Saul (2012: x) suggests here that 'it only makes sense to ask which notion of
saying is right for a particular purpose'. She assesses saying in the context of her
search for the appropriate definition of lying. On her construal, 'lying' through the
use of metaphor, malapropisms, or linguistic errors, is not lying. For her purpose,
saying is consistently minimal. But, surely, were we to adopt a contextualist stance on
what is said, the definition of lying would have to change too. This shows that we can
slide the problem, so to speak, along the 'minimal-radical contextualist' scale,
opening up the possibility of different combinations of construals of the truth-
conditional content.

Opening up the possibility for such dimensions as that for defining a lie, orthogonal to the one pertaining to the degree of pragmatic contribution to what is said,[9]
has to be clearly distinguished from the relativist positions where meaning is relative
to the context of interpretation or the context of assessment: '[t]o be a relativist about
truth is to allow that a sentence or proposition might be assessment-sensitive: that is,
its truth value might vary with the context of assessment as well as the context of use'
(MacFarlane 2005: 305).[10] Clearly, relativism is also a position that can be adopted in
conjunction with the selected point on the scale of the minimal—pragmatics-rich
content, or, to use the imagery adopted above, it can slide along the minimal-
pragmatics-rich scale. But, clearly, this two-dimensionalism does not result in one
proposition that is subjected to the truth-conditional analysis; instead, we have
dependence on the context of assessment and therefore different truth conditions
and truth values pertaining to one and the same situation of discourse.

---

[8] See here the discussion in the literature concerning knowledge attribution, for example in the Bank
Case (after DeRose 1992 and subsequently e.g. Stanley 2005; Blome-Tillmann 2013; Lutz 2014): 'I know the
bank will be open tomorrow' can be spoken truly when the *stakes are low* (for example when it is not
important to deposit the cheques tomorrow) but falsely when the *stakes are high* (when not depositing the
cheques would cause an overdraft and a failure to pay important bills).

[9] *Nota bene*, the term 'contribution' is used intentionally and it serves the particular purpose of
signalling that information about meaning that does not originate in the structure of the sentence or the
lexicon need not be regarded as 'enrichment' of the sentence's logical form. This perspective is further
developed in the discussion of Default Semantics in Section 2.2.

[10] See also MacFarlane 2014 and for a comparison with contextualism Davis 2013.

Considered from the perspective of the requirements of a linguist interested in discourse meaning, relativism appears to be a rather weak position.[11] It does not allow us to assess moves in a dialogue, neither does it allow any formal treatment—or at least treatment with a reliable predictive power—of cross-sentential phenomena, be it anaphora, bridging, implicature tracing, and so forth. For the purpose of a theory of discourse meaning it can be utilized only when we flip the perspective from pluri-propositionalism to the situation of assessment as a point of departure, which will give us one proposition, appropriate for the assessment conditions that are in place. But then, it is clear that we enter the domain of radical contextualism and the relativist adventure becomes futile anyway. To trivialize after Davis (2013: 19), 'what is the point of uttering a sentence if one thereby asserts such a wide array of content?' There is no point, and they are not 'asserted' *tout court*: they can be taken as asserted, and this is a very different perspective to adopt.

Let us finish with a disclaimer. Intuitive truth conditions are not a psychological construct to be consigned to the analyses of particular intentions of particular discourse participants. They form a robust theoretical concept and a robust tool that is used in approaches to discourse that enjoy a fairly reliable predictive power. It is true that conversation does not always proceed according to even the best of generalizations: neither Gricean maxims, nor Horn's principles nor Levinson's heuristics offer exception-free guidance to utterance understanding.[12] Intentions can be misrepresented, or interlocutors can be subject to various conditions that make their recovery of meaning erratic. But I believe that the types of miscommunication constitute a different subject of inquiry from constructing a theory of discourse meaning. The first relies on case studies and particular instances; the latter necessitates attention to regularities and has to result in a normative account. *A fortiori*, we leave the first to be pursued by psycholinguists, neurolinguists and clinical linguists and focus instead on a Model Speaker and Model Addressee, assuming successful and faithful (reasonably faithful, appropriate for the task at hand) recovery of intentions, bearing in mind that the objective is a theory of meaning in communication with a sufficiently high predictive power.

2.1.2 *Misplaced faith in logical form*

Logical form used to be a convenient starting point for doing semantics. When there was no good promise of a solution in syntax to a puzzle about meaning, logical form often became endowed with elements or decorations that helped provide such a solution. In addition to the standard indexicalist solutions such as Stanley's covert variables or Larson and Ludlow's Interpreted Logical Forms discussed in Chapter 1,

---

[11] On the weakness of relativism as a stance about meaning see also Cappelen and Hawthorne 2009.
[12] See also Asher and Lascarides 2013 on non-Gricean, strategic communication.

we have 'local' solutions to particular problems such as Barker's (2012) recent suggestion that quantificational binding in English does not rely on c-commanding and anaphora requires a semantic rather than a syntactic solution. What an explanation of binding requires is invoking scope requirement (that a quantifier has to take scope over a pronoun that it binds) and reconstructed linear order: '[q]uantifiers take scope by projecting into a separate layer of composition involving *continuations*' (Barker 2012: 630). This allows one to resolve the dependency for example in (6).

(6)   His$_i$ mother seems to every$_i$ boy to be a genius.
                  (adapted from Barker 2012)

In the case of quantificational binding this stepping beyond syntax is not radical; arguably it can be kept within traditional formal semantics. In the case of quantifier domain restriction in (7) it has to go the whole hog to the actual context and therefore to pragmatics.

(7)   Every seat is reserved.

Next, continuing with 'localist' solutions, by which I mean solutions that apply to a particular problem rather than fix the semantics for the language *en masse*, one can appeal to the power of the lexicon. The power of the lexicon is the topic for Chapter 4 but suffice it to exemplify this strategy here by Chierchia's (e.g. 2004, 2013) derivation of implicatures from the properties of words such as 'every' or 'not'. He proposes that inferences to a superset and subset as in (8) and (9) 'are rooted in the compositional part of the grammatical system' (2013: 3).

(8)   Every cat has sharp claws. >> Every cat has claws.

(9)   Every cat is cute. >> Every Siamese cat is cute.

It seems quite plausible that what Grice tried to capture under the general label of a context-free implicature (GCI) is better considered on a one-to-one basis and accepted as lexical meaning in some cases, while relegated to context-dependent inference in others.

Moving fast towards radical contextualism, logical form also appeared to be a good peg for hanging additional, syntactically unaccounted for aspects of meaning on. Unarticulated constituents were added to it freely as the so-called free enrichment and were motivated only by the requirements of arriving at the intended meaning. But just as modest impositions by indexicalists, so the radical impositions by contextualists proper have more and more often been considered an unnecessary burden for the theory of utterance meaning. Vicente and Groefsema (2013) rightly observe that instead of enrichment, one can appeal to constraints on building conceptual structures. For their argument they chose Dynamic Syntax (Kempson *et al.* 2001) and Conceptual Semantics (Jackendoff, e.g. 1983, 2002) but analogous reasoning has been employed in Default Semantics in the past two decades and *a fortiori* applies here: we do not add elements to the logical form but instead we compose a semantic/conceptual representation directly. The advantage of Default Semantics over those proposals is that it spells out this composition *not* as constraints on the sentence-driven representation but rather takes the idea one step further. It builds representations out of linguistic and non-linguistic components, without privileging either type. As a result, the logical form of the uttered sentence may surface in the merger representation as one of its contributing components or, in the case of (rather frequent) indirect ways of conveying a message, it does not figure in the final output at all. This gives it an advantage over Vicente and Groefsema's construal as it attains a higher level of cognitive reality—complicating the compositional account infinitely of course but at least striving to represent the right kind of meaning irrespective of these theoretical hurdles: the primary meaning intended by the Model Speaker and recovered by the Model Addressee. To repeat: 'model' affords it normativity and thus the necessary predictive power. Vicente and Groefsema's proposal is broadly in line with Default Semantics and can easily be extended to reach this level of cognitive reality.

Building representations out of inputs of different status is thus not new. To give a very different example, in Layered DRT (Geurts and Maier 2003), discourse representation consists of layers of information of different status, such as asserted, presupposed, or implicated. Like in Default Semantics, these contribute to the discourse representation. But unlike in Default Semantics, what is represented is sentence-based discourse meaning: a presupposition can inform binding relations but cannot in itself be represented in preference to the syntactic element of the discourse. To give another example, Ginzburg's (2012) conversation-oriented semantics (KoS) builds conversational interaction into grammar by relying on clues that are not in the syntax such as the structure of moves in conversation, question under discussion (known in the literature as QUD), the purpose of a particular turn in the dialogue, or the effect of grounding.[13]

Now, as was discussed in Chapter 1, saving the logical form through indexicality is open to various problems, most critical of which is the fact that indexicality cannot be delimited in either of the two standard ways. First, we cannot discern a class of indexical expressions to be contrasted with non-indexical ones: expressions that do not standardly fall in the class of indexicals can behave like indexicals (see e.g. Clapp 2012). In (10), even the metaphorical interpretations of 'the city' and 'asleep' can be handled in this manner.

---

[13] It is perhaps noteworthy that Ginzburg (2012) also uses the term 'interactive semantics'—coined independently for the semantics of dialogue. In the body of the theory, however, his interactive semantics of KoS does not bear further resemblance to the essentially Gricean, intention-based Default Semantics.

(10)   The city is asleep.
       (from Recanati 2012b: 190)

Meanings are flexible but context imposes a limitation on this variability. Irrespective of which approach to indexicality we choose, the class of indexicals cannot be delimited. Second, even when we acknowledge the fact that, *pace* Kaplan, there is no clear indexical/non-indexical distinction in the language system, in that even pure indexicals like 'I', 'now' or 'here' can adopt different meanings, including the meaning where they 'stand for the character only', so to speak, rather than for the content, the problem arises how to delimit the variation of these 'occasion-indexicals'. 'Fixers' postulate some devices, be it covert variables in the logical form (Stanley 2000) or, for example, variadic functions that allow us to manipulate predicates' adicity (Recanati 2002; Jaszczolt 2007a), to capture on the level of the logical form this indexicality *en masse* in the lexicon, restricted only by the constraints of the context. The *ad hoc* status of this 'fixing' was discussed at length in Chapter 1, so suffice it to say that unless we find an independent reason for this fixing, it will be difficult to justify it either in the methodology or in the metaphysics.

One option would be to extend indexicality to include expressions that are context-sensitive but in a slightly different way from that in which indexicals are context-sensitive. Let us take the example of relative adjectives such as 'tall'. Recanati (2012c: 69) proposes the following:

'The variable is introduced in the semantics, via the lexical entry for the item, while in the case of pronouns and indexicals, the lexical item occurring in the syntactic structure is itself (like) a variable.'

Enrichment is governed there by the lexicon; it is 'bottom-up' and obligatory. But then the problem arises as to how to delimit this class of expressions that require bottom-up obligatory enrichment (saturation) as opposed to just occasional, free, top-down pragmatic enrichment. Is there a set of truly non-indexical lexical items? If so, how is their context-free conceptual content delimited? These are the questions that begin to emerge once we relax the indexical/non-indexical distinction in the direction of words with less context-sensitive meaning: there does not seem to be an obvious point where one ought to stop.

Let me explain. The elements that enter the compositional process are not immune from contextual variation. Recanati (2012c: 77) calls them 'modulated senses'. But if the components themselves are 'modulated', then they must be affected not only by factors external to the sentence but also by other elements in the sentence itself. Coming back to example (10): does the modulated sense of 'city' in 'the city' affect the sense of 'asleep' or does the modulated sense of 'asleep' affect the sense of 'the city'? The outcome will be different on these two scenarios. If 'the city' comes to mean 'the inhabitants of the city', then 'asleep' retains the standard sense. Looked at differently, if the intention is to retain the standard (traditionally, 'literal', *pace* the vagaries of the term) sense of 'asleep', then 'the city' stands for its inhabitants. But if we start with the standard sense of 'city', then 'asleep' acquires a metaphorical interpretation: quiet, slow-paced, a dark landscape with extinguished lights in the windows, and so forth. All in all, the view does not seem to be tenable at this level of generalization in that we do not know what constituents are being affected and how. Recanati (2012c) maintains that the entire process is still compositional and grammar-driven:

'Even though free pragmatic processes, i.e. pragmatic processes that are not mandated by the standing meaning of any expression in the sentence, are allowed to enter into the determination of truth-conditional content, still, in the framework I have sketched, they come into the picture *as part of the compositional machinery*. Semantic interpretation remains *grammar-driven* even if, in the course of semantic interpretation, pragmatics is appealed to, not only to assign contextual values to indexicals and free variables but also to freely modulate the senses of the constituents in a top-down manner. Semantic interpretation is *still* a matter of determining the sense of the whole as a function of the (possibly modulated) senses of the parts and the way they are put together.'

Recanati (2012c: 77)

But, to repeat, if words are affected top-down, then words around these words are affected in a way that depends on how other words are affected. So, we cannot say that grammar remains a reliable matrix while constituents are affected; this 'affecting' creates a new grammatical structure—a conceptual structure.

In fact, Recanati (2012b: 176) admits that words are semantically flexible in this 'syntagmatic' way in that their meaning varies 'as a function of the other words' they combine with. In other words, he admits both top-down and lateral influence. However, invoking the finiteness of context as the explanans will not do. In order for the construal to work, one has to have an algorithm that captures the conditions under which a constituent becomes subjected to contextual alterations—the conditions that would delimit what this constituent is on a given occasion. Is it a lexical item, a phrase, a clause, a complex sentence, or, when assigning the overall sense of a multi-sentential unit, is it a paragraph in written text, topic unit in speech, the entire discourse, and so forth? So, while we don't wish to slide to what Recanati (2012a: 148) dubs 'holistic guesswork' discussed in Chapter 1, grammar-driven composition will not suffice either. Instead, we have to invoke a conceptual structure—a merger of information whose compositionality does not *preclude* but instead *depends on* constituents that 'constitute themselves', so to speak, for the purpose at hand from linguistic and extralinguistic resources employed for the particular purpose. There is some neuropragmatic evidence that there is a context-free starting point to this process though, in that words do have determinate context-free senses; this can be inferred from the area of the activation in the brain (Pulvermüller, e.g. 2010). This reliance on the starting point is what makes the entire enterprise of formalizing meaning feasible.

It is important to acknowledge that compositionality can be maintained together with the view that lexical meaning is heavily context-dependent. The essence of compositionality is building propositions from component parts—ultimately from the lexicon and the structures in which it is used. But the meanings of words are up for grabs: we can legitimately ask a question here as to whether some form of a neo-classical theory, with its reliance on definitional properties, or alternatively a heavily use-based theory, is more cognitively real, and then choose the winner. This discussion will be the topic of Chapter 4. What is important at this point is to flag the fact that since compositionality is predicated of intended and recovered propositions (from now on dubbed discourse-bound propositions), the approach to the lexicon has to follow suit and reflect discourse-bound word meanings. It is only with these caveats in place that we can start building semantic representations.

Equally, adopting the intended content of an act of communication as the object of semantic analysis does not have to mean abandoning the assumption of compositionality. The main outcome of this construal will be that the logical form of the sentence is not the adequate unit of investigation in that it will not give us the semantic representation of the intended proposition. As we saw in Chapter 1, there have been numerous attempts to fix this problem, but neither of them was radical enough to capture the primary intended message in the form of a formal representation. To repeat, 'fixers'' approaches to semantic underdetermination stop half-way in postulating enrichments to the logical form. They retain a separate treatment of indirectly conveyed messages in the form of pretty much traditional standard Gricean implicatures. Needless to say, this strategy sometimes hits the target but quite often it misses it. When the main message is indeed communicated in such a way that an elaboration of the logical form of the uttered sentence represents it faithfully, we have a perfect match. But when the main message is communicated indirectly, we have a miss in that any enrichment will produce a superfluous representation that does not correspond to any cognitively real meaning. So, it seems that there are two options for formal representations of meaning: either stay close to the logical form of the sentence and (more often than not) miss the object of inquiry, or bite the bullet and attempt to represent the main, primary intended message, taking on board the variety of ways in which it may be conveyed and the variety of sources of information that have to be accounted for in a semantic representation so radically conceived. To repeat, this reconciliation of context- and intention-dependence of representations with compositionality is by no means a new idea. As was discussed in Chapter 1, Recanati's (e.g. 2004) contextualist approach relies on an interactive, pragmatic, or *Gestaltist* compositionality. Default Semantics takes it further in attempting semantic representations of such context-bound intended meanings.

Now, in all these accounts the role of context has been presented in rather negative terms: contextual variation of meaning is a feature of natural language use that we have to put up with; it is a nuisance for semantic theory but it cannot be ignored. This seems to me now to be a relic of the old Montagovian formal theory—a relic that ought to be shed. In fact, contextual variation is to be welcome in that contexts provide a shield, a 'bumper' that allows us to ignore the meanings that a word or a construction would have had in a different situation of discourse. We can safely cushion off the discourse at hand, and the utterance in this discourse that gives rise to a proposition under investigation, without worrying about the possibly unlimited uses that the words and the sentence itself might have on a different occasion of use. This appears to be a welcome change of the outlook: *context helps the formalization rather than obstructs it*. Precisely in this vein Lasersohn (2012: 188) argues that context-dependent interpretations are perfectly compatible with compositionality where the latter is understood as homomorphic interpretation:

'In all these cases – puns, double entendres, metalinguistic interpretations, and intensional contexts – we find that substitution of what would ordinarily be a synonym fails to preserve truth value, precisely *because* in these contexts words that are ordinarily used to talk about the same thing are instead used to talk about different things. It is this contextual shift in interpretation which allows us to preserve the idea of homomorphic interpretation. In other words, far from being problematic for compositionality, contextual variation in interpretation is precisely what *rescues* the claim that interpretation is compositionally assigned from apparent counterexamples.'

His statement, however, is merely programmatic—important for the revindication of context in a compositional contextualist semantics but a programmatic foundational tenet nevertheless. The essential component will be the implementation, showing *how* a compositional representation can be attained, starting from contextual variance. Associating interpretations with contexts does not yet give us predictive power: it does not guarantee systematicity. And here is where Lasersohn's view reveals essential shortcomings:

'Even if the only way to identify propositional content of a sentence in context requires heavy appeal to pragmatics, this does not show that this content violates compositionality principles.'

Lasersohn (2012: 188)

This 'heavy appeal' is then reanalysed as 'invoking pragmatic concepts', such as relevance, salience or plausibility (p. 185). Surely, this is not enough to secure a compositional semantics. What is needed is a systematic account of how such salience or plausibility works—an account that predicts certain interpretations, given the available sources of information. And this is where Default Semantics provides the missing *how*, laid out in detail in Section 2.2.

As I am writing this at the end of 2014, there seems to be little doubt that reaching meaning composition through the standard Fregean route is a futile enterprise unless we tamper with the semantic representation to the degree that makes the project circular: meaning turns out compositional because we manipulate the logical form until it appears compositional. Similarly, non-representational accounts tamper with the metalanguage until compositionality appears to be there.[14] The disillusionment with a quest for a simple semantics is all-pervasive and is well expressed in Kaplan's 'Dthat' (1978: 671):

'During the Golden Age of Pure Semantics we were developing a nice homogenous theory, with language, meanings, and entities of the world each properly segregated and related to one another in rather smooth and comfortable ways. This development probably came to its peak in Carnap's *Meaning and Necessity*. Each *designator* has both an intension and an extension. Sentences have truth-values as extensions and propositions as intensions, predicates have classes as extensions and properties as intensions, terms have individuals as extensions and *individual concepts* as intensions, and so on. The intension of a compound is a function of the intensions of the parts and similarly the extension (except when intensional operators appear). There is great beauty and power in this theory.

But there remained some nagging doubts: proper names, demonstratives, and quantification into intensional contexts.'

Three and a half decades later, these 'nagging doubts' have increased into all-pervasive scepticism in that it appears that it is not even possible to isolate specific areas of language such as referring expressions or intensional contexts that pose problems for the Pure Semantics; take any linguistic expression or construction, Pure Semantics simply is not there. The 'nagging doubts' amount to more than finding out what aspects of meaning qualify for positing hidden indexicals or other fixing devices discussed in Chapter 1. They permeate more than quantifier domain restriction, the semantics of sentential connectives, the semantics of time and modality; they amount to even more than descending to the semantics of the lexicon with its vagueness and occasion-meanings would allow us to handle. The problem with semantics starts with the fundamental question as to what it is that enters a compositional analysis. Until we have resolved this fundamental question of the appropriate approach to the components and composition of meaning in natural language, no improvements in formal methods of representing meaning will take us any closer to understanding what natural language meaning is and what a semantics of natural language should do or what it is for. Against this background of aims and problems, the path opted for is the semantics of linguistic interaction that builds on the account of interactive compositionality developed in Default Semantics and concerns itself with discourses and with their building blocks: acts of communication.

Let me give one quick example of how this perspective fares with the traditional debates. For Kaplan (1978), saying 'that' and pointing does not have to result in the

---

[14] For a detailed discussion and examples from dynamic semantics see Jaszczolt 2005a, Chapter 3.

intended demonstratum. For Donnellan (1966), it does. From the point of view of the semantics of linguistic interaction developed here, these debates are beside the point in that the utility of the concepts of the intended and the achieved demonstratum (if they do have any utility) is not reflected in the semantic representation. To repeat, our concept of meaning is confined to *cases where the intended and grasped content match in the aspects relevant for the discourse at hand.* The rest is psychology and as such would obfuscate the normativity of the outcome.

2.2 Putting it right: The semantics of linguistic interaction

2.2.1 A précis of Default Semantics

The progressing pragmatization of the representation of meaning owes its success to several intertwined factors. One of them is the longstanding dissatisfaction with the attempts to patch up formal semantics of natural language sentences by applying the ill-fitting mould of Fregean compositionality of meaning, producing well-known problematic results such as hidden constituents of the logical form or annotated logical forms discussed in Chapter 1. Another obvious source, especially in post-Gricean circles, is the attempt to capture the meaning that is intended by the speaker, making use of the so-called 'intuitive' truth conditions.[15] Yet another is the dissatisfaction with isolated sentences as units of analysis, moving instead towards coherent discourses.[16]

It is against the background of this theoretical scene that Default Semantics began to be developed in the late 1990s, moving forward especially the first two of the barriers mentioned above, namely the kind of compositionality that is appropriate for analysing natural language, the notion of intuitive truth conditions, but also embracing the third point, namely viewing semantics as a theory of discourses rather than sentences. Default Semantics (Jaszczolt, e.g. 2005a; 2010; henceforth DS) sits comfortably in the contextualist camp in its radical flank, but also goes significantly beyond some of its assumptions. Its objective is to model utterance meaning as intended by the Model Speaker and recovered by the Model Addressee. As was discussed in Section 1.5.3 this question of 'whose meaning' a theory should model is subject to ongoing discussions which frequently result in conflicting interpretations of Grice's Cooperative Principle, allowing for either a normative or an intensional, speaker-oriented interpretation.[17] In addition, post-Gricean approaches opt either for the speaker's or for the addressee's perspective.[18] DS adopts the normative perspective for modelling utterance meaning,

---

[15] See Carston 1988, 1998, 2002; Recanati 1989, 2004 among many others.

[16] See Kamp and Reyle 1993; Kempson *et al.* 2001, among others.

[17] See Saul 2002 and Davis 1998, 2007 respectively.

[18] See Levinson 2000 and Sperber and Wilson 1995 respectively, with the proviso that Levinson's theory can also be read as normative.

in the sense of behavioural norms pertaining to rational communicative behaviour. Its preoccupation is somewhat orthogonal to that of post-Gricean debates in that it does not take a stance, for example, on the question of how many maxims/heuristics one should postulate in explaining linguistic interaction—a question that exercised neo-Griceans and in particular relevance theorists.

I don't find this question particularly interesting. Whether one postulates one two-pronged principle that relies on the equilibrium of processing effort and cognitive effect as relevance theorists do (Sperber and Wilson 1995), or two counterbalancing principles à la Horn (1984, 1988), or even three principles à la Levinson (1987, 2000), who acknowledges the importance of the manner of expression, has little bearing on the overall explanation, perhaps with the proviso that the more well-defined heuristics we have, the easier it is to computationally implement the theory and the better its predictive power, as the implementation of Levinson's (2000) three heuristics in Optimality-Theory Pragmatics demonstrates (Blutner 2000; Blutner and Zeevat 2004). Instead, DS focuses on identifying a *unit* that is most worthy of a semantic analysis, followed by identifying the *sources of information* that provide the addressee with this unit and the *processes* that uncover the intended information or, on some occasions, co-construct the semantic content in the interaction.

DS differs from other extant contextualist approaches in its understanding of the interaction between the logical form of the sentence and the semantic representation of the utterance or discourse. Unlike other contextualist accounts, it does not recognize the level of meaning at which the logical form is pragmatically developed, enriched, or modulated, to use some of the standard terms, as a real, interesting, and cognitively justified construct. First, there is no evidence that such a developed logical form does indeed correspond to the intended content: it may do, on some occasions, but evidence suggests that it rarely does so.[19] Next, as was concluded in Chapter 1, there is no reason to assume that the output of the syntactic processing ought to be regarded as a frame into which we fit the remaining 'bits of meaning' in constructing a conceptual representation—and it is the conceptual representation that is constructed in a DS-theoretic analysis. Semantic theory ought to be a theory of linguistic interaction and as such ought to model the main intended meaning, the most salient conveyed content. Overwhelming empirical evidence suggests that to bequeath the logical form with this privileged status is unjustified and that vindicating developed/enriched/modulated logical forms to the status of a theoretical object is one of the biggest mistakes on the part of contextualists, preventing them from embracing the true primary meaning, independently of the form in which it has been conveyed: (i) direct, (ii) direct but incomplete, (iii) indirect but conventional, or (iv) indirect and in need of inferential recovery.

---

[19]   See e.g. Chapter 1 and Nicolle and Clark 1999; Schneider 2009.

Several decades on, we are a long way away from Grice's clear-cut distinction between what is said, defined as the truth-conditional aspects of utterance meaning, and implicatures. The post-Gricean community of scholars identified a battery of pragmatic processes that help produce the said/explicit content. Metaphor has now been reanalysed as belonging to the explicit rather than implicit domain,[20] substantially improving on Grice's proposal that metaphorical meanings are implicated—implicated not by what is said but by what is 'made as if to say'.[21] But even this move does not take us far enough into the domain of main, intended content. If the explicit, truth-conditionally evaluable content accommodates shifts from standard concepts such as VACUUM CLEANER to newly constructed concepts as in (11), then, surely, it can also accommodate other kinds of meanings, meanings with a different provenance, as long as they play the role of the intended content, communicated as primary meaning.

(11)   (about a dog eating bits of food from the kitchen floor) Fido is a reliable vacuum cleaner.

For example, the teacher's reply in (12) communicates (12c) rather than (12a) or (12b) as its primary content. There is no reason to adopt (12b) as a privileged theoretical object.[22]

(12)   Child: Can I go and get my phone from the locker?
        Teacher: The lesson has not finished yet.

(12a)   The lesson has not finished yet.

        (= minimal proposition but not primary meaning)

(12b)   The lesson at which the child is present has not finished yet.

        (= modified proposition but not primary meaning)

(12c)   The child can't go and get the phone from the locker.

        (=implicit proposition but primary meaning)

It is for this primary, salient, intended meaning that DS provides a conceptual representation. This conceptual representation has the status of semantic representation and it is for the analysis of this meaning that truth conditions are employed. Needless to say, such representation need not be isomorphic either with the minimal

---

[20] See Carston 2002.
[21] In this way Grice tried to avoid the problem with the commitment to literal content which, clearly, in the case of metaphors, is not present.
[22] This idea was first expressed in Jaszczolt (1992) and was subsequently called the *Parsimony of Levels (POL) Principle*: 'Levels of senses are not to be multiplied beyond necessity' (Jaszczolt 1999: xix).

or with the modified logical form of the uttered sentence in that it can—and on many occasions, does—pertain to the primary content that is conveyed implicitly. In this sense, in Jaszczolt (2005a) DS was called *the semantics of acts of communication*.

A semantic representation so understood is called in DS merger representation. This representation is assumed to have a compositional structure. Compositionality is there a methodological but also an epistemological and metaphysical assumption, based on the argument from productivity and systematicity of conversational inter-action patterns. The word 'merger' and the Greek letter sigma (Σ) that symbolizes summation, reflect the fact that information coming from different sources merges to produce one semantic structure. DS is still very much a theory in progress but at the current stage of its development, information is being allocated to the following sources: (i) world knowledge (WK); (ii) word meaning and sentence structure (WS); (iii) situation of discourse (SD); (iv) properties of the human inferential system (IS); (v) stereotypes and presumptions about society and culture (SC).[23] WK provides information coming from the physical laws and facts, such as that metals shrink in low temperatures as in example (13), allowing for the connective *and* to be inter-preted as *and as a result*.

(13)   Trams are out of service. The temperature fell below -20 degrees Celsius and the rails shrank.

    $\to_E$ The temperature fell below -20 degrees Celsius and as a result the rails shrank.

WS is responsible for the output of the syntactic processing of the sentence. SD is the context of utterance. Next, IS stands for the properties of mental states that allow us to effortlessly recover certain default meanings. For example, the property of inten-tionality allows us to assign the highest degree of informativeness where there is more than one option of interpretation: *de re* over *de dicto*, referential over attributive, presupposing over non-presupposing, and so forth.[24] These default meanings are automatic interpretations that are available in some contexts. Likewise, SC allow for the automatic retrieval of information, bypassing the need for an inferential process.

In brief, merger representation Σ contains information about the primary meaning as intended by the Model Speaker and recovered by the Model Addressee. This primary meaning is represented as the result of interaction of different processes that draw on the five sources listed above. All five sources of meaning have equal status: they do not 'embellish' or 'fill in' the logical form produced by WS. Instead, infor-mation retrieved from WS can give rise to a representation that is not in any way

---

[23] This revised version of DS was first proposed in Jaszczolt 2009a.

[24] Meanings that stem from intentionality of the mental states that underlie acts of communication have been discussed widely in the literature—in DS they have often been discussed since the 1990s and the reader is referred to the relevant sources (Jaszczolt 1997, 1999, 2005a, 2012f; Haugh and Jaszczolt 2012).

isomorphic with the logical form of the uttered sentence, neither does it have to resemble it in contents.

Now, a semantic representation obtained through composing information coming from various aspects of the situation of discourse is still sometimes labelled a 'logical form'. This terminology could arguably be adopted on the proviso that, as Stainton (2006: 186) puts it, 'there are some things that have logical form but are not expressions of spoken languages'. However, bearing in mind the long history of the term logical form, and in more specific intra-theoretic discussions also its specific construal abbreviated as LF, it seems more appropriate, *pace* Stainton, to differentiate a semantic representation that corresponds to a conceptual unit of primary intended message (the main speech act that is intended and recovered) from the translation of the syntactic unit (a sentence) into a metalanguage that results in its logical form. Following the tradition in DS, the semantic representation of such a conceptual unit pertaining to the main speech act is therefore called a merger representation rather than a logical form.

Next, DS identifies a mapping between the sources of information and the processes that are active in producing a merger representation. This mapping is not bi-unique but is fairly robust. World knowledge (WK) and stereotypes and presumptions about society and culture (SC) are associated with automatic, default interpretations called jointly **social, cultural, and world-knowledge defaults** (SCWD)[25] but they can also trigger a process of pragmatic inference, called **conscious pragmatic inference** (CPI)—'conscious' so as to make it clear that any processing that occurs below the level of conscious awareness is regarded as a different category. Next, situation of discourse (SD) also triggers conscious pragmatic inference (CPI): here there is a one-to-one mapping (albeit not a bi-unique one) from the source to the process. **Word meaning and sentence structure** (WS) is a label both for a source and for a type of process. This allows the model to be compatible with the modular accounts on which language processing proceeds through specialized, dedicated mechanisms with the modules identified somewhat differently in different accounts,[26] as well as with the connectionist models where the WS process can be interpreted weakly as nothing more than reading off the linguistic source of information. WS is associated with the logical form of the uttered sentence, with the proviso that the incremental nature of discourse interpretation allows for situations where parts of the logical form may already interact with the outputs of other sources. Since DS is a semantic theory rather than a psycholinguistic theory of processing, the exact models for such interaction fall outside its remits; it is interested in the semantic

---

[25] The need to incorporate sociocultural considerations in pragmatic theory is now widely recognized, not only in accounts of GCIs and linguistic politeness. See e.g. Ariel (2010: xiv, 212–13).

[26] See Section 2.2.3 below.

representation as a product and engages with the psychology of processing only to the extent that is necessary for giving a compositional account of a conceptual structure. Finally, the source IS, properties of human inferential system, gives rise to automatic, default interpretations that, to repeat, can be traced to the structure and operations of the brain. These interpretations are called **cognitive defaults** (CD). Here there is a one-to-one correspondence between the source and the process. The components of Σ, encased in square brackets, are then indexed for the type of process that is responsible for this particular component of meaning, and as a result we obtain a compositional representation: compositional in the sense of summing up the composition process, the result of the interaction of different processes that draw on different sources. As it is a theory in progress, neither the set of sources nor the set of processes are envisaged as final; they simply represent the most adequate division of the field of available sources of information and interacting processes achieved in the current state of the theory.

In accordance with the semantic rather than psycholinguistic objectives, DS also advocates the principle of the so-called *methodological globalism* (Jaszczolt 2005a). Recent literature in pragmatically-informed psycholinguistics has featured extensive discussions of the global vs. local character of implicatures (see e.g. Geurts 2009, 2010), asking such questions as whether there are embedded implicatures, or more generally whether implicatures are produced incrementally or post-propositionally. Various powerful examples have been brought in to support the sides in the debate. From the perspective of DS, such debates, however, are founded on a wrongly posed question. It is not methodologically correct to ask whether implicatures are local or global, looking at types of linguistic constructions. Rather, in some situations, the unit that gives rise to an implicature will be a subsentential element, while in others it will be an entire sentence or a string of sentences. Inferential bases are *flexible*: when we take a particular construction uttered in different circumstances and on different scenarios, it can give rise to different implicatures on the basis of units of different length.[27] To invoke again the example of the scalar quantity implicature, while in (14) the quantifier 'some' alone would typically produce the sense 'not all', in (15) 'some say' is normally taken as a formulaic expression (cf. 'rumour has it') and as such constitutes a *unit* in processing and functions as an *inferential base*.[28] As a result, the implicature does not normally arise.

(14)   A: Did everyone bring a present?
       B: Some children did.

(15)   Some say that you and Jack are a couple.

---

[27] See Jaszczolt 2012c and Section 4.2 below.
[28] The proposal of flexible inferential bases is developed in Section 4.2.

Viewed from this perspective, the localism/globalism debate ceases to be of any interest for experimental testing: no experiments can decide whether implicatures (or pragmatic enrichments) are local or global because this is *a wrong question to pose*: they are local or global *not* in virtue of the construction they pertain to but in virtue of the situation in which they arise.

This also puts into question Levinson's (2000) rigid, system-based GCIs. For Levinson, generalized implicatures are invariably systematized into local enrichment that, barring the fact that they are supposed to be widely cancellable, is strikingly akin to lexical meaning. For example, the GCIs in (16)–(21) are local and strong, written into the properties of lexical and phrasal units, and have to be considered as cancelled when they do not surface. They are there in virtue of the I-heuristic: 'What is expressed simply is stereotypically exemplified'. '$\to_{GCI}$' stands here for 'conversationally implicates via a GCI'.

(16)   bread knife $\to_{GCI}$ knife used for cutting bread

(17)   kitchen knife $\to_{GCI}$ knife used for preparing food, e.g. chopping

(18)   steel knife $\to_{GCI}$ knife made of steel

(19)   a secretary $\to_{GCI}$ female one

(20)   a road $\to_{GCI}$ hard-surfaced one

(21)   I don't like garlic $\to_{GCI}$ I dislike garlic (triggered locally by 'don't like')
                                            (adapted from Levinson 2000: 37–8)

By contrast, in DS such pragmatic senses are left to occasion meaning: they arise or they do not arise, and when they do, they arise automatically as SCWDs (examples (16)–(20)) or CDs (example (21)) on some occasions and for some speakers, and via CPI on others and for others. Moreover, they can arise very locally, or on the basis of longer structures, or finally outright post-propositionally. A small necessary dose of psychologism notwithstanding, the flexibility of this way of composing meaning cannot fail to appeal.

To sum up, DS adheres to the general heuristic that allows us to model meanings in context:

Localism/Globalism Heuristic:

Default and inferential interpretations operate on a unit that is adequate for the current situation of discourse, ranging from a morpheme to the entire discourse.

I discuss this heuristic in Section 4.2 when I propose a concept of a dynamic ('fluid') character.

DS has a clear advantage over Grice's globalism and Levinson's localism. CDs and SCWDs do not constitute enrichment of the logical form provided by WS. To repeat, since all the processes have an equal status, meanings that result from such processes can also 'override' the logical form. This affords a rather significant change of perspective on utterance meaning. The sources of meaning trigger partial outputs that merge to produce a merger representations. In this sense, *the question of localism or globalism disappears altogether*: all there is, is a summation of information that is arrived at through different routes in different contexts. It is not interesting that pragmatic aspects of meaning as in (16)–(21) are 'additions' to the lexical meaning obtained via WS. Instead, it is interesting that all these aspects of meaning contribute to Σ.

Next, it has to be remembered that in addition to the main message speakers commonly intend to communicate a range of other meanings. In DS, just as the primary meaning can be explicit or implicit, so the secondary meanings can be implicit or explicit. As is discussed in Chapter 3, salient meanings cut across the explicit/implicit divide. By the same token, the primary/secondary meaning distinction advocated in DS is orthogonal to the standard Gricean and post-Gricean distinction between what is said and what is implicated.

To pursue the disclaimer that DS is not a theory of processing, it has to be remembered that a normative theory that adopts Model Speakers and Model Addressees as its agents and recipients cannot, and need not, encompass analyses of individual acts of communication. For example, utterance (22) can trigger an automatic process of the recovery of the referent that yields the author of the ancient Greek epic poems *The Iliad* and *The Odyssey*, or an automatic process that results in the retrieval of a character from *The Simpsons*, or a process of conscious inference involving assessing the situation in order to retrieve the correct, intended referent.

(22)   Johnny and Sam were talking about Homer, sitting in front of the TV.

Semantic theory is not interested in which interpretation was actually retrieved on a particular occasion; it is interested in the principles of composition of meanings, given particular bits of information and particular resources that process this information. It is this that gives it its predictive power.

The progressing pragmatization mentioned at the beginning of this section can be best seen when we compare DS with its parent theory, DRT (Kamp and Reyle 1993). DS is loosely modelled on DRT in that it employs its language, extending and amending it to fit the purpose of representing conceptual content of varying, linguistic and non-linguistic, provenance. Formalization is assumed to be possible when we attain the level of understanding at which algorithms can be produced for the interaction of various fragments and aspects of information. But its main goal is representing conceptual structure. In this goal it resembles Jackendoff's (e.g. 2002; Culicover and Jackendoff 2005) Conceptual Semantics: like Conceptual

Semantics, it makes use of formal methods but avoids the confines of formal languages.

DS has been applied to a variety of types of constructions and phenomena, beginning with definite descriptions, proper names, and propositional attitude reports (e.g. Jaszczolt 1997, 1999, also with reference to Polish); negation, discourse connectives (Lee 2002, also with reference to Korean); presupposition, sentential connectives, number terms, temporality, and modality (e.g. Jaszczolt 2005a, 2009, 2013a, Jaszczolt *et al.* 2016), the latter two also with reference to Thai (Srioutai 2004, 2006; Jaszczolt and Srioutai 2011); conditionals (Elder 2014; Elder and Jaszczolt 2013); various speech acts in English and in Russian (Schneider 2009); subsentential speech (Savva 2017); and racial slurs (Sileo 2016). The applications testify to the versatility of the framework in that one can represent even most problematic phenomena regarded as tough testing grounds for semantic theories.

This is how it works in practice. For example, (23a), a likely primary meaning of the incomplete but highly predictable conditional construction in (23) can be given a merger representation as in Figure 2.1.

(23)   If you leave the tea on a wobbly table...

(23a) $\to_{PM}$ If you leave the tea on a wobbly table, you will spill it.

The representation features discourse referents in the top row, followed by a list of discourse conditions, where the material in square brackets is obtained via the processes marked in the following index. For example, $[e_1 \to e_2]_{CD, \, CPI_{pm}}$ stands for the conditional thought, the antecedent of which is recovered via CD (the 'if' clause) and the consequent via CPI. The index 'pm' stands for 'primary meaning' in that CPI is a process that is also active in the construction of secondary meanings. ACC is an operator on propositions (merger representations) that accounts for temporality: for example, $ACC_\Delta^{tf} \vdash \Sigma_1$ reads as 'it is acceptable to the degree delta, pertaining to the tenseless future that it is the case that Σ_1', and $[ACC_\Delta^{tf} \vdash \Sigma_1]_{ws}$ signals that the meaning of the antecedent is retrieved via WS. The account of temporality developed in DS regards time as inherently modal where past-, present-, and future-time reference are analysed using degrees of epistemic detachment from certainty, at the same time postulating that such modal 'building blocks' are ultimately universal semantic components of temporal concepts.[29]

---

[29] Representing temporal reference was developed in detail in Jaszczolt 2009a.

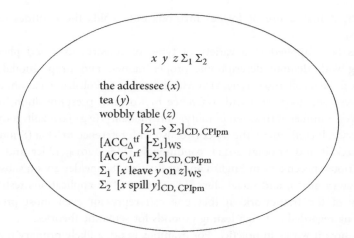

Figure 2.1 Σ for the likely primary meaning of example (23): 'If you leave the tea on a wobbly table, you will spill it.' (adapted from Elder and Jaszczolt 2013)

Next, remaining with conditional constructions, primary meaning communicated implicitly can be exemplified as in (24a) for (24). The merger representation is given in Figure 2.2.

(24)   If you'd like to put on your helmet.

(24a)   →$_{PM}$ Please put on your helmet.

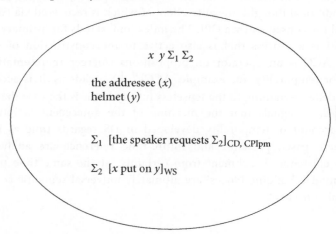

Figure 2.2 Σ for the likely primary meaning of example (24): 'Please put on your helmet.' (adapted from Elder and Jaszczolt 2013)

For the purpose of this discussion we shall not descend to the details of building representations for specific linguistic constructions or phenomena; this would require repeating the detailed construction rules laid out in extant literature, possibly even going back to the parent theory of DRT. Figures 2.1 and 2.2 serve the purpose of illustrating the general principles of interactive composition. The purpose of this inquiry is a more philosophical one and consists of demonstrating the advantage of such an interactive outlook on meaning and on meaning construction. We obtain the representation of primary meanings as produced in linguistic discourse—meanings that need not be explicitly uttered or need not be uttered completely, at the same time preserving the normative character of the theory and thereby its predictive power.

There are ample remaining questions and ample possibilities of further applications in the process of which the principles of building merger representations can be improved and made more precise. But the pressing questions that remain for the current project concern the role of grammar and lexicon: we will now focus on the WS source and the WS process and, in agreement with what seems to be currently in the focus of the analyses of natural language meaning, will try to delimit information that can legitimately be ascribed to the lexical system of the language and to its grammar (in Section 2.2.2 and Chapter 4), so as to be able to address a bigger question, that of the lexicon/grammar/pragmatics trade-offs in constructing discourse meaning.

Until we are in a position to offer an algorithmic account for the truth-conditional content construed as the intended and recovered content, the theory retains its hypothetical status, partly supported over the past two decades or so by representations of various types of constructions that are particularly resistant to traditional semantic compositional treatment. This method of analysis requires a disclaimer though. Constructing a theory of discourse meaning via building algorithms does not mean restricting one's methods to conceptual analysis—or, what some experimental pragmaticists rather derogatorily call 'introspection'. Such understanding is far from the truth. As the research in DS demonstrates, one uses methods that are most appropriate to the purpose at hand. While theory construction has to rely on the overall conceptual analysis, the analysis of particular language constructions is informed by databases compiled out of language corpora (see e.g. Elder and Jaszczolt 2013; Elder 2014; Jaszczolt *et al.* 2016; (Savva 2017). Moreover, the feasibility of adopting a particular type of content as the object of inquiry, notably the content that pertains to the intuitive proposition, benefits from experimental support that demonstrates its cognitive plausibility as compared with more narrow construals.[30]

2.2.2 *The metaphysics of grammar*

If we compose salient meanings of diversified provenance, should not the principles of this composition be called 'grammar'? Isn't it what grammar really means: a

---

[30] The literature on this topic is substantial and growing. See e.g. the papers in Noveck and Sperber (eds) 2004 for early accounts and Hansen and Chemla 2013 for a recent study of the dependence of truth value judgements on context shifts.

'systematic account of the structure of a language; the patterns that it describes' (Matthews 2014: 163)? According to the same definition from this trusted source (*ibid.*), the understanding of the term 'grammar' is '[o]ften restricted to the study of units that can be assigned a meaning'. In DS, these units pertain to conceptual representations of parts of the content that together form one conceptual representation: merger representation. This is not a novel idea: conceptual structure is pervasive in theorizing about meaning (cf. Jackendoff, e.g. 2002, 2011). Equally, it is opposed to linguistic structure as the true locus for some structural and semantic universals (cf. Evans and Levinson 2009). What has emerged as an intriguing and challenging topic of inquiry is the question of how to reconcile a grammar of thought with the grammar of natural languages. The question as to whether the language of thought is different from natural language will for the purpose of this discussion be regarded as tangential: be that as it may, we will remain Fodorian on the structural similarities between the two (but not necessarily on anything else). So, what 'grammar' should we pursue? One recent approach (Hinzen and Sheehan 2013) suggests a very semantics-rich and metaphysical outlook on grammar: grammar enables reference (p. 119),[31] it comes with the concept of TRUTH and the SELF (p. 336). On this construal, grammar appears to be, so to speak, a universal semantic facilitator of engaging with reality: we start with reality to be able to employ a concept, and proceed through grammar in its role of a 'cognitive infrastructure' for thinking (p. 261). The authors claim that 'grammatical semantics' so construed is universal and that it obviates the need for Jackendoff's conceptual structure in that there is no need for parallel architecture. But this conclusion seems to be a little too hasty. It is not clear that the conceptual structure they envisage can work as a standalone fix for a cognitive infrastructure for thought. On the one hand, it is too broad in that it claims to include metaphysical concepts that seem to function without its help such as the SELF, TRUTH, and INTENTIONALITY. On the other, it is too narrow in that, as my discussions so far have made clear, no grammar of this kind can handle interactions with reality in a normative way: we need the 'unsaid', the components of meaning that do not obviously yield to such generative linguistic treatment. The simplest fix would be to say that the grammar pertaining to the language system is, so to speak, 'semantically incomplete': it can throw up meanings, but it may not; it can produce compositional structures but sometimes it simply does not. Equally, it produces meanings that more often than not are *not the primary meanings* of this discussion. What we need is a grammar that would result in merger representations: *a grammar of Σs*. It is not certain that angling generative grammar to perform this task for conceptual structure would be possible: some units, although they enter a compositional process themselves, are simply not compositional in this way. Suffice it

---

[31] Cf. 'If the grammar didn't operate on a given lexical concept, the concept would never become referential.' Hinzen and Sheehan (2013: 119).

to say that SCWD and CD appear to have these characteristics: cognitive defaults contribute information that is not an effect of compositional processing. They arise in virtue of the human mental architecture; highest degree of informativeness, such as referential as opposed to non-referential reading, or *de re* as opposed to *de dicto*, or presupposing as opposed to non-presupposing reading arise, so to speak, by fiat, in that the mental states corresponding to these meanings come with a higher degree of intentionality. At the same time, we have to make a provision for non-default meanings. I have written on this topic at length,[32] so for our current argument suffice it to say that while the output of IS or SC enters a compositional process, the input is *never* compositional in the case of IS because in virtue of the construal of this source it always yields a CD process, and need not be compositional in the case of SC because it may produce an input via SCWD rather than conscious inference (CPI). In the latter case, assuming propositionality and compositionality of the thoughts involved in the reasoning seem to be the only way to proceed. Jackendoff's (2011) and independently Evans and Levinson's (2009) arguments that conceptual structure evolved long before language and is independent of language make this position particularly appealing. They are fuelled by evidence in favour of recursion as a phenomenon that belongs with cognition rather than with language: it is not unique to syntax and it is not unique to language.

The noncompositional status of some components of Σ can now be immersed in a broader picture of human interaction with reality. In particular, if conceptual representations can contain components that are not themselves compositional, can we extend this reasoning further and possibly admit also representations that are not conceptual at all? Gauker's (2011) anti-Kantian proposal fits snugly here. He puts forth a hypothesis that concepts do not inform perceptions. In addition to conceptual representations, there are also perceptual and non-conceptual representations and they play a part in problem-solving:

' . . . there is a kind of cognition that employs representations that are not conceptual but which are more than merely an impetus to thought, because they themselves are the medium of a kind of problem-solving. It can guide behavior without the intervention of conceptual thought at all. The representations involved are similar to perceptual representations in the way they represent, but they are not all perceptions *per se* because what they represent is not confined to perceptible scenes present before the senses. I will call this kind of cognition *imagistic* cognition.'

Gauker (2011: 145)

The idea is not all new. If we delve into German phenomenology, we can find there various kinds of vehicles through which thought is externalized (Husserl 1900–1901; see also Jaszczolt 1992, 1999). Acts of consciousness display intentionality; that is,

---

[32] See e.g. Jaszczolt 1997, 1999, 2002b.

they are directed at an object, and through meaning-giving acts (called objectifying acts) we obtain a semantic interpretation.[33] Knowing the object of the act of consciousness requires fulfilling intentions which can be achieved by thought, perception or imagination. The phenomenological provenance of 'non-perceptual representations' is thus diaphanous. But it is important to revive these ideas in a new form and a new context. In DS, this allows us to complete the picture of semantic representations in two ways. First, we can add perceptual (and non-conceptual) representations as a component of (conceptual and compositional) Σs, and second, we can envisage the model of cognition on which (conceptual and compositional) merger representations are not the only representations involved in human communication; there may also be representations that are not conceptual and whose compositionality, if any, would require redefining composition as a form of reflection of the structure of the world. How far we can proceed with this metaphysical compositionality is however an open question in that non-conceptual representations need not be based on perception. Just as they can reflect the physical world, so they can reflect mental reality. And at this point the circle closes and we have to admit that they are either compositional in the same way as conceptual representations are (whatever it would have to mean) or not compositional at all.[34]

Everett (2012: 35) asks: '... if language is shaped by communication, cultural values, information theory and the nature of the brain as a whole, what is there left for a universal grammar to do?' The answer will now have to subsume a substantial reanalysis of universal grammar, attending especially to its metaphysics.

2.2.3 Default Semantics and a dedicated module: A disclaimer

In his 'Default Semantics and the architecture of the mind', Capone (2011) asks why, how and when default processing identified in DS takes place. On his interpretation of DS,

'... default semantics heuristics are the systematic response to environmental problems that have recurred and, because of their recurring quality, require dedicated mechanisms and more specialised solutions.'

Capone (2011: 1747)

---

[33] Contrast this with Wittgenstein's §329 of his *Philosophical Investigations* (1953): 'When I think in language, there aren't "meanings" going through my mind in addition to the verbal expressions: the language is itself the vehicle of thought.'

[34] There are other proposals on the market that link conceptual structure with reality, such as the embodied cognition account, at the same time retaining the methodological requirement of compositionality but predicating compositionality of a thought. See e.g. Feldman 2010 for Embodied Construction Grammar. Suffice it to point out for the purpose of our construal that extralinguistic sources of information, not always conceptual and compositional themselves, are also invoked there in the compositional process.

He brings these automatic processes in line with Gigerenzer's (e.g. 2000, 2008) 'fast and frugal heuristics' understood there as strategies that evolved in response to the interaction with the environment. Humans rely on 'the mind's adaptive toolbox' (Gigerenzer *et al.* 1999: vii) that allows them to acquire 'social rationality'—the ability to gauge from cues to the best course of action. This rationality is bounded by cognitive strategies on the one hand, and by the structure of the environment on the other, which act, as he says, like 'a pair of scissors' (Gigerenzer 2000: 125), where both blades are needed for human intelligence. The concept that best reflects this duo is 'satisficing' (Simon, e.g. 1982: 249): a blend of 'satisfying' and 'sufficing' in order to go ahead in a rational manner.[35]

Now, while it is conceivable that SCWDs are short-circuited inferences, CDs are not: they are basic, simple, not derivable from any other more rudimentary way of arriving at the relevant meanings. This is so because they pertain to the specific property of mental states: intentionality, and therefore strong informativeness, produces them. For example, the default *de re* interpretation stems out of what Capone (2011: 1744) calls in a Kantian manner an '*a priori form* of our interpretation process'.

Next, how does this account fare with respect to the question of the modularity of mind, and more specifically, the idea propounded in some post-Gricean literature that there are mechanisms dedicated to comprehension, called by relevance theorists (Sperber and Wilson, e.g. 2002) mind-reading?[36] Relevance theorists mean by a module 'a domain- or task-specific autonomous computational mechanism' and they propose a comprehension module, founded on the principle of relevance that says that human cognition tends to aim at maximizing relevance. More particularly, they envisage a sub-module of the general ability of mind-reading that evolved as an adaptation and that accounts for inferential processing of stimuli. Now, domain-specificity can be understood either as specificity with respect to contents or specificity with respect to function (Carruthers 2006). *Pace* faculty psychology, Gigerenzer (2000: 200) opts for function: social exchange, mate search, parenting. Then, '[t]he module dedicated to solving each of these problems needs to integrate motivation, perception, thinking, emotion, and behavior into a functional unit'. Comprehension module is clearly on the wrong side in this classification: it assumes faculty psychology. DS, on the other hand, can be construed as either siding with relevance on the specialization of comprehension (and possibly its sub-specializations), or as non-modular altogether: note that the sources make use of various processes and that one and the same source (SC) can result in an automatic processing (SCWD) or a

---

[35] In a 'satisficing search', which is one of the three optimal problem-solving methods discussed by Simon, one is interested in developing search algorithms that minimize the necessary search effort on the route to the first goal (in that 'all goals are equally desirable' (*ibid.*)).

[36] See also Wilson 2005 and for an introduction Clark 2013.

conscious one (CPI). Mapped onto a neural networks model, it appears that the processes signify that meaning recovery and collective meaning co-construction are sometimes inferential (CPI), at other times automatic (WS, SCWD), and yet at other times stem out of simply being human, that is from intentionality—the 'directed-ness', 'aboutness', or 'referentiality' of mental states. Where exactly this leaves us is unclear and perhaps need not be clear in this project; formal contextualist semantics is not an exercise in psychology. However, multiplying sub-modules to explain the variety of tasks involved in comprehension does not seem to be a promising way to go unless it is independently supported by conceptual argumentation from a different domain or, better, by neurolinguistic evidence. At present we have neither. On the contrary, specialized behaviour seems to be well explicable in connectionist frameworks and evidence for it is mounting. But we will have to leave the issue open at present and relegate it to a separate future venture.

All in all, Capone's project of explicating DS-theoretic defaults seems to encounter several problems along the way. First, CDs are primitives that are hard-wired, just as intentionality is hard-wired, and as such do not undergo any such reduction—probably not even when looked at in the evolutionary perspective. Second, if DS were to fit the mould of modularity, it is likely to be faculty modularity rather than social function modularity à la Gigerenzer. Most importantly, however, as it stands, DS contains no claims that would place it in the modular camp. It contains neither the assumptions, nor logical inferences, nor empirical evidence to warrant a commitment. To conclude on a methodological note, there are plenty of routes to explaining shortcuts in reasoning besides declaring a module.[37]

Any further comparisons with Relevance Theory would be premature. Relevance theorists have never developed any account of sources of information. As Capone (2011: 1749) observes, '[w]hile Relevance Theory confines itself to adding pragmatic increments to semantic templates, Default Semantics gives us the principles whereby such integration can be effected'. It gives precisely the principles on which algorithms are to be constructed, building upon the idea of compositional merger representations. Looked at the current state of development of Relevance Theory, a comparison would involve a category mistake: relevance adheres to a syntax-driven object of study that consists of the (often) developed logical form of the sentence, making only very slow in-roads into primary meaning *en masse* by allowing metaphorical concepts on this level of (truth-conditional) representation. DS does not share this historical ballast: to repeat, it focuses on the main meaning, be it explicitly or implicitly expressed, and on a conceptual representation of this object of inquiry.

---

[37] For arguments against massive modularity see also Gibbs and Orden 2010.

2.2.4 Lexicon/grammar/pragmatics trade-offs: An example

2.2.4.1 *Ways to temporality*   Expressing temporal reference of a state or event can be accomplished in a variety of ways, both within a particular language and looked at cross-linguistically. One temporal concept can be expressed by different means across languages, and, equally, there are various means available for speaking about time within one single language. These ways range from the use of lexical and grammatical markers of time (WS process), through automatically assigning salient interpretations to overtly tenseless expressions (CD or SCWD), to relying on the addressee's active, conscious inference of the temporal location of the situation in the particular context (CPI).

Conceptualization of time has both universal and culture-dependent aspects. There are universal concepts that underlie thinking about time such as memories, current experiences, and anticipations, as well as mental ordering of events and states. We talk about what happened or will happen, or about current states of affairs, either as known facts or as possibilities. This is the philosophical and largely phenomenological component. On the level of linguistic expressions, 'time talk' demonstrates that languages afford a diverse array of means for referring to the past, the present, and the future. These means include grammatical markers of time such as tense, aspect, or modality, lexical markers such as temporal adverbs, temporal connectives, and other particles, as well as evidential markers. In addition to these overtly present devices, there are also pragmatic means: inducing inference or inducing an automatic, default interpretation based on discourse structure or the scenario. Overtly tenseless expressions can obtain tensed interpretations either when such interpretations are salient to the interlocutors in the particular context or when they are salient and default for that construction in that language in general. To repeat, securing a recovery of such a reading can be achieved either by relying on the addressee's active, conscious inference of the temporality of the situation in the particular context (CPI) or by relying on the automatic, unconscious assignment of the reading by the addressee (CD, SCWD). In this context, I address the question as to whether one can discern universal discourse principles on which such a selection, or trade-off, between the types of devices can proceed.[38] English, for example, relies predominantly on tense and temporal adverbials in expressing temporality. Thai, on the other hand, has optional markers of tense and aspect, random use of adverbials, and relies largely on situated meanings, inferred from the shared background assumptions or assigned subconsciously as default interpretations.[39]

In what follows I demonstrate how temporal reference is represented in DS and how it results from the processing of various overt and covert indicators mentioned

---

[38] This discussion makes use of some material from Jaszczolt 2012a.
[39] See Srioutai 2006; Jaszczolt and Srioutai 2011.

above. I demonstrate how we can account for cross-linguistic differences in conveying temporal location by allocating information about temporality to different sources of information about meaning and to different processes that interact in producing a representation of the primary, intended meaning. It is the universal applicability of these sources, their mutual trade-offs, as well as the universal status of the pragmatic processes that allow us to reconcile diversity and universalism about language. First, I discuss the diversity of means for expressing temporality in discourse and illustrate it with pertinent examples. Next, the question of *pragmatic universals* and *processing universals* is briefly taken up, followed by constructing a few merger representations for temporal expressions that exemplify this diversity of linguistic means on the one hand, and reliance on conceptual universals on the other.

2.2.4.2 *Vehicles of temporal reference*   Let us begin by placing the topic in a broader perspective. The diversity of ways of expressing meaning is not confined to temporal reference but persists throughout the conceptual system. Meanings that are expressed overtly in one language, by the lexicon or grammar, may be expressed in another through pragmatic inference or default assignment of meaning to a construction.[40] What is important is that this diversity of expression is a widespread fact rather than an exception and therefore should be regarded as such by any explanatorily adequate theory of meaning. For example, basic knowledge of propositional calculus entrenches in many people the conviction that concepts such as conjunction, disjunction, implication, equivalence, and negation are so fundamental that they are necessarily lexicalized in all languages. And yet, not all languages have clear equivalents of the English *and, or, if... then, only if,* or *not.* In Wari', a Chapacura-Wanham language of the Amazon, and in Tzeltal, a Mayan language spoken in Mexico, there is no direct equivalent of the disjunction connective *or.* In Maricopa, a Yuman language of Arizona, there is no direct equivalent of the conjunction connective *and.* In Guugu Yimithirr, an Australian aboriginal language, there is no direct equivalent of the implication connective *if.*[41] In this context the questions we have to address are as follows: (i) If the language doesn't have a word or grammatical structure for expressing a certain concept, does it still have other means for expressing it? And if so, (ii) How can we make sure that these 'other means' are given adequate attention in representing meaning?

Continuing on the topic of connectives, it appears that their lack or profusion in a language is no obstacle to the universality of the corresponding concepts. As von Fintel and Matthewson (2008: 170) observe:

---

[40] See also Sbordone (2016), on such trade-offs in the domain of gradable adjectives.
[41] See Mauri and van der Auwera (2012), and Evans and Levinson (2009).

'... while perhaps none of the logical connectives are universally lexically expressed, there is no evidence that languages differ in whether or not logical connectives are present in their logical forms.'

This permissibility is also the methodologically preferred starting point as far as the vehicles of temporality in discourse are concerned as it allows us to search in different domains of language system and language use. For this purpose, we now move to the expression of temporality in the example of two phenomena: (i) the evidentiality/temporality mix and (ii) the tense-time mismatches. To exemplify (i), in Matses, a Panoan language spoken in the Amazon region, there is an evidential system that requires that the source of information is overtly specified whenever a past event is reported on the basis of inferential evidence (see Fleck 2007). In particular, it is specified in a sentence how long ago the event took place, as well as how long ago the speaker obtained evidence. Fleck calls this inflectional solution *double tense*. A relevant verbal inflectional suffix in Matses combines temporal and evidential information as in (25). *Erg* stands for 'ergative', and *Dist.Past.Inf-Rec.Past.Exp* for 'distant past inferential' combined with 'recent past experiential'. The conveyed temporal information is that the speaker discovered the hut a short time ago, while it was made a long time ago.

(25)   mayu-n   bëste-wa-**nëdak-o**-şh.
       non.Matses.Indian-*Erg*   hut-make-*Dist.Past.Inf-Rec.Past.Exp*.3
       'Non-Matses Indians (had) made a hut.'
                                              (adapted from Fleck 2007: 590)

Matses has three past tenses: recent, distant, and remote, and three evidential distinctions: direct experience, inference, and conjecture (see Fleck 2007: 589). The marker *nëdak* expresses the distant past, referring to any temporal interval from between about a month ago to the speaker's infancy, combined with the inferential evidence, while *o* marks recent past, normally from immediately before the time of speaking to up to a month ago (although a more extended scale is also used in some contexts), combined with experiential source. Altogether we obtain *nëdak-o* which combines two items of temporal reference: distant past, that of the making of the hut, and recent past, that of the discovery or obtaining information. Analogously, markers for other combinations, such as that for recent past inferential or distant past experiential, are available in the language, making up nine markers for the past-time reference in total.

Fleck suggests that the fact that these distinctions are present only for referring to the past can be partly explained by the observation that they are less important (although perhaps not unnecessary) in the case of the future or the present. What is interesting for our purpose is that what is expressed as compulsory double tense in Matses would normally be achieved through a grammar/lexicon means in English, or grammar/pragmatics when the time of obtaining evidence is obvious from the context. In addition, when we also consider the three-way distinction in marking past tense, we require an additional grammar/lexicon or grammar/pragmatics mix in English, which may result, for example, in a grammar/pragmatics/lexicon mix for expressing the combination from (25), as in the rather crude attempt in (26).

(26)   Tom built a house [a long time ago]. [I [have just] realized/deduced from what you were saying that he did].

It is easy to envisage discourse scenarios in which the material in square brackets, outer or inner, could be redundant. All such differences in what languages grammaticalize or lexicalize as far as temporal reference is concerned add more fuel to the argument that, to put it in the form of a slogan, *whatever information content there is in an utterance has to be present in its meaning representation, independently of how it got there*, i.e. independently of what sources or what processes are responsible for it.

Example (25) has a conceptual representation as in Figure 2.3, where the information 'a long time ago' and 'as I have just deduced' (or something to that effect) is obtained via WS. For the clarity of argument, I do not represent the nuances of the ergative structure and regard 'bëste-wa' as a unit and 'mayu-n' as the 'subject' in the sense of the actor.

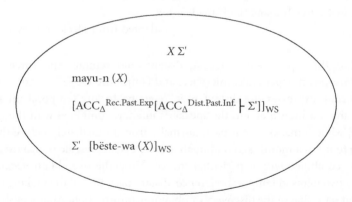

$X \Sigma'$

mayu-n (X)

$[ACC_\Delta^{\text{Rec.Past.Exp}}[ACC_\Delta^{\text{Dist.Past.Inf.}} \vdash \Sigma']]_{\text{WS}}$

Σ' $[\text{bëste-wa } (X)]_{\text{WS}}$

Figure 2.3 Σ for example (25): mayu-n bëste-wa-**nëdak**-o-şh (adapted from Jaszczolt 2012a: 116)

In the English equivalent (26), this double temporality and source of evidence is either not intended or, in some circumstances, may be inferred via CPI_{pm} or taken for granted (SCWD).

Let us move to phenomenon (ii), tense-time mismatches. These are pervasive in many languages, and it is so for good reasons. For example, when a speaker uses present tense with future-time reference, a phenomenon that is sometimes called *tenseless future*, the choice is likely to be motivated by the intention to emphasize the high probability of the future event or a potential difficulty in altering the plan or schedule as in (27).

(27)   On Monday the Prime Minister is in Glasgow.

The so-called *futurate progressive* as in (28) exemplifies a similar phenomenon.

(28)   On Monday I am planting trees.

Vivid, or historic, present obtained through present tense forms used with past-time reference as in (29) is yet another example of the discussed mismatch.

(29)   This is what happened to me yesterday: I come to the office and see this guy standing by my desk and smiling. I say to him, . . .

From the conceptual, or semantic, point of view, it is more appropriate to call the phenomenon the *past of narration* in that the grammatical form is used to refer to past eventualities—by analogy with *futurate* progressive or tenseless *future*.

   In short, future or past temporality need not map onto future or past verb forms in English. Moreover, there are languages in which temporal reference is not grammatically marked (Mandarin) or this marking is optional (Thai). This fact constitutes further supporting evidence for the claim that all information about temporal reference has to be treated on an equal footing, no matter what its provenance. I present below how this can be represented in DS. We need here a 'theoretical whip' that would tame and subjugate this diversity and we will see that DS stands up to the task.

   At this point of our exposition of DS, it is diaphanous that compositionality has to be accepted as a property of conceptual structure, and thereby, on the construal of semantics adopted here (the semantics of linguistic interaction), also as a property of semantics. In this context, let us consider the idea of semantic universals. Von Fintel and Matthewson (2008: 142) invoke the Strong Effability Hypothesis and Translatability Thesis, both attributed to Jerrold Katz. The Strong Effability Hypothesis says that 'Every proposition is the sense of some sentence in each natural language.' This is, needless to say, wishful thinking for a formal semanticist and it doesn't take much evidence to disprove it. Next, the more relaxed Translatability Thesis says that 'For any pair of natural languages and for any sentence S in one and any sense σ of S, there is at least one sentence S' in the other language such that σ is a sense of S'' (p. 143). This thesis, again, is much too strict as we can see from the fact that languages widely use the lexicon/grammar/pragmatics trade-offs. It is only workable when we substitute the term 'utterance' for 'sentence' and construe semantics in a radical contextualist way. On the other hand, von Fintel and Matthewson (2008: 191) note that 'languages often express strikingly similar truth conditions, in spite of non-trivial differences in lexical semantics or syntax'. This for them signals the plausibility of semantic universals understood as (a) universal semantic composition principles, which, however, are rather problematic to discern, or (b) Gricean principles of utterance interpretation.

Now, Evans and Levinson (2009) contend that processing principles are precisely the universals we are looking for. But here we have two options. We can look for these principles in the domain of formal semantic/pragmatic generalizations or rather, or also, in the domain of processing generalizations. For example, if we were to go along with dynamic semantics and incorporate more and more information from context into formal representation, we would be opting for the first strategy. If we were to go along with post-Gricean, and therefore intention-based, contextualism in semantics and incorporate results of pragmatic inference in the truth-conditional representation, we could still opt either for a focus on the final representation or a focus on the kinds of processes that lead to this pragmatics-rich representation. Evans and Levinson go with the latter. As they say, '[f]or our generativist critics, generality is to be found at the level of structural representation; for us, at the level of process' (*ibid.*, p. 475). In short, the methodological question is whether universal principles should include generalizations about processing. As the earlier exposition of DS showed, DS does include them but only as triggers of chunks of the compositional structure Σ rather than as the locus for generalizations about meaning *per se*. In this we shall differ quite substantially from Evans and Levinson.[42]

Tense-time mismatches in English exemplified in (27)–(29) repeated below provide a suitable testing ground for DS in that not only temporality cannot be derived directly from the grammatical tense but also the temporal reference that is standardly associated with that tense is not the case there.

(27)   On Monday the Prime Minister is in Glasgow.

(28)   On Monday I am planting trees.

(29)   This is what happened to me yesterday: I come to the office and see this guy standing by my desk and smiling. I say to him, . . .

(27) and (28) are rather problematic for those formal semantic accounts in which temporal reference is closely associated with the tense of the sentence (see e.g. the 'feature TENSE' in DRT). In DS, where the grammar has no privileged status over other sources of information, such mismatches are not a problem. Sentence (27) has the representation as in Figure 2.4. To repeat, the superscript 'tf' stands for 'tenseless future' and gives the value to ACC_Δ.

---

[42] The difference is augmented by the fact that DS does not subscribe to modularity. See Section 2.2.3.

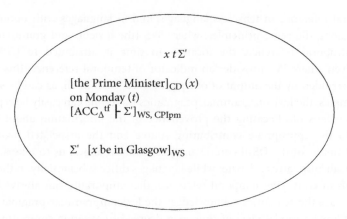

Figure 2.4 Σ for example (27): 'On Monday the Prime Minister is in Glasgow.' (adapted from Jaszczolt 2012a: 117)

Example (28) obtains a representation as in Figure 2.5. The temporality is conveyed through CPI$_{pm}$. The superscript 'fp' stands for 'futurate progressive'.

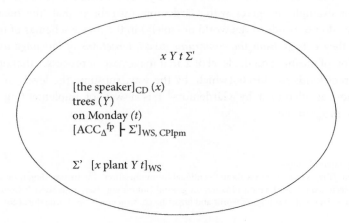

Figure 2.5 Σ for example (28): 'On Monday I am planting trees.' (adapted from Jaszczolt 2012a: 117)

Example (29), involving the past of narration, can be represented analogously: CPI$_{pm}$ accounts for the past-time reference in spite of the grammatical form of the verb (given by WS). Since Σs represent entire discourses, following the procedure adopted in DRSs of the parent theory DRT, all the sentences in this narration will appear in one representation.

Temporal reference in tenseless languages and in languages with optional tense proceeds along the same principles: where WS (the lexicon and grammar) do not provide temporal reference, the location in time is attributed to CPI, CD or SCWD. Even where WS provides an indicator of temporal reference, this reference can be overridden by the output of other processes.[43] All in all, as can be seen from these examples, the lexicon/grammar/pragmatics trade-offs can easily be represented in DS by means of allocating the provenance of the information about temporal location to the appropriate contributing source and the associated process. The additional bonus of the DS-theoretic analysis is that it allows us to take a stance in the universalism/relativity debate: while languages differ substantially in their choice of methods of conveying temporal reference, the temporality can always be represented because the semantics acknowledges the lexicon/grammar/pragmatics trade-offs and adopts a modal view of time as a degree of epistemic commitment to an eventuality—a DS-theoretic ACC with a value for Δ provided by one of the sources of information acknowledged in the theory.

The semantics of linguistic interaction so construed testifies to the need for bringing together the insights of cognitive linguistics in building semantic representations that have the status of mental representations and formal semantic theory that provides tools for a truth-conditional analysis, affording the theory its predictive power. For example, it agrees with Gärdenfors (2014b: 3) that 'the meanings of expressions do not reside in the world or (solely) in the image schemas of individual users but they *emerge from the communicative interactions of language users*.' The composition of meaning on the level of Σ that makes use of processes that operate on very different kinds of objects (which, by the way, subsume the levels of meaning construction as identified by Gärdenfors[44]) is a way of implementing such an interactive programme.

---

[43] See e.g. Jaszczolt 2009a.

[44] These are: Praxis (interaction without intentional communication); Instruction (linguistic, cf. language games or speech acts); Coordination of common ground (informing, asking questions); Coordination of meanings (negotiation of meanings of words and linguistic constructions). See Gärdenfors (2014b: 6).

3

Defaults in context

'He sipped his brandy a second time and said it was made pleasingly *rounded* by the thickness of the vessel which he was far too polite to call a cup. He understood, he said, for the first time, that certain brandies must have been taken, from the earliest years, in vessels of this thickness, which served to counterfeit viscosity and were therefore, as it were, part of the taste.

In short, the drink was rough enough to blind a sailor.'

Peter Carey, *Parrot and Olivier in America*
(2010, London, Faber and Faber, p. 447)

3.1 Salient meanings and default meanings

In Chapters 1 and 2 I defended a version of contextualism that is founded on a notion of primary meaning that reflects the meaning intention of a Model Speaker as recovered by a Model Addressee. I called it Salience-Based Contextualism. At the same time, I avoided the pitfalls of meaning eliminativism by acknowledging that words come with salient meanings that are sometimes independent of the situated content. In what follows I attempt a reconciliation of the idea of context-free salience and the context-internal salience, where the latter is captured in DS as default, automatic interpretations arrived at via CD and SCWD.[1] The first question that arises is: *Are salient lexical meanings and default utterance meanings compatible concepts?* In DS, automatic (a.k.a. default) interpretations and inferential interpretations are regarded as alternative routes that potential addressees follow in recovering the intended message. It has to be emphasized that defaults are *process-based* rather than *language-system-based*: defaults arise only for *some* speakers, and even for these, only on *some* occasions, notably when the message is recovered automatically, while *others*, and again on *some* occasions, employ a conscious process of inference. This is how the DS-theoretic defaults differ from system-based defaults proposed by Grice and by Levinson as their respective GCIs. In DS, there is no cancellation of

---

[1] This chapter contains a further development of my view on salience that originated in Jaszczolt 2011.

defaults. They are just one of two possible routes to utterance meaning, sometimes employed, and on other occasions not made use of.

If we take, for example, the utterance in (1), repeated from Chapter 2, the contextual salience clearly differs from context-free salience: while watching *The Simpsons*, regular viewers will automatically associate 'Homer' with a character in the cartoon.

(1)   Johnny and Sam were talking about Homer, sitting in front of the TV.

The referent is salient, and the meaning of 'Homer' is arrived at through a default process, but the referent is not salient in virtue of the context-free association with 'Homer'—at least not for most well educated speakers (granted, it may be such for some). At the same time, as Giora's (e.g. 2003, 2012; Peleg and Giora 2011) experimental evidence demonstrates, irrelevant meanings are also activated to a greater or lesser degree; they give rise to the phenomenon of 'graded salience' at the level of the lexicon. It is therefore necessary to incorporate this phenomenon into a compositional account of utterance meaning—the primary meanings of DS. This reconciliation of context-free and context-bound salience will necessitate an account that is characterized by a fair amount of psychologism, which is a topic taken up in Section 3.3.

To adopt a historical perspective, Grice's GCIs[2] are interpretations that normally ensue unless context supresses them. They are propositional and are understood as implicated thoughts. What interested Grice was the *relation* between such common implicata and the uttered sentence; what did not interest him was the *process* by which such implicata came into being. The task of a contextualist in the current intellectual climate is very different: even if we do not aim at a psycholinguistic theory of discourse processing, we must address the question of the compositionality of the main message, and therefore the question as to how and at what point in the process of discourse interpretation such meanings arise. In Chapter 4 we will make a more precise suggestion concerning the unit that gives rise to automatic meaning construction. For now, let us focus on the concept of salience itself. In (2)–(5) we have examples of interpretations that go beyond the literal content of the lexical items. But on closer inspection, this is achieved in very different ways.

(2)   Some ($\rightarrow_E$ some but not all) people like Ian McEwan.

(3)   The hospital ward has a new nurse ($\rightarrow_E$ female nurse).

(4)   The freezer broke and ($\rightarrow_E$ and as a result) all the food was wasted.

(5)   Use the silver polish ($\rightarrow_E$ polish for cleaning silver) for these ornaments.

In (2), we have a standard Horn scale in virtue of which 'some' comes to communicate 'some but not all'. In terms of DS, this is, however, an interpretation of 'some'

---

[2] Grice 1975; see also Horn 2004.

that arises for many contexts but *in virtue of this context and in virtue of the situation of discourse*. If we attribute the enrichment to the lexical item itself, we have to face a problem with cancellation in contexts in which 'some' means just that: *some* (and possibly all) as for example in (6).

(6)   If you want to be head of department, some of your colleagues will have to support the nomination.

It appears that the 'not all' reading, where present, is arrived at on the basis of a unit larger than the word itself. Sometimes even the entire phrase 'some of your colleagues' does not guarantee the scalar reading when juxtaposed with deontic modality as in (6). It is therefore more prudent to contend that scalar readings are sometimes automatic, sometimes inferential, and at other times do not arise at all. All in all, it appears that scales are a much less theoretically interesting phenomenon than the attention afforded to them would suggest.

Next, names of professions such as 'nurse' or 'secretary' are said to invoke the default reading of 'female nurse' or 'female secretary'. Levinson (2000) regards these as presumptive meanings that are local, incrementally arrived at GCIs. There is no question that, alas, these occupations are predominantly taken up by women and therefore it is justifiable to surmise that such enrichment to the presumed gender may in many contexts arise automatically. But, again, it does not arise in all contexts and as such is better described as an automatic interpretation—a DS-automatic, that is, automatic for the situation and the interlocutors at hand, rather than automatic at large, for any interlocutors and any contexts. Moreover, 'secretary' describes a fairly wide range of positions and in some work scenarios the female default will not be the case. Instead, the male default may ensue or there may be no gender-related automatic reading. When there is one, it appears that it is best captured as a SCWD in that it reflects our inculcated presumptions about culture and society.

Example (4) testifies to the causal reading of the conjunction *and* that has often been discussed in the literature as a case of default interpretation, along with the temporal *and*. There is quite a strong tendency to attribute causal and temporal readings to juxtapositions of sentences in the case of which such relations are diaphanous. In DS, we often ascribe them to the SCWD in that it is the knowledge of physical laws that triggers this, often automatic, reading. DS also accommodates the situations in which the addressee, say, a child, has to perform conscious inference (CPI) in order to recover the causal or temporal link.

'Silver polish' in (5) is a standard compound. And yet, Levinson (2000) discusses such cases under the umbrella term of a presumptive meaning (his GCI). To repeat, his examples include 'bread knife', 'kitchen knife', and steel knife'[3] and they are

---

[3]   See Levinson (2000: 5) and examples (16)–(18) in Section 2.2.1 above.

brought in to testify to the variety, but at the same time predictability, of the kinds of semantic links between the adjectival and the nominal component of the compound. This seems to be stretching the defaultness and the domain of pragmatic explanations somewhat too far. Pragmatic meanings have to be 'soft' meanings as contrasted with the content that is derivable from the language system; they have to be either cancellable, as it is in the case of Grice's and Levinson's GCIs, or they have to be triggered by context, as it is in the case for DS-theoretic automatic interpretations (context-driven defaults). But these compounds are clearly stronger than that: their meaning is very hard to cancel; it consists of more than presumptions about intended interpretations and as such falls not in the domain of defaults but rather in the domain of lexical semantics.

All in all, it appears that automatic interpretations can be stronger or weaker and they can be ascribed to different kinds of processes that render the overall meaning of an utterance. On Levinson's account, their provenance is supposedly accounted for by allocating the examples to the relevant heuristics. (2) is processed via the Q-heuristic ('What isn't said isn't'). In other words, if there is a stronger expression that could have been used but was not, there are strong grounds for inferring that the same sentence with a stronger term substituted for the weaker one would render falsehood. (3)–(5) succumb to the I-heuristic ('What is expressed simply is stereotypically exemplified'). In other words, where the richer meaning is obvious, it need not be spelled out. But then, Levinson's (2000: 5) next example (our (7), repeated from (21) from Chapter 2) is also supposedly governed by the I-heuristic.

(7)   I don't like garlic.   ($\rightarrow_E$ I dislike garlic.)

The I-heuristic is thus applied to a mixed bag of cases: social stereotypes that need not always hold, physical laws that are known to some but not to others, strong meanings associated with lexical compounds, as well as interpretations of entire phrases such as that in (7). It is a mixed bag indeed, not only as far as the provenance of meanings is concerned, but also with respect to the strength of this meaning and the properties of the unit on the basis of which it arises. It is difficult to see how one can arrive at a normative account by proceeding in this way. At best, one can attempt a perfunctory description of the facts of conversation but certainly not an explanation, a theory with predictive power.

All in all, conversational defaults are a fact of everyday discourse and as such they deserve an explanation. However, they do not constitute one uniform phenomenon. They have different provenance, different strength, and arise at different places in the incremental process of interpretation—'different' even with respect to one and the same sentence uttered in different contexts, or even in one and the same context but assessed by different participants. We have here context-sensitivity as well as assessment-sensitivity but *not merely* with respect to the truth that has been so widely discussed in the literature (Predelli 2005a, b; MacFarlane 2005, 2014). It is context- and assessment-sensitivity with respect to the interpretation process itself, and thus extending much further beyond the widely discussed cases.

Next, the question arises if the label 'default' is suitable for such interpretations. As far as DS is concerned, the matter is merely terminological: interpretations that are arrived at automatically, without help of the conscious process of inferring, merits the label 'default interpretation'. However, the strategic importance of this terminological choice should not be underestimated either. Ever since Grice proposed the concept of the generalized implicature there have been vivid discussions in the literature concerning the legitimacy (*qua* psychological plausibility) of his default, context-free pragmatic meanings. Grice's project was relatively easy to defend as a philosophical, as opposed to linguistic-pragmatic, pursuit that aims at generalizations about facts of conversation *tout court*. It is perhaps a quirk in the progress in social sciences that this philosophical idea was then taken up by linguists and developed into an eccentric hybrid in the form of Levinson's heuristics, where the attention to processing began to be an essential part of the theory. It is at this point that problems arose: one cannot have language-system-governed GCIs and at the same time psychologically real GCIs; the first would have to be algorithmically delimited, and the latter would have to be much, much weaker than Levinson's GCIs and not *normally* cancellable (albeit *in principle* defeasible, to account for cases of miscommunication).

And this is where the DS-theoretic revindication of the term 'default' comes in. The fact that there are no system-based presumptive meanings à la Levinson, and the fact that there are no sentence-based GCIs à la Grice do not yet mean that there are no kinds of meaning that merit the label 'default'; there is an important qualitative difference between effortless, automatic interpretations and effortful, inferential ones and this is what the label is brought in to capture in DS.

Default meanings have a long and respectable tradition in philosophy, logic, and linguistics. Default reasoning, the term that captures the automaticity of conclusions, has permeated the writings of Humboldt, Jespersen, and Cassirer among many others. Closer to the present, Bach (1984: 40) presents it as reasoning that contains a defeasible step that is taken without the aid of thinking, decision-making: ' . . . you just take it unless you think something might not be OK'. This phenomenon of human reasoning is also associated with default logic: C can be concluded if A has been concluded and B can be assumed (although B cannot be proven). It adds to it the feature of subdoxasticity: DS-theoretic defaults are automatic, common-sensical, and, of course, salient.[4]

---

[4] On default reasoning see also Reiter 1980; Veltman 1996; Thomason 1997; Benferhat *et al.* 2005; Allan and Jaszczolt 2011; Jaszczolt 2006a; and for an overview Jaszczolt 2006b and 2009c.

It is the term 'salient' that requires more attention in that, in our discussion so far, it has applied to contextual salience (the DS-theoretic defaults) as well as to lexical, context-free salience (Giora's 'graded salience'). We need both, though, and both are pragmatic, nonmonotonic. We process lexical items via nonmonotonic reasoning.[5] This assignment of meanings to lexical items draws on many sources that pertain to our experience, properties of the human inferential system (and as such, the structure and operations of the brain), knowledge of language, purpose at hand, as well as various other external and internal factors. As such, it is not easy to put into a mould of any formal analysis. But all we need at the present point in the argument is the recognition of the fact that just as there is a contextual salience, so there is lexical salience and it is therefore justifiable to ascribe the first to SCWD and the latter to WS.

Now, CD poses a problem in this binary distinction in that, while it normally yields informatively strong interpretations associated with a high degree of intentionality of the mental state associated with the speaker's utterance, as in the case of the *de re* over *de dicto* reading of a belief report or the referential over the attributive reading of a definite description, it is also in principle associated with informatively strong, context-independent interpretations of lexical items. For example, in the case of the identity between the hypernym and the subordinate term 'cow', it is likely that the subordinate reading is retrieved.[6] In the case of vague terms exhibiting typicality effects such as 'red', the prototypical 'red' ('reddy red') is likely to be activated.[7] This phenomenon is best ascribed to the property of intentionality and *a fortiori* the strongest aboutness and the strongest informativeness—or, in DS-theoretic terms, the CD process. In short, CD will interact with WS in assigning meanings to lexical items that are defeasible but strong. These salient meanings can have different provenance, coming from the sources identified in DS.

So, the problem with lexical salience is not yet solved: just as CD can yield a salient lexical meaning, so can SCWD. This is also predicted by the well-discussed theories of prototypes. To give an example, just as CD can produce a context-free meaning of 'reddy red', so SCWD can produce a context-free meaning of 'nurse' as 'female nurse', or 'teenager' as, say, 'rebellious young boy or girl, dressed to imitate pop stars'. How do we reflect this fact in the merger representations of DS? The answer is, we do not, and for good reasons. First, the addressee often does not know what salient meanings go through the speaker's head while composing the message. Second, these salient meanings do not have to match those of the recipient of the message. Third, as Giora demonstrates, these meanings are not necessarily relevant for the message at hand:

---

[5] See e.g. Asher and Lascarides 1995 on default inheritance; Pustejovsky 1995 on abductive inference; Giora 2003 on graded salience; Allan 2011 on probabilistic inference.

[6] Note that this process is not treated here as ambiguity resolution.

[7] See e.g. Berlin and Kay 1969.

'...more salient meanings – coded meanings foremost on our mind due to conventionality, frequency, familiarity or prototypicality – are accessed faster than and reach sufficient levels of activation before less salient ones. According to the graded salience hypothesis, then, coded meanings would be accessed upon encounter, regardless of contextual information or authorial intent.'

Giora (2003: 10)[8]

Defined in this way, they do not always enter the composition process captured in Σ. When they do, they are subsumed under a suitably flexible concept of 'word meaning'. The latter is the topic for Chapter 4 but the question to be discussed there is a very different one: given that there are such defeasible lexical meanings that do contribute to the compositional process captured in Σs, why do we then ascribe them to WS rather than CD/SCWD? In general terms, if their provenance is in fact CD or SCWD, why do we allocate them to the lexicon rather than to the pragmatics of processing? In Chapter 4 we will ascribe them to the lexicon—a flexible semantic storage that will make it redundant to descend to any attempts at lexical decomposition which are, in any case, doomed to fail, as the history of lexical semantics well forewarns. For now, this is the gist of the answer.

Returning to salient meanings, it is now clear that the term 'lexical salience' itself has two different uses: lexical salience independently of context (including, of course, cases of salience 'in spite of context' where the salient activated meaning is not employed in the composition process) and lexical salience triggered by context. We have here focused on the first, demonstrating that it is compatible with the understanding of salience in DS but only on the qualification as 'context-free' salience. It is compatible but attains relevance for the DS when this salience is utilized in the composition of meaning. Since '[w]hat is foremost on one's mind need not necessarily be foremost on another's' (Giora 2003: 37), what is foremost on one's mind cannot be assumed by one to be retrieved by another, and as such does not enter the picture of discourse interaction. Instead, it remains in the domain of the psychology of processing and only becomes a concern for a semanticist of a contextualist orientation when it happens to correspond to mutual, shared assumptions. In the words of Haugh (2008, 2011), defaults in conversation result from emergent intentionality: they rely on the process of co-construction of meaning.[9] Therefore, it follows that conversational defaults will subsume Giora's salient meanings when this salience becomes shared by the interlocutors due to the process of assimilating the understanding of words (ws) as conversation progresses, or the process of construction of complex concepts during social interaction.

---

[8] See also the discussions in Jaszczolt and Allan 2011.
[9] See also Tomasello, e.g. 2008, 2009 on the origins of human communication in shared intentionality and cooperation.

But from the point of view of the theoretical distinctions we defend here, context-free salience is also useful in another way in that it testifies to the need to revise the literal/non-literal distinction along the lines we pursued in Chapter 1. As Giora (2003: 33) observes on the basis of her experimental data:

'Though literal meanings tend to be highly salient, their literality is not a component of salience. The criterion or threshold a meaning has to reach to be considered salient is related only to its accessibility in memory due to such factors as frequency of use or experiential familiarity'.

Bearing in mind that neither conceptual analyses nor experimental research have succeeded in isolating a 'literal core' from which interpretation would depart, this empirical support for the context-independent activation testifies to a more function-based approach to word meanings, and as such will also support our decision to subsume SCWD/CD-driven and CPI-driven word meanings under the WS source in Chapter 4.

3.2 Primary meaning vis-à-vis the explicit/implicit distinction

Salience plays an important but multi-faceted role in DS. On the one hand, it features in the default, automatic but at the same time context- and interlocutors-dependent components of interpretation that are arrived via CD and SCWD. On the other, it features in our reinterpretation of word meaning in the spirit of what we can call 'illocutionary literality': while there are no literal meanings *tout court* that can be clearly separated from non-literal meaning, there are salient meanings that are clear, primary for an addressee due to his/her particular experience, but need not be relevant for the purpose at hand. Yet again, there are salient word meanings that are salient in virtue of shared experiences of the interlocutors and as such contribute to the co-construction of meaning and the compositional process of discourse interpretation.

There is also another, fourth, way in which salience features on this account. Merger representations of DS model primary meanings, that is, meanings that are recovered as main messages intended and communicated by the speaker. Such primary meanings, to repeat, cut across the explicit/implicit divide: they can be explicitly or implicitly communicated. This distinction into primary and 'other', secondary meanings as orthogonal to the explicit/implicit content is dictated precisely by this characteristic of salience: the main message is the most salient one, albeit not necessarily the most explicitly communicated one. It need not be a default reading; it can rely on some aspects that are arrived at by default, but also some aspects that are arrived at inferentially. Consider (8). The primary meaning makes use of a referential reading of the description (a default one, via CD) but it pertains to the implicit content in this context.

(8)   (Fiona and Jack stand in front of a window display in a local bookshop, looking at a new novel by Ian McEwan, *The Children Act*. Fiona says:) Ian McEwan is my favourite writer.

The likely primary message (but, of course, not the only one) is here that Fiona would like to buy the novel or would like Jack to buy the novel for her. The proper name acquires the strong referential reading via CD (suggesting some form of acquaintance with the person or, more likely, his works of fiction), while the overall message is recovered via CPI. It is the most salient message in our fourth sense of salience (salience$_4$).

At this point the 'fixers' in the contextualist camp[10] would ask for external evidence that a primary/secondary meaning distinction that is orthogonal to the explicit/implicit one has a *raison d'être* in a truth-conditional theory of meaning. Strong arguments have been provided through conceptual analyses such as those in Chapters 1 and 2. Next, there is also evidence from the psychological reality of what is said, collected through a questionnaire method.[11] Finally, some can be provided by investigating the property of cancellability. It is the latter to which I now turn.

In order to further support the category of primary meaning as it is construed in DS, one has to demonstrate that it is not the explicit/implicit distinction that makes a difference for cancellability but rather the primary/secondary one. Salience will help us do precisely that. Grice (1975: 39–40) proposed various well-known criteria for delimiting conversational implicatures, among which is cancellability: what is said is not cancellable, while what is implicated is. Some notable exceptions made his followers revise the criterion (Weiner 2006; Blome-Tillman 2008) but, essentially, the test withstood the trial of time and can still be used as a reliable criterion for the distinction we want.[12] In what follows, I summarize briefly Grice's cancellability test, move on to a rejection of some recent attempts to undermine it, and then apply it in turn to the explicit/implicit distinction as adopted by 'fixers' and to the primary/ secondary distinction adopted in DS. The test is shown to uphold the latter distinction. As a side corollary, the primary/secondary distinction in turn testifies to the utility of the test.[13]

According to Grice (1978: 44), there are two ways in which a putative conversational implicature can be cancelled. First, a putative implicature is explicitly cancellable when an utterance implicating p can be followed by 'but not p' or 'I don't mean to imply that p' without contradiction. The cancellation is explicit in that it takes

---

[10]   See Chapter 1.

[11]   E.g. Nicolle and Clark 1999; Schneider 2009 referred to in our previous discussions.

[12]   But see Capone 2009 on cancellability of the relevance-theoretic construct of an explicature (argued against in Chapter 1).

[13]   The arguments in what follows are developed from Jaszczolt 2009b.

place in the actual situation of discourse.[14] In practice, such a potential implicature is either cancelled or is prevented from arising in the first place. The other way pertains to contextual cancellability that arises whenever there are imaginable scenarios on which this potential implicature would not arise. The difference thus consists in juxtaposing actual acts of cancellation with the theoretical possibility that such an implicated meaning simply is not the case: two very different tests indeed. On first glance, explicit cancellation is more reliable in that it can easily be tested against speakers' judgements, while contextual cancellation, arguably, leaves room for tweaking the scenarios in such a way that the implicature in question is absent.

The main observation for our purpose, however, has to be that cancellation so conceived is not limited to Grice's GCIs. There are also potential particularized implicatures when the phenomenon is looked at from the perspective of the speaker (albeit, in agreement with Horn's (2004) slogan that speakers implicate and hearers infer, we would call them 'potential inferences'). Returning to (8), we can easily imagine Fiona continuing as in (8').

(8') Ian McEwan is my favourite writer. But I am not suggesting we should buy this book now. Let's get it for the Kindle.

The test, useful as it is, easily extends to such context-specific potential implicatures and as such does not help in arguments in support of the GCI/PCI distinction.

Grice's test came up for scrutiny in Weiner's (2006: 128) apt scenario in which an implicature is allegedly not cancellable. Instead, every attempt to cancel it will result in strengthening it even more.

'Suppose that Alice and Sarah are in a crowded train; Alice, who is obviously able-bodied, is sprawled across two seats, and Sarah is standing. Sarah says to Alice, "I'm curious as to whether it would be physically possible for you to make room for someone else to sit down.".'

It is obvious that on this scenario Sarah is not in fact curious about Alice's ability to move; rather, she ironically reproaches her for her selfish behaviour. Now, on Weiner's scenario, Sarah continues as follows: 'Not that you *should* make room; I'm just curious.' (p. 128). The conclusion follows that the attempted cancellation fails, and so the reliability of Grice's test collapses with it.

The argument is, however, unsound. Grice does not say that a particular imagined cancellation phrase *must* work, just that, on one hand, there are actual cancellation phrases that do work, and on the other, that we can imagine scenarios in which cancellations would work. The latter still holds. When due attention is given to the fact that the sentence functions as an implicit request, uttered ironically, then the cancellation phrase would look very different indeed. First, irony necessitates a

---

[14] See e.g. Haugh and Jaszczolt 2012 on the topic of ascribing intentions to speakers and Levinson 2000 who argues for the omnipresence of such explicit cancellation.

substitution of a different, often opposite, meaning in order to obtain the intended content.[15] This would give us something to the effect of (9).

(9)   I know that you are capable of moving a bit to make some room for others to sit.

Applied to this content, the cancellation as in (10) conforms to Grice's test, albeit its awkwardness testifies to the entrenchment of indirect request as a conventional, common way of executing this speech act.

(10)   But this is not a request to move.

Irony is thus not the best test case to dislodge Grice's criterion.

Next, Blome-Tillmann (2008) rightly observes that the explicit and the contextual cancellability ought to be kept apart and formulates the pertinent criteria of Explicit Cancellability and Contextual Cancellability. But he adds a rather curious requirement that both criteria have to be operative in order for the meaning to be classified as an implicature:

'Grice thought that since each of these two principles articulates a necessary condition on the presence of conversational implicatures, they provide us with a useful test for when such implicatures are *not* present: if the consequent of at least one of the two principles is not satisfied, Grice contended, then we can be sure that we are not dealing with a case of conversational implicature.'

Blome-Tillmann (2008: 157)

It is difficult to see how Grice's observation that implicit content can be cancelled in two ways can be legitimately made into a rigid two-pronged requirement. It is also difficult to see how explicit cancellation can be fitted into the same criterion as the 'thinking up' of scenarios. They are very different kinds of tests indeed. One pertains to situated meanings (Mey 2001, 2007), meanings of utterances in context, and the other to the meaning potential of the sentence. It seems that there is a simpler way out in this case, focusing on the properties of irony, which will also provide a more general principle for addressing outer, before inner, layers of interpretation.[16]

---

[15] See Kapogianni 2013 for a new typology and a discussion of the cancellability of irony.

[16] As I point out in Jaszczolt 2009b, Grice (1978: 44) himself observes that the test is not sufficient and has to be taken in conjunction with other criteria for implicature status. For example, assessment-relativity ('This tie is green' (in certain light conditions)) can result in cancellation but does not justify calling the cancelled meaning an implicature. Similarly, vagueness and non-literality ('I bought Lidia a lion ($\rightarrow_E$ a toy lion) for Christmas') allow for cancellation that does not signal an implicature status. The implication thus goes: when a meaning is an implicature, it has to be cancellable. The strengthening to a bi-conditional does not work:

'Now I think that all conversational implicatures are cancellable, but unfortunately one cannot regard the fulfilment of cancelability test as decisively establishing the presence of a conversational implicature. One way in which the test may fail is connected with the possibility of using a word or form of words in a loose or relaxed way.'   (Grice 1978: 44)

More importantly, however, Blome-Tillmann revises the requirement of the conjunctive test introducing 'Explicit* Cancellability', stating that the explicit cancellation phrase has to work only for some contexts. Had the mistaken assumption of a conjunction of tests not been adopted in the first place, confounding of Grice's explicit would not have had to take place. But *pace* what now appears to be unnecessary revision, what we have here is a valuable attempt at saving Grice's criterion. Doubts about its potential dispelled, we can now move to applying it in order to test the salience of explicit vis-à-vis primary meaning.[17]

First, we shall briefly assess differences in cancellability for the explicit/implicit divide adopted by 'fixers'. As was discussed in Chapter 1, since the mid-1980s one of the dominant themes in post-Gricean pragmatics has been to identify the types of contributions to what is said that have not been identified by Grice. When 'fixing' the semantic representation was in full swing, different kinds of contribution were identified. In brief, those pragmatic aspects of meaning that modify the logical form of the uttered sentence result in the explicit content, while the pragmatic processes that produce a separate thought with a separate logical form result in an implicit content.[18] In the scenario in (11), (11a) is the explicit content, while a proposition along the lines of (11b) is the most salient implicature: the recital was not appreciated by the audience and as such not a success (symbol '$\to_I$' stands for 'implicates').

(11)   (Jack and Fiona talk about Fiona's piano recital)
        Jack: Was the performance a success?
        Fiona: Some people applauded.

(11a) $\to_E$ Some but not all people applauded.

(11b) $\to_I$ The recital was not very good.

On this scenario, (11b), the implicit content, functions as the primary meaning. (11a), on the other hand, is weaker and can be regarded at best as one of the secondary meanings communicated in (11). Let us consider the cancellability of

---

[17] In Jaszczolt 2009b, I have also remarked on the important distinction between cancellation and simple self-correction. In (i), the second sentence can perform either of the two functions: revoking the potential reading 'exactly twenty pounds' or self-correcting.

(i)   I spent twenty pounds on books today. In fact, I spent twenty pounds and sixty pence.

The choice can be dictated by the content and/or the context, as well as by the availability of expressions that could be substituted for 'in fact'. For example, the negation marker in (ii) makes the self-correcting reading the only (or at least the strongly preferred) choice.

(ii)   I spent twenty pounds on books today. No, I spent twenty pounds and sixty pence.

[18] Part of this vintage debate is the search for the criteria for distinguishing the said/explicit from the implicit. See Carston 1988, 1998 and Recanati 1989.

the primary, implicit meaning. Once the enrichment in (11a) goes through, (11b) is very difficult to cancel. We could attempt (11c).

?(11c)   Some but not all people applauded. But this does not mean the performance was not good: most left in a hurry to catch the last train.

Possible in principle, (11c) sounds very odd as an answer to the question on the quality of the playing. It is simply irrelevant as an answer and as such violates the principles of conversational coherence.

Now, cancellation of (11a) is normally possible and easy, as (11d) demonstrates.

(11d)   Some people, in fact everyone, applauded.

But it is more difficult when the primary meaning in (11b) goes through. Following (11d), the implicature that the concert was not particularly good would not normally ensue unless after cancelling the secondary meaning we 'bring the implicature back', so to speak, strengthening it by repeating it as explicit content as in (11e).

(11e)   Some people applauded. In fact, I think everyone did but I still think my playing was awful.

On this scenario, the secondary, explicit content is cancellable without difficulty.

Even from this modest example a tentative conclusion can be drawn that it is not the explicit vs. implicit status of a message that affects cancellability but rather its salience. Implicatures that are well entrenched are not cancellable, while explicit content that results from pragmatic enrichment is cancellable when less entrenched. Needless to say, this allows us to surmise that the implicature in (11b) cannot be easily cancelled because it constitutes the primary meaning. Let us consider another example: a scenario that is well discussed in the literature and derived from Bach (1994). A little boy cuts his finger and cries, to which his mother reacts as in (12).

(12)   You are not going to die.

'Fixers' present the explicit content as (12a).

(12a) $\rightarrow_E$ The boy is not going to die from the cut.

On the other hand, DS opts for modelling the main intended meaning that in this case corresponds to an implicature resembling that in (12b) or (12c).

(12b) $\rightarrow_{I/PM}$ It is nothing serious.

(12c) $\rightarrow_{I/PM}$ There is no need to worry.

Again, as in the previous example, an attempt at a cancellation produces dubious results, as (12d) demonstrates.

[?](12d)   You are not going to die but it looks serious. We should rush you to the
hospital.

The cancellation only goes through if the idiomatic expression 'you are not going to
die' is understood literally. Otherwise, it produces a clash with respect to the
illocutionary and perlocutionary content.

In Jaszczolt 2009b, I also discussed evidence from biased questions by Reese and
Asher (2010). Sentence (13) conveys a bias towards a negative answer in virtue of the
presence of the negative polarity item 'ever'.

(13)   Is Fiona ever satisfied?

Negation in questions has the opposite effect: (14) signals an affirmative answer, and
(15) does so even more emphatically due to the presence of 'too' (as opposed to
'either').

(14)   Isn't Fiona angry?

(15)   Isn't Fiona angry too?

Next, (16) conveys a question and an assertion by making use of a question tag.

(16)   Fiona isn't angry, is she?

They point out that the conveyed 'biases' are not GCIs in that they are not cancellable, as (17) demonstrates.

[?](17)   Is Fiona ever satisfied? I am not suggesting she is never satisfied, I am just
asking.

Salient meanings of biased questions are difficult to cancel across the board.
Compare example (18), adapted slightly from Reese and Asher (2010: 155). By
asking a biased question, B saliently conveys that he/she disagrees with A, strongly
implicating (18a).

(18)   A: I have no beliefs on the matter.
        B: Aren't you a member of the Communist Party?

(18a)   →_{I/PM} Your political beliefs are biased towards communism.

The implicit meaning in (18a) is the primary meaning. Therefore, according to our
predictions it should be difficult to cancel—and it indeed is, as (18b) demonstrates.

(18b)   A: I have no beliefs on the matter.
        [?]B: Aren't you a member of the Communist Party? I am not suggesting you
        have political beliefs though.

Let us now consider implicatures that serve the purpose of secondary meanings in
order to check if they are equally entrenched. For this purpose, we will modify the

dialogue in (11), adhering to the same scenario, borrowed from Ian McEwan's novel *The Children Act*, as in (19).

(19)   (Jack and Fiona talk about Fiona's piano recital)
       Jack: Was the performance a success?
       Fiona: Yes, it was. The room was full and I got a standing ovation.

The explicit content resembles that in (19a). This content is also the primary meaning of Fiona's message. To repeat, merger representations of DS model discourses and hence $\to_E$ can capture multi-sentential contents.

(19a) $\to_{E/PM}$ Fiona's piano recital was a success. The concert room was full and she received a standing ovation.

As is usual in discourse, (19) is likely to come with a range of stronger or weaker secondary meanings, which in this case correspond to implicatures. (19b) can be easily envisaged to be one of them. '$\to_{SM}$' stands for 'communicates as secondary meaning'.

(19b) $\to_{I/SM}$ Fiona is happy with her performance.

But the secondary meaning in (19b) can be easily cancelled, as (19c) demonstrates.

(19c)   (Jack and Fiona talk about Fiona's piano recital)
       Jack: Was the performance a success?
       Fiona: Yes, it was. The room was full and I got a standing ovation. But I am not happy with my performance. It wasn't expressive enough.

So, unlike implicatures serving the purpose of primary meaning, implicatures that serve the purpose of secondary meaning seem to be quite easy to cancel.

   Let us try another example. (20) has explicit primary content as in (20a) and let us assume that on this scenario (20b) is a likely secondary meaning.

(20)   Fiona pushed Jack and he fell.

(20a) $\to_{E/PM}$ Fiona pushed Jack and as a result he fell.

(20b) $\to_{I/SM}$ Fiona was angry with Jack.

Again, the cancellation of (20b) is relatively easy, as (20c) exemplifies.

(20c)   Fiona pushed Jack and he fell. But she didn't do it deliberately, no matter what everyone thinks under the circumstances.

The meaning in (20b) is much less entrenched than the primary explicit meaning in (20a). When explicit content functions as primary meaning, cancellations are not easy in that the enriched meaning is often quite entrenched due to the frequency, conventions, or predictability. Most of all, the speaker normally assesses correctly the common ground and does not risk miscommunication. For example, cancelling the causal reading of 'and' in (20a) is rather difficult, as (20d) demonstrates.

?(20d)   Fiona pushed Jack and he fell. But he fell not because she pushed him but because he slipped on the wet floor.

To repeat, it is the fact that the explicit content functions as primary meaning that makes it so entrenched.

Analogous examples of cancellations can be thought up for other possible secondary meanings, such as 'Fiona has a bad temper', or even taking a different turn, 'Fiona couldn't have done it deliberately'. It is precisely the status of these implicatures as secondary meanings that makes them less entrenched.

Let us return briefly to the case of explicit content that functions as primary meaning. Clearly, when the explicit content does not require any significant departures from sentence meaning, the entrenchment can be predicted, and so can the difficulty with any attempted cancellation, as (19) and (19a) demonstrated. But even in the case of a more significant pragmatic contribution as in (20a), the cancellation in (20d) was shown to be difficult. It is pragmatically ill-formed in that it exposes the first conjunct as irrelevant and clearly misleading. On the other hand, explicit content, when it corresponds to an enriched logical form of the uttered sentence as proposed by 'fixers', can be more easily cancelled when it functions as secondary meaning, as was exemplified in (11e).[19]

To sum up, we have now considered four types of possible cancellation: cancellation of implicit content functioning as primary meaning, cancellation of explicit content functioning as primary meaning, cancellation of implicit content functioning as secondary meaning, and cancellation of explicit content functioning as secondary meaning—the latter on the scenarios where cancellation is, or is not, blocked by the implicit primary meaning. It can be concluded that the primary/secondary meaning distinction withstands the cancellation test: primary meanings are entrenched and as such difficult to cancel, while secondary meanings are by definition weaker, and as such, predictably, less entrenched and *a fortiori* easier to cancel.

Digression: Remarks on the method of conceptual analysis

We have used several pertinent scenarios in this argument and at this stage the methodological question arises as to whether testing the primary/secondary distinction vis-à-vis the explicit/implicit distinction using the cancellability test ought to be subjected to a more extensive empirical study—either using real examples from corpora of spoken language in order to see what kinds of cancellation we do find and what kinds we do not, or perhaps using a method of questionnaires with a battery of pertinent scenarios that would allow us to arrive at a quantitative result. It

---

[19] Throughout this discussion, the expression 'cancelling the content' means cancelling its status as an intended message.

appears, however, that it would be a gross overkill: empirical testing is required when predictions have the status of a plausible hypothesis. On the other hand, when a conceptual analysis demonstrates that salience and entrenchment, and by the same token weakness and cancellability of meanings, go hand in hand, it would be a waste of time and resources, as well as a methodological fallacy, to employ the method of falsification in trying to come up with a hypothesis to the contrary that could then be proven wrong. Sadly, precisely this error has befallen post-Gricean pragmatics: Grice's observation that implicatures are cancellable was unduly extended to the post-Gricean distinction between explicit but enriched vs. implicit content.[20] What was quite forgotten was that Grice himself would call such enriched or modified explicit content implicatures, and hence the characteristic of cancellability would apply to them, so there is no reason to uphold Grice's original take on the cancellability of implicatures or to juxtapose them with a post-Gricean 'explicit content'. What was also forgotten was that Grice was interested in saving the truth-conditional approach of meaning, so he didn't give much regard to the exact status of what falls outside his construct of the truth-conditionally evaluable what is said. As a consequence, the fact that some implicatures pertain to the main intended content, that is, the fact that primary meanings can be implicit, or to put it differently again, that there are indirect speech acts, fell outside his considerations at the time. One cannot simply take his cancellability test and apply it to the post-Gricean domain of 'fixers'; instead, it is necessary to realize that we are adopting it for a very different object indeed, that is the object of main intended meaning and secondary intended meaning. In this situation the results of our little tests simply could not render a different result—one has to admit it almost at a pain of circularity: salience and enrichment go hand in hand, just as weak meaning and cancellation do. So much the worse for those who did not spot this obvious correlation between 'salience at all costs' and entrenchment, while insisting on the correlation between entrenchment and fixed propositions. And, of course, so much better for those of the speech-act orientation who sever the link between salience and explicitness and point out the obvious.

Let me give one example of experimentation that suffers from testing a theory that is clearly not worth testing, in that conceptual analysis alone, of the type pursued in DS, reveals its flaws. Doran *et al.* (2012) follow the lead of other equally misled experimentalists who attempt to discredit GCIs by showing that GCIs are not always part of what is said. As we concluded in our earlier argument, this is simply unnecessary. They attempt to show what is obviously true and as such not in need of wasting resources or time on, namely that aspects of meaning that are commonly classified as GCIs are not automatically incorporated in the explicit content. They

---

[20] See e.g. Burton-Roberts 2006 who assesses the cancellability of *explicature*, that is, of a level in-between Grice's minimal what is said and Grice's implicature.

obtained the values between 15 and 63 per cent, depending on the *type of construction*, understood by them as the *type of GCI*. In particular,

'With respect to truth-conditional meaning, we found that no GCI type was consistently incorporated into what is said. By the same token, we also found that no GCI type was consistently excluded from what is said. Thus, we can conclude that for each GCI type, participants only sometimes incorporated the corresponding implicature into what is said, suggesting that speakers *are* able to access an interpretation exclusive of GCI – that is, one in which the GCI does not affect the truth-conditional meaning of the utterance.'

Doran *et al.* (2012: 145)

This finding is entirely predictable and corresponds to the fact that is simply necessary, as can be shown through a conceptual analysis alone.[21] Argumentation and exemplification alone demonstrate that Levinson's understanding of GCIs is too strong if what one looks for is a psychologically plausible category rather than, as he intended, a construct that would fit into a description of the power of a language system. The only way in which we can preserve the role of GCIs in the theory of meaning that aims at psychological plausibility with respect to meaning construction is to accept that, yes, it is true that there are context-free pragmatically derived meanings, the automatic, default meanings of DS, but these cannot be listed once and for all. They are context-free in that they arise *modulo* evidence to the contrary, but they do not arise *always*. For example, the referential or *de re*, or presupposing readings arise in virtue of the properties of the human inferential system (intentionality of mental states) but they do not always arise. It is therefore more accurate not to dub them 'context-free' *tout court* but perhaps 'context-free$_{CM}$', where the subscript '$_{CM}$' stands for Cognitive Minimalism proposed in Section 1.6.1 above: there is a default, made-up and assumed context that dictates such seemingly context-free meanings.

Having asked a wrong question, Doran *et al.* failed to notice an arguably more important corollary of their finding, namely that GCIs may not constitute a category in themselves. In fact, one can use their evidence to argue precisely to this end; their GCIs are characterized by significant differences in their salience, recoverability, and also entrenchment. It seems only natural to take one further step and opt for salience as the main criterion for attributing the status of primary or secondary meaning, abandoning the *what is said*/GCI/PCI distinction.

End of digression

---

[21] In Jaszczolt 2009b, I have also pointed out that mere exemplification that is common practice in theoretical linguistics fits with an adequate method of inquiry. Evidence of acceptability comes from intuitions, understood by Chomskyans as speakers' cognitive states that result from linguistic competence, and by Devitt (2006, 2010), for example, as subconscious, unreflective judgements that constitute the central processor's responses to stimuli. So, while the definition and origin of the intuitions is a debatable matter, their status in theoretical linguistic analyses is well defended.

To follow up on the method of analysis, we need two final disclaimers. First, what I have demonstrated here is not that cancellability provides a necessary and sufficient criterion for distinguishing primary and secondary meaning but rather that there is a strong correlation between salient, primary meaning and its entrenchment, analysed here as its resistance to cancellations. Next, and related, the question arises as to whether piling up counterexamples would be compatible with this method. Devising scenarios in which the putative intended meaning is cancelled is an easy task but it would necessitate introducing another variable into the argument, namely the difference between the meaning intended by the speaker and the meaning recovered by the addressee. And then the DS-theoretic concept of primary meaning, meaning intended by the Model Speaker and recovered by the Model Addressee, would no longer apply. Instead, we would be entering the domain of psycholinguistics, discourse misunderstandings, conversation breakdowns, and mismatches of information backgrounds, excluded here for very good reasons attended to in Chapter 2. Cancellation patterns would be very different indeed but we would also enter an entirely different domain of inquiry. The question of psychologism in DS is indeed an important one in that it has to be asked whether the latter is to be admitted at all, or, rather, following Frege, it is to be considered a 'corrupting intrusion', infecting theoretical investigations with the deficiencies of human mind and human behaviour. While at first glance adopting the desideratum of normativity and the perspective of the Model Speaker and the Model Addressee may suggest that we follow the Fregean line, it will emerge that modelling discourse where the object of study is *salient meaning independently of its form and provenance* requires a much more nuanced attitude to this 'contamination' with psychologism. This is the topic to which I now turn.

3.3 Psychologism: A 'corrupting intrusion'?

A normative approach to discourse meaning such as DS that stays away from miscommunication, deficiencies in recognizing common ground, conversational breakdown, deficiencies in the knowledge of the language or the shared customs of language use, ought not to be troubled by the psychology of language. But at the same time it cannot stay clear of the requirement of psychological plausibility of its heuristics and generalizations, or indeed the concomitant utilization of these heuristics in modelling discourse, say in the form of merger representations. This construal of the playing field requires a well-thought-out attitude to the question as to how much psychology of processing is to be included. The obvious methodological stance would be to answer: as little as it is necessary for building adequate representations; components of meaning in the compositional analysis have to be allocated to the correct processes and the components themselves have to be accurate: words, phrases, sentences, or some constituent fragments, and so forth. That is why throughout this project we are attending to the allocation of information to the relevant processes, justifying the decisions where questions ensue.

Arguably, this methodological stance testifies to the underlying rejection of psychologism: we are not in the business of talking about the 'messy' aspects of conversation, but instead pursue compositionality and lay down the rules, norms, or heuristics for this pragmatic, interactive composition. Following Frege's attempts at purifying logic and mathematics from the psychological perspective, psychologism has been understood precisely as a contamination as opposed to purity, the subjective as opposed to the objective, the unscientific as opposed to scientific, the unreliable as opposed to the reliable, the speculative as opposed to the proven, and so forth.[22] While in modern sciences the pejorative connotations are no longer appropriate in that psychology has scientific methods for dealing with what is seemingly chaotic in human behaviour, the methodological requirement of limiting the psychological aspect of a semantic theory seems to remain a condition *sine qua non*: by delimiting the object of study to regularities and generalizations, we only let in 'the mental' when it underlies this obedient conversational behaviour *and* adds to the explanatory adequacy of an account of it.

Formal analyses of language borrow from Frege the disinclination towards subjective mental representations, or particular, actual thought processes with all their convoluted, situated aspects. In his *Begriffsschrift*, Frege (1879a, b) presented an analysis of the logical form of judgements that gave rise to a breakthrough in the understanding of logic. It consisted of the well-known now function-argument analysis, where a function from objects to truth values gives the meaning of a predicate. Logic is no longer concerned with actual human reasoning but instead is understood as a mathematical system.[23] In *Grundlagen der Arithmetik*, Frege (1884a) reinforces the ban on psychologism by pointing out that the object of logic is to be freed from the subjective, from the psychological; the way thinking subjects arrive at definitions or valid proofs are the psychology, while the definitions and valid proofs themselves belong to logic. He writes:

---

[22] This is a further development of a discussion of psychologism that originated in Jaszczolt 2008.

[23] Frege's influence must not be overestimated though. Already in 1847 Boole's *The Mathematical Analysis of Logic* opened up a path to this paradigm shift by freeing the symbolic algebra from the interpretation of the symbols and focusing instead on 'the laws of their combination' (Boole 1847: 3). In a sense, the true origins of modern logic can thus be traced to Boole, as the famous opening passage of the introduction to this little treatise well indicates:

'They who are acquainted with the present state of the theory of Symbolical Algebra, are aware, that the validity of the processes of analysis does not depend upon the interpretation of the symbols which are employed, but solely upon the laws of their combination.'

(*ibid.*)

On the function-argument analysis see also Baker and Hacker 2003; Green 2006; or Stalmaszczyk 2006.

'The description of the origin of an idea should not be taken for a definition, nor should the account of the mental and physical conditions for becoming aware of a proposition be taken for a proof, and nor should the discovery ["Gedachtwerden"] of a proposition be confused with its truth! We must be reminded, it seems, that a proposition just as little ceases to be true when I am no longer thinking of it as the Sun is extinguished when I close my eyes.'

Frege (1884b: 88)

Next, in his *Grundgesetze der Arithmetik*, vol. 1 (Frege 1893: 202), psychological considerations in logic are called 'corrupting intrusion' in that *'being true* is quite different from *being held as true'*. In *Logic* (Frege 1897/1969: 243), the 'logical' is clearly contrasted with the domain of 'ideas and feelings' in that:

'Logic is concerned with the laws of truth, not with the laws of holding something to be true, not with the question of how people think, but with the question of how they must think if they are not to miss the truth.'

Frege (1897/1969: 250)

The importance of this new concept of logic for linguistic theory cannot be overstated in that very soon predicate logic was to become the metalanguage in which the formal analyses of natural language meaning were conducted,[24] using model theory and truth conditions, the latter successfully adopted into linguistics from Tarski by Davidson (1984).[25]

These were the origins of the application of formal logic as a tool for linguistic analyses. We have now moved on to adopting the truth-conditional method, as well as various formal languages derived from predicate logic and its extensions, to a more 'pragmaticky' object of study which in the radical Salience-Based Contextualism of DS pertains to the 'model discourse meaning': the meaning intended by the Model Speaker and recovered by the Model Addressee. The obvious question arises, how does such a model of discourse interpretation as DS fare with Frege's anti-psychologism? Does the ban on psychological considerations extend to radical contextualism in the analysis of natural language meaning? In Jaszczolt (2008: 36) I argued that psychologism was necessary in semantics at the pre-theoretic stage at which we delimit the object of study and the methods:

'... psychologism in truth-conditions-based pragmatic theory is necessary in order to formulate food for experimentation on at least the following fronts: [1] the perspective which should be adopted: that of the speaker, the addressee, or a Model Speaker – Model Addressee interaction; [2] the unit on which the pragmatic inference or default enrichment operate; [3] the definition and delimitation of default interpretations vis-à-vis conscious pragmatic inference; and [4] what counts as the main meaning to be modelled. This considerably narrows down the playing field.'

---

[24] See Montague 1974; Partee 2004. [25] See also Jaszczolt 2002a, Chapters 3, 5.

I am no longer certain that this is indeed the case. The pre-theoretic use of psychologism is not yet psychologism in natural language semantics; it is, so to speak, methodological psychologism or a form of *metapsychologism*. On the one hand, if we follow Travis's (2006b: 125–6) supposition, taking *any* stance on the topic of logical laws is already a form of psychologism in that it is permeated with the stance on *how people grasp logical laws*. So defined, psychologism also affects Frege's works cited above. On the other hand, by extension, one can argue that adopting any stance on how psychological considerations interact with a given area of scientific inquiry also is a form of psychologism. If so, psychologism permeates the entire DS-theoretic enterprise, and in fact the entire contextualist, post-Gricean project in semantics and pragmatics of natural language. At the same time, normativity of DS keeps psychologism at bay in that it is not the actual understanding of a real, physical utterance and the actual intentions of a real speaker that we are concerned with. The latter would be the domain of psycholinguistics that includes an inquiry into the reasons for miscommunication and conversation breakdown—a domain that we have carefully kept apart from a normative and formalizable theory of discourse meaning that is characterized by its methodological requirement of compositionality and its desideratum of predictive power. Model speakers and model addressees are theoretical constructs that gather together the human conversational experience that leads to generalizations and heuristics. As such, DS is psychology-free. But in virtue of the very object of study, the meaning of the conversational interactants, the participants in the conversation, DS is permeated with psychologism: we model not meaning in abstraction but meaning as used in acts of communication.

There is a further step in this argument though. As we have argued throughout these three chapters, the meaning of acts of communication is pretty much all there is: the only semantic theory that is worth pursuing is a theory of *meaning in linguistic interaction* in the title of this book. This is so for multiple reasons to do with compositionality, salience, psychological reality (note the metapsychologism again), discussed at length throughout Chapters 1–3. But it is mostly to do with the problems with delimiting semantics as a study of meaning pertaining to the language system alone, discussed in more detail in Chapter 4 in the domain of word meaning. It seems that if we adopt the stance that the semantics of linguistic interaction is all there is, then, surely, the entire question of psychologism begins to look inapplicable to linguistic semantics: all there is to meaning is how speakers of a language use this language; there is no meaning in abstraction from discourse. As we argue in detail in Section 4.1, DS grants that there are context-free$_{CM}$ concepts. But these concepts are fluid to the extent that the literal/non-literal distinction cannot be discerned.[26] While WS pertains to syntactic structures of the language used for communication, the

---

[26] See Sections 1.4 and 4.2.

composition of meaning takes place on the level of conceptual structures (mental representations) and these structures do not obey the syntactic constraint; they do not necessarily follow the logical form of the uttered sentence, *pace* various attempts by 'fixers' to make them appear to do so. Merger representations of DS demonstrate how such syntactic-constraint-free conceptual structures can be built, and so do, albeit in a different way, some extant approaches in the cognitive linguistics paradigm.

Now, if conceptual structures constitute the most adequate, and perhaps the only, level for semantic analysis, then the question about psychologism does not apply. There would have to be an object of inquiry that, after subtracting psychologism, gives objectivist and 'pure' normative semantics. We have shown that it is the semantics of linguistic interaction that is the core; there is no possibility of any 'subtraction'.

In a way, we are moving in this argument in the direction opposite to Frege's: he laid the foundations for new, subject-free logic, capturing valid arguments for a formal language, whereas we start with the formal language as a means of description but use it *not* to capture patterns of deduction (or at least, not only and not in abstraction) but rather various human convoluted means of reasoning, as well as shortcuts through reasoning—the *nonmonotonic logic of human conversational interaction*. DS attempts to capture these patterns and as such has one advantage over the cognitive paradigm in that it does not break away from the methods of formal semantics; it adopts the salient, primary meanings as the object of study, rendering representations that may have nothing or little in common with the logical form thrown up by WS, but at the same time uses the formal language modelled on predicate logic and its modal and temporal extensions and assumes the compositional structure.

Rounding up, let us assess one more quotation from Frege against the background of this discussion of contextualist semantics:

'If a geographer was given an oceanographic treatise to read which gave a psychological explanation of the origin of the oceans, he would undoubtedly get the impression that the author had missed the mark and shot past the thing itself in a most peculiar way. (...) The ocean is of course something real and a number is not; but this does not prevent a number from being something objective, and this is what is important.

Reading this work [see below, KJ] has enabled me to gauge the extent of the devastation caused by the irruption of psychology into logic ...'

Frege (1894: 209)

This passage derives from Frege's review of Husserl's *Philosophy of Arithmetic, I* where Husserl offers a psychological treatment of number. Phenomenology was of course the main target of Frege's 'purification' from the subjective. But looking at the history of research on acts of communication, through late Wittgenstein, speech-act theorists Austin and Searle, to post-Gricean forms of contextualism, we have to acknowledge that they all benefit from the phenomenological insights into intentionality of mental states and the discussion of how meaning is endowed and externalized (see Husserl 1900–01). In Husserl's *Logische Untersuchungen*, the co-existence of the psychological and the formal is natural and well-motivated. On the one hand, we have the aboutness of mental acts that endow meaning, on the other we have the first attempt at a categorial grammar (Husserl's Investigation IV, *ibid.*). The intentionality of acts of consciousness then informs speech-act theory, while a formal analysis of language informs formal semantics. It appears that Frege's ban ought not to percolate to natural language semantics where the objects of inquiry are mental representations and the methods are formal and where the construal of the composition of meaning on the cognitive level is as good as it gets: 'psychologically contaminated' meaning is the only meaning there is.

But here is where the semantics of linguistic interaction obeys Frege's desideratum: in *Der Gedanke*, Frege (1918–19: 342) says that the domain of logic is not 'investigating minds and contents of consciousness owned by individual men' but rather 'the investigation of *the* mind; of *the* mind, not of minds'. Fregean *thought* is construed on similar principles: '[a]lthough the thought does not belong with the contents of the thinker's consciousness, there must be something in his consciousness that is aimed at the thought' (*ibid.*). This more concessive stance subsumes Grice's idealized meanings$_{NN}$, Levinson's presumptive meanings, DS-theoretic model meanings and merger representations, and even Husserl's meaning-giving acts; they are all about *the* mind and *the* meaning in idealized acts of communication. In this sense, we are all Fregean after all.

A digression: Minimalism and contextualism—co-existence or choice?

In Chapters 1 and 2, we assessed the rationale for minimalist, contextualist, and indexicalist 'fixers' and DS-theoretic, primary-meaning-driven (and as such, speech-act-driven) stances on the truth-conditional content. We also pointed out that the question of the compatibility of minimalist, including here Grice's own, and contextualist approaches has been well rehearsed in the literature (see e.g. Saul 2002), leading to a consensus that the programs can co-exist in that they concern different domains of inquiry. For example, Grice is interested in model interactants (the feature also adopted in DS), while Borg in her minimal semantics is interested in the language system delimited by its modularity and adherence to deduction. However, the current discussion on psychologism sheds some doubt on this auspicious picture. One can proceed by asking the question: Do psychological considerations permeate all of the stances? If the answer is 'yes', then the co-existence may not be a defensible stance. It can be rescued when all we find is metapsychologism, the methodological psychologism discussed earlier in this section; to repeat, metapsychologism concerns the choice of theoretical assumptions, objects of study and desiderata. If, however, we also glean psychologism proper, then, so to speak, 'being a minimalist in the morning and a contextualist in the afternoon' may not be an internally consistent enterprise.[27] To be consistent, one would have to demonstrate that the two have distinct objects of inquiry, like, say, pursuing a project in historical syntax in the morning and (synchronic) syntactic theory in the afternoon. They inform each other but their aims are distinct. In the case of Meaning$_{NN}$, Insensitive Semantics, Minimal Semantics, Truth-Conditional Pragmatics, Default Semantics, and various forms of indexicalism, however, meaning is pursued with a greater or smaller recourse to context. They are all founded on a proposition, a unit that undergoes a truth-conditional analysis. And as such, they have to allow for some dose of intervention from the situation of discourse: be it free enrichment or just filling in slots provided by the grammar. As will be argued in Chapter 5, grammar does not provide a reliable explanans for a minimal, allegedly system-based construal; indexicals serve many different purposes, and the indexical/non-indexical distinction, looked at from the perspective of the units that in natural languages serve as indexicals, turns out to be nothing more than philosophers' fiction. There is no clear demarcation line between the minimal and the contextual construal. They all 'psychologize' meaning, be it by resolving reference and disambiguation or by doing more than that.

If this is the case, then the question arises, what 'dose' of psychologism is the correct one. Facing a gradation rather than a binary split into minimalism and contextualism, there seem to be two methodologically plausible solutions: the smallest, pertaining to the least 'corrupting intrusion', or the largest, where we capture the intended meaning, making it as sensitive to the speaker's intentions as necessary.

The smallest dose within the proposition-based accounts will not do, in that, to repeat, to obtain a proposition it has to be founded not only on the meanings derived from the language system but also has to make use of situation-dependent, albeit grammar-triggered, meanings. But what if propositionalism were to be abandoned, like in Bach's (2001) radical minimalism? We would still have filling in of slots that correlate with stable semantic roles; the ones provided, as he says, '*by* context' (say, 'I'), not '*in* context' (say, 'she'), by the speaker's intention (p. 32).[28] So, again, the object of study is still some rudimentary speaker's meaning rather than meaning in the language system alone. But without propositions even for simple sentences such as 'She is happy' and without the associated possibility of a truth-conditional analysis, this proposal falls out of our domain of inquiry; instead, the object of study that fits with our above list would be Bach's (1994: 273) implicitures. They 'go beyond [his minimal, KJ] what is said, but unlike implicatures, which are additional propositions external to what is said, implicitures are built out of what is said'. And this is contextualism through and through and psychologism through and through. The

---

[27] See also the discussion of Cognitive Minimalism in Section 1.6.1.
[28] My emphasis.

answer to our question about the 'dose' of contextualism would then have to be that, out of the two options, it is the largest rather than the smallest, where we model the real, primary, salient, intended meanings.

In answer to our main question concerning compatibility, it has to be concluded then that psychologism permeates all of the approaches to meaning that adopt the truth-conditional analysis and, if we were to use the, to use Frege's word, 'corrupting intrusion' as a criterion in resolving the question of compatibility, the answer would have to be negative. Whether psychologism *ought to* be regarded as a criterion of this compatibility is, of course, a question for metasemantics for which we have given here a positive answer. On the other hand, whether psychologism works as a criterion of adequacy of semantic theories themselves is an entirely different metasemantic question to which the answer was found to be negative.

End of digression

3.4 Concluding remarks

Salience is what linguistic interaction is built on. Thoughts are conveyed directly and indirectly, strongly or weakly. We can control the way in which they are conveyed and we can control the strength with which they are conveyed because we know how information is *normally* conveyed and we come to the situation of discourse with a baggage of previous experience, generalizations and abstractions over this experience, as well as anticipations of conversational goals. Salience, culminating in automatic retrieval of meaning, is present in discourse on two levels. First, it is a characteristic of lexical meanings and belongs to WS in that words are flexible and trigger memories of their past uses. Second, it is a characteristic of the process of the recovery of the intended meaning of utterances and discourses and as such belongs to the level of Σ, the level of merging information. As a foundation of communication, salience requires a unit of analysis that would capture it but surpass the divisions into the manners in which salience is achieved. We found such a unit in primary meanings that cut across the explicit/implicit divide that has been so entrenched in post-Gricean theories. We have also provided evidence in support of this construct, coming from cancellability tests and its psychological plausibility vis-à-vis alternative construals. We have also found it to be the methodologically most preferred candidate for the meaning to be modelled.

4

Delimiting the lexicon

'What kind of mask is everyone wearing? I thought these people were on my side. But the mask is all that's on my side – that's it!'

Philip Roth, *American Pastoral* (1998, London, Vintage, p. 353)

4.1 Dynamic words

In his *LOT2: The Language of Thought Revisited*, Jerry Fodor's pursuit of mental representations of meaning results in a common-sense claim, but the one that is often laboriously arrived at, that 'reference is the only primitive mind-world property' (2008: 16). Adopting this tenet as a theoretical assumption gives us a springboard for what we want to do in this chapter: assess what exactly it is that the lexicon of a natural language brings into the process of interpretation of meaning in discourse. In the DS-theoretic terms, we want to know what the 'W' in the WS source contains and what the 'W' in the WS process operates on. We have to start with the observation that the above statement is not exactly accurate in that there is no 'W' source in DS; there is a WS and it is so for a reason: the lexicon contains information about the *structures it enters into* (on the construction grammar accounts),[1] or, as generativists claim, the *structures that it allows to create*. Although argument structure is approached very differently in generative accounts of grammar on the one hand, and in construction grammar on the other, they all agree on one point of principle: the lexicon and the structure are not merely levels of analysis in a linguistic hierarchy; they are more intimately connected. It is so independently of whether we portray them as linguistic structures permitted by the language system and clearly delimited by its formal syntax, or as constructions that language users create, delimited by the purposes of discourse and by conversational practices.[2] As is evident from the previous three chapters, in spite of its formal, proposition- and truth-conditions-based foundations, DS leans towards the cognitive orientation of construction grammars as far as the dynamic construal of the object of these formal analyses is concerned. This makes it

---

[1] Construction grammar provides an explanation here in the form of the *lexicon/syntax continuum*.

[2] See e.g. Ludlow 2011 for the discussion of the first paradigm and Croft 2001 for the latter.

Meaning in Linguistic Interaction. Kasia M. Jaszczolt.

eclectic, in a way (but positively so), as regards its objects vis-à-vis its methods. The debate surrounding the power and adequacy of syntactic theories (and even paradigms) will not concern us here; our interest in it will be only tangential. Instead, we will focus on the lexicon as it is used in natural language discourse, with its flexibility and productivity, its fluid standards of correctness and the flexible definitions for the corresponding concepts. The question we want to address can be broken down into the following two, more theory-internal, questions:

(i)   What components of information that participates in the construction of merger representations can be attributed to WS?

and

(ii) What are the criteria for attributing information to WS as opposed to other sources?

Let me give an example. In (1), the word 'country' has the meaning 'the inhabitants of the country', or 'the citizens of the country', or 'the majority of the working population of the country'.

(1)   The country is tired of the austerity measures.

The word 'country' is not used strictly literally, but neither is it an obvious metaphor: 'country' is often used as an abstract term or a collective term for its inhabitants rather than a term referring to the physical, geographical location. The question is, how does the addressee know how to process the word 'country' on hearing the sentence? Where does this information come from? Is it there, in the lexicon, or does it emerge from the composition of the sentence meaning, or perhaps does it come from the context: from the salient default meaning or the salient occasion meaning of the term? In DS-theoretic terms, is this information obtained via WS or rather via SCWD or CPI?

In one way or another, the question of the delimitation of the lexicon is currently pursued within semantics of different orientations (see e.g. Asher 2011; Borg 2010, 2012) as well as in the philosophical literature (e.g. Ludlow 2014). In this chapter we state the question in terms of the sources and processes of DS and attempt to pursue it in the following way. We begin with the working assumption adopted in Chapter 1 that the highest degree of concession one can afford to the lexicon, such as occasion-sensitivity of meaning (Travis 2008), founded on what we now call meaning elim-inativism (Wittgenstein 1953), would be a weak position to fall back on and ought to be adopted only when it is clearly demonstrated that no account that admits some form of 'core meaning' of a word or regularity to its use can be made to work. In Section 4.1.1 I show why this is the best strategy to adopt. Next, I discuss problems with the 'core plus meaning shift' approaches (Section 4.1.2) and address the question of the utility of the concept of salience in the lexicon (Section 4.1.3). In what follows, I move to the role and concept of context, addressed through the problem spelled out in (ii) above, namely the boundaries between sources and the content of the processes identified in DS, moving to the proposal hinted at in various places in this book, namely that context identifies the units for a semantic analysis—the so-called 'fluid characters' (Section 4.2). Next, I return to the problem signalled in my earlier reference to Fodor, namely the semantic status of reference, in particular asking the question about the role of the lexicon (and WS) in acts of referring in linguistic interaction, juxtaposed with the roles played by other sources and other processes identified in DS (Section 4.3). Conclusions follow, reinforcing the role of lexicon/grammar/pragmatics trade-offs, but at the same time justifying the boundary between them—and *a fortiori* between WS, CPI, and SCWD in DS.

4.1.1 *Where lexicon ends and pragmatics begins*

While Fodor may be correct in saying that 'reference is the only primitive mind-world semantic property' (2008: 16), one must remember that he is talking about the language of thought:

'There may be no good reason for supposing that English has a semantics at all; perhaps the only thing that does is Mentalese. If that's right, then what are usually called "semantic level" representations of English sentences (or representations of their "logical form") are really no such things. Rather, they should be taken as representing translations of English into Mentalese. The translation of a sentence in Mentalese is, of course, no more a representation of that sentence than is its translation in French. To suppose otherwise would be to commit what in the old days they called a "category mistake".'

Fodor (2008: 219)

This possibility is perfectly compatible with the view of compositionality developed within DS when we assume that merger representations are conceptual representations and as such represent thoughts—propositional thoughts held in the language of thought but expressed via natural language lexicon and grammar, but also via the situation of discourse and some assumptions shared among the interlocutors. But what is interesting is that this view remains perfectly fine even when we assume that the language of thought *is* a particular natural language in which we speak; all we have to do is shift compositionality to the level of performance and the level of merger representations. Now, where does this leave us as regards natural language lexicon? It leaves us with precisely these two options: either there are concepts that need not stand in one-to-one correspondence with the lexical items of the language used in the discourse in question, or concepts are word meanings but there is something else: concepts that pertain to other vehicles of meaning, concept shifts that are triggered by those other vehicles. In other words, we have to conduct the analysis either on the level of concepts of the language of thought, or on the level of the use of words. In a 'conceptual analysis' that is founded on natural language discourse, we have only the latter option open to us.

Let us assume for the moment that there are core 'literal' meanings that provide a template, or a starting point, for any interpretation of utterances in discourse. Metaphorical meanings are then produced in the process of departing from such literal cores—for example through *ad hoc* concept construction—a dynamic, online process triggered as and when the situation signals that such a meaning is intended. These processes are then either free from any formal constraints (Carston 2002) or proceed according to rules that can be set out as abstractions over concept formation as in Asher's (2011) type composition logic (TCL). The latter includes complex lexical types, to reflect an ambiguity in the sense of fulfilling different grammatical functions—for example 'fall' in (2) and (3).

(2)   This was a dangerous fall, you could have injured yourself.

(3)   The surface is wet and slippery—no wonder you fell.

Such rules will also include relations between senses, for example between 'stop' and 'finish' which support slightly different sets of grammatical patterns as in (4) and (5).

(4)   John has finished the garden/the kitchen.

*(5)   John has stopped the garden/the kitchen.
       (from Asher 2011: 230)

In this example, Asher proposes that the difference can be captured by the sets of type presuppositions the words come with. Unlike 'stop', 'finish' in transitive constructions presupposes that the agent's activity directly affects the object. The problem is that the all-pervasiveness of various context-driven departures from such lexical rules makes the formalization very difficult and the proposal is in danger of slipping into a contextualist view such as Carston's *ad hoc* concept construction or Recanati's free, top-down modulation:

'Radical pragmaticists like Recanati claim that contextual effects are to be found everywhere. The view I have elaborated here is more cautious, but TCL predicts discourse effects to be possible wherever there is underspecification in lexical and compositional semantics. Given the discussion of the coercion data, lexical underspecification might be quite common.'[3]

Asher (2011: 245)

However, abstractions over such processes of making a word fit an uncommon mould, or one of several available moulds, do not yet allow us to build a semantics

---

[3] Coercion means an effect a word exerts on another word, making it alter its ordinary meaning. For example, 'finished' in 'I finished a book' coerces the argument into playing a role of an event: commonly reading a book, or in some cases writing a book.

as we understand it, that is the semantics of linguistic interaction. They allow us to attempt a formal semantics of a minimalist kind that would pertain to the available, well-formed structures of a particular natural language. But even this is problematic in that every novel type of coercion will fall outside the system already built, unless we attempt to capture it, so to speak, even before it occurs. The feasibility of such an abstraction is weak indeed. Further, it has to be remembered that the standard problems with the compositionality of natural language semantics (such as intensional contexts) still remain, which makes this route less attractive than the routes of interactive, pragmatic compositionality in DS or the compositionality in Mentalese proposed by Fodor.

In many ways, Asher's TCL is not far away from the minimalist view on which words have simple meanings but the slots into which they fit in the structure are governed by rich rules. Borg (2010, 2012) calls this 'organizational lexical complexity' and the resulting approach 'organizational lexical semantics' (OLS). This is how it works according to Borg (2012: 196):

'"Want" means *want*, then, but the lexicon contains more information than this, containing in addition rules which tell us the kinds of arguments the term can take and the rules of composition relevant to those different arguments. As on the current proposal, this additional information is not meaning constituting: one could know the meaning of "want" without knowing the kind of arguments the expression requires. This ignorance would no doubt be reflected in all kinds of errors but it seems they would be errors about how "want" works not about what "want" means.'

The idea is that, in agreement with Fodor, words don't decompose but instead the structures that they enter into are harnessed into semantic regulatory principles such as for example 'if x is a dog, x is animate'; 'if x is blue, it is coloured', and so forth—a principle well known from Carnap's (1952) meaning postulates.

Sadly, the solution seems to fail for the same reason for which meaning postulates had failed, and for the same reason for which Asher's TCL ultimately falls back on radical contextualism: the contextual effects are too strong and too omnipresent; they are strong to the extent that almost anything goes in lexical composition as long as one is sufficiently creative to invent an appropriate scenario. Moreover, it is not clear what advantage we gain from assuming that word meaning can be separated from 'knowing how to use it': if I understand 'want', then, surely, I understand that the want/desire/wish has an *object*, that I can want/desire/wish to obtain this (material or abstract) object *from someone*, or that that I want/desire/wish it *for someone*. While language constructions pertaining to such concepts differ from language to language, the concepts seem to be intricately connected with the meaning of 'want' and, *pace* Borg, they do contain structural information—structural on the level of mental representations (for example DRSs or Σs) but also reflected in the structure of the sentence. To exemplify the three '*want* concepts' mentioned above, let us compare

(6)–(8) with their Polish equivalents in (9)–(11). Relevant grammatical features are listed in the translation.

(6)   I want an ice-cream.

(7)   I want you to buy me an ice-cream.

(8)   I want Lidia to eat an ice-cream.

(9)   Chcę   loda.
      want-*Pres.1Sg*   ice-cream-*Acc*

(10) Chcę,   żebyś   kupił   mi   loda.
      want-*Pres.1Sg*   that-*Subj.2Sg* buy-*Past3SgM*   me-*Dat* ice-cream-*Acc*

(11) Chcę,   żeby   Lidia zjadła   loda.
      want-*Pres.1Sg*   that-*Subj* Lidia eat-*Past3SgF* ice-cream-*Acc*

Wanting *something* is associated with the accusative case in Polish; wanting it *from* someone triggers a controlled PRO construction in English and a complement clause in Polish, and analogously with wanting it *for* someone.[4] The exact constructions will differ from language to language but it is difficult to imagine a convincing support for a view that separates the structures—be it on the level of universal grammar or on the level of conceptual representation of linguistic practice—from the concept of *want* itself.

All in all, not only do the attempts at a normative, rule-based system fail because of the all-pervasive freedom to circumvent such rules in a context, but, independently, they fail because building them into the words does not yield to sufficient generalization and abstraction, and *not* building them into words misses essential components of the concepts themselves.

4.1.2 *Against meaning shifts*

It appears that meaning shifts, from the abstracted core to the context- and situation-specific intended sense, will not work. This explains the curious appeal that meaning eliminativism has had, returning periodically to the forefront of semantics and philosophy of language: Wittgenstein's meaning as use or Travis's occasion-sensitivity exorcize such problems by appealing to the *hic et nunc* of the discourse, above any abstractions and systems. But this does not yet give us a semantics. Ludlow (2014) provides here an interesting step, saying that semantics need not be precise: word meanings are inherently dynamic and underspecified and the very fact that we

---

[4] In generative linguistics PRO ('big pro') is an empty category that takes the subject position of a non-finite clause.

use them affects ('adjusts') them: 'human languages are things that we build on a conversation-by-conversation basis' (p. 3) and 'we are using our conversation to make adjustments to the language itself, perhaps to clarify the claims that will only follow later' (p. 4). The view also entails the dynamic construction of the lexicon: the language faculty, assumed on Ludlow's view, provides the basic 'skeleton' upon which words are built by discourse participants in a collaborative process by means of 'lexical entrainment' (Clark, e.g. 1996).[5] This dynamic and essentially rule-free view allows for a semantic theory to be kicked up to the level at which in DS we have the merger of information: the semantics is the semantics of utterances, not sentences. Foreseeing 'a theory which computes the semantic values of utterances (or, if you prefer, tokens)—not sentences construed as abstract objects', Ludlow's proposal remains at a stage of an attractive but undeveloped manifesto. As he says, 'this is a distinctively anti-Kaplanian assumption which I won't defend here' (Ludlow 2014: 112).[6] This is precisely where semantics of discourse interaction such as DS takes up the task, with the proviso that DS distinguishes the level of dynamic types—a level between Ludlow's types and tokens—introduced in what follows as fluid characters.

Now, if a semantic theory can be built upon such assumptions, and it has predictive power, then these assumptions are justified. The problem is that it is very difficult to see how allowing so much freedom to word meanings can still lead to a normative theory: it probably cannot. And if we have no normativity, we have no predictive power, and we have no formalization (*nota bene*, also rather flippantly rejected by Ludlow). It seems that we are now left with only one option: if we want a semantic theory that allows for the freedom of context-dependence and at the same time recognizes the fact that there *are* word meanings, that, to put it crudely, the word 'dog' is much more likely to refer to dogs than cats or food processors, we have to start with the assumption that words stand for concepts but that these concepts are situation-specific *not* because they shift according to some clear rules or that they are constrained by the possibilities of the grammar; neither are they situation-specific because they are built in the process of language use. Rather, they are dynamic simply

---

[5] *Entrainment* is a term used by Clark to describe the emergence of meaning in the process of joint action—a view with which DS is very sympathetic:

'Picture Helen and Sam each looking at the diagram of a maze and talking about it on the telephone. The horizontal passages in this maze can be described as rows, lines, columns, or paths, and so can the vertical passages. But once Helen has described the horizontal passages as *rows*, that sets a precedent. From then on, Sam must use *rows* for the horizontal passages and some other term – say, *columns* or *lines* – for the vertical ones. The reason: Helen's precedent becomes the jointly most salient solution to Sam's next reference to the passages, and Sam must conform or risk misunderstanding (. . .). Entrainment of terms like this is ubiquitous in conversation – powerful evidence for precedent as a major source of coordination in language use.'

Clark (1996: 81)

[6] We are going to go further and 'pragmaticize' Kaplan's approach in the domain that is the closest to Kaplan's (1989a) own concerns, namely pure indexicals, in Chapter 5.

because they are susceptible to new uses in virtue of past uses; the generalization over past uses does not produce an abstract concept but instead paves the way towards new uses. In this sense, Clark's and Ludlow's co-construction is the closest match. But what they miss is an account of how this co-construction is delimited. To repeat, Carnap's postulates or Borg's organizing principles will not suffice because they belong to a wrong level of analysis. Instead, situation-driven inference and society-, culture- and science-driven default interpretations seem to serve the purpose well, and so do the architecture-of-the-brain-driven cognitive defaults. They will tell us that 'the country' can stand for its inhabitants, its geographical location, or even for its underpaid working population as in example (1) above (SCWD or CPI); they will tell us that the definite article signals the strongest informativeness and hence the presupposing reading in that we are talking about the interlocutor's shared location, United Kingdom (CD);[7] finally, they will testify to the importance of the lexicon/grammar/pragmatics trade-offs but, unlike meaning eliminativism, will not obliterate the differences between them by subsuming kinds of information specific to CD, SCWD or CPI under a corrupted and unrestrained WS.

It seems that Allan's (2011) distinction between monotonic and nonmonotonic inferences triggered by lexical items points in the same direction. In (12) and (13), 'lamb', 'goat', 'leopard', and 'fox' all share a meaning 'the product of the animal in question'.

(12)   Harry prefers lamb to goat.

(13)   Jacqueline prefers leopard to fox.
         (from Allan 2011: 180)

This meaning is non-cancellable and can be described as a result of a monotonic process of reasoning—albeit in practice it is likely to be arrived at automatically, by default. At the same time, (12) and (13) differ in that the first triggers the reading 'the meat of the animal in question' while the latter 'the pelt of the animal in question', rendering the interpretations as in (12') and (13') respectively.

(12')   Harry prefers lamb ($\to_E$ eating lamb) to goat ($\to_E$ eating goat).

(13')   Jacqueline prefers leopard ($\to_E$ wearing leopard skin) to fox ($\to_E$ wearing fox fur).

---

[7] This is what Vicente (2012) seems to mean when he postulates that words have rich semantics, in the sense of rich conceptual structure; occasion-sensitivity à la Travis will not suffice unless every sense is in itself rich, comprising both encyclopaedic and world knowledge. However, his rather programmatic view seems to be open to the same objection as any other component-based view: how do we discriminate between what is in such a conceptual structure vis-à-vis the meaning potentials that are to be left out? Knowability of such structures poses another problem.

This part of the meaning is defeasible and as such a result of a nonmonotonic process. It is rather difficult to envisage scenarios on which the meat-of and pelt-of readings would be reversed. However, it is not difficult to imagine a specific scenario where different interpretations ensue, as in (12") and (13"), albeit with the proviso that the plural form is more natural here than the generic bare noun. Imagine that Harry works on a farm, Jacqueline works in a zoo, and their main task is to feed the respective animals.

(12")   Harry prefers lamb ($\to_E$ feeding lambs) to goat ($\to_E$ feeding goats).

(13")   Jacqueline prefers leopard ($\to_E$ feeding leopards) to fox ($\to_E$ feeding foxes).

At the same time, unless a specific scenario is available, it seems likely that the interpretations in (12')–(13') will arise automatically. As such, they are then attributable to 'WS+SCWD' in that it is the knowledge of the social customs of eating lamb and wearing leopard skin that affords these sentences such salient meanings (although, to move with the times and acknowledge animal rights, we ought to assume faux fur in this case!)

The phenomenon is analogous to that of the case of prototypes discussed in Section 3.1, viz. 'teenager' or 'red'. We surmised there that the first produces a stereotype of a young boy or girl, rather rebellious towards parents and society, and perhaps dressed to imitate pop stars.[8] The latter triggers the prototype of 'reddy red': blood-coloured red.[9] We said then that in their role of prototypical meanings, these meanings need not necessarily be accounted for in merger representations because they do not always contribute to the compositionally built intended utterance meaning. But what interests us now in this chapter is the case when they *do* contribute. What process do we ascribe them to in DS? It seems natural to ascribe the typical sense of 'teenager' to SCWD and the typical meaning of 'red' to CD. But a methodological question arises as to what exactly we gain through splitting the hair and dividing the meaning of the lexical item between two different sources. One advantage would be a compositional account of word meaning—the monotonic and the nonmonotonic, corresponding to the linguistic core and the separate psychological core, the latter including 'bloody red' as well as 'red for a cow' in the case of 'a red cow'—or even, in agreement with our muddying of the literal/non-literal distinction, 'red' for 'seeing red'. On the other hand, in doing so we are necessarily left out with the WS that will simply not work: the WS on which word meaning, devoid of the contribution of such salient interpretations of the lexicon, is not likely to be delimited either by conceptual analysis or by experimentation. As evidence for the first we can refer to the failures of the attempts at semantic decomposition several

---

[8] See Kamp and Partee 1995 for an attempt at a compositional analysis.
[9] For the seminal account see Berlin and Kay 1969.

decades ago,[10] and for the latter, experiments in neuroimaging that demonstrate that neuronal activation groups concepts coarsely, suggesting that they are construed broadly, to include the metaphorical and speech-act-specific uses of words and complex expressions (Pulvermüller, e.g. 2010, 2012). It seems therefore more theoretically accurate, and also methodologically prudent, to retain the concept of word meaning as sufficiently flexible to subsume such influences of context-driven inferences as well as automatic interpretations of different provenance. In short, as was anticipated in Section 3.1, we place such meanings in the lexicon and as such in WS, without descending to any deeper level of granularity (W) of lexical semantic description.

4.2 Fluid characters

4.2.1 Indexicality and language use

In a nutshell, utterance interpretation can rely on the meanings of words to a different degree. Sometimes the standard, salient$_{CM}$ meaning does all or most of the job—salient in the speaker's lexicon storage, assessed independently of the context of use. At other times the adjacent words exert what Recanati (2012b) calls 'lateral influences'; yet at others the context triggers an interpretation that substantially differs from the context-free salient meaning. One aspect of this gradation of context-dependence is associated with the tightness of the collocations formed on particular occasions of use. What it means is that while in one context a word will function as an independent entity from the point of view of semantic composition, on other occasions the composition will not reach this level of granularity but instead will stop at clusters. In idioms, some complex metaphors, proverbs, and other standardized (and even more so, fully conventionalized) collocations it seems most appropriate to conceive of the complex that enters the interactive composition as a unit, in that going below the level of the complex would not be reflected in the compositional representation anyway. What is interesting is not that such idioms, complex metaphors, formulaic expressions, and so forth exist; this is common knowledge in semantics, pragmatics and sociolinguistics. What is interesting is that one and the same expression can function as such a unit on one occasion, while affording a full composition on the word level on another. In what follows I address the question of the construction of such units and the fact that, seen across contexts, they appear to vary, and discuss the consequences from this fact for the strict Kaplanian notion of a character, a linguistic meaning of an expression. I conclude by a pursuit of a notion of context that is commensurate with my new, dynamic ('fluid') concept of a character.

---

[10] See Jaszczolt 2002a, Chapter 2 for references and discussion.

To begin with, the problem is this. Philosophers are fond of rigid distinctions such as that into directly referring expressions and expressions that perform a referring function only in some contexts of use. Indexicals, such as personal pronouns and some adverbs ('now', 'here', 'yesterday'), and referentially unambiguous proper names belong to the first category, while definite descriptions belong to the latter. Such rigid classifications rely on a formal semanticists' wishful thinking that expressions can be put into clear semantic categories with respect to their referring role. Next, they want to regiment the role of context. To take the most notable example, in his version of two-dimensional semantics, Kaplan (1989a) makes a distinction between character, which is the value of an expression that comes from the language system, and content, the semantic value this expression has in a particular sentence. On the one hand, there are expressions that have a context-sensitive character which allows them to have a fixed content that does not differ with circumstances of evaluation. These are indexicals, such as for example personal pronouns or the adverbials 'here' and 'now'. On the other hand, there are expressions that have a fixed character, allowing for the content that differs with circumstances of evaluation. These are non-indexicals, e.g. common nouns. But all is well if one is happy to abstract from the actual use of words. When one looks at how, say, personal and demonstrative pronouns and common nouns are used, then it is clear that they do not correspond so neatly to Kaplan's categories; the indexical/non-indexical distinction appears to be philosophers' fiction. I will return to this topic in more depth in Chapter 5 when I discuss the behaviour of the first-person 'indexical' vis-à-vis other ways of expressing the self but for now we shall focus on another problem with Kaplan's distinction, namely the problematic discernibility of a character. When we try to build a semantics on the level of conceptual structures and intuitive truth conditions, characters become complicated. While the distinction itself, into linguistic meaning and content proper, is definitely worth saving, linguistic meaning (and hence our WS) poses some problems that we have already mentioned: how do we know that the processing of utterance meaning in the particular discourse proceeds on the level of words as building blocks? Sometimes it does, but at other times it does not. Even pronouns 'I' and 'you' in formulaic expressions such as ' . . . or shall I say' or 'if you like', 'if you pardon the expression' do not seem to trigger the search for content; they function, so to speak, as characters alone, without attempting to pick out the speaker as the referent. These are exemplified in (14)–(16).

(14)   He is rather slow, or shall I say he is a child with severe learning difficulties.

(15)   It is still peanuts if you'll pardon the expression.

(16)   I went in with a bone of complaint, if you like.[11]

---

[11]   Examples (15) and (16) come from Elder's (2014) database compiled out of the British component of the International Corpus of English (ICE-GB). See Elder 2014 and Elder and Jaszczolt 2013 for a discussion.

Now, if what really matters for a theory of meaning is the *uses* to which we put words and structures, then it is only natural that we would want to extend Kaplan's otherwise insightful solution in such a way as to make it applicable to the *functions* words have rather to the symbols in isolation. Such a desideratum merely puts a stamp on what contextualists have been progressing towards in the past two decades, namely the recognition of what we can call 'degrees of indexicality': all words are context-dependent to some degree, arguably all words are potentially modifiable by the context, and as such they aspire to the category of indexicals. Some are 'more indexical', so to speak, than others, but the indexical/non-indexical distinction does not hold when one looks at meaning in use.

As was discussed earlier in this chapter, there is a tendency in contextualist debates to consider quite seriously meaning eliminativism. With the revival of interest in lexical pragmatics, evidence has been mounting that there is no part of lexical meaning that can be legitimately abstracted from the context of discourse. As was observed in the discussion of Asher (2011), even if we allow for some default senses, they will have to be fuzzy and easily changeable through procedures that are not easy to formalize. As a result, any natural language semantics will have to conform to, and reflect, this changeability of word meaning. It seems therefore prudent to pursue and adapt the ideas of those who focused on this changeability for that part of the lexicon that is clearly semantically changeable, and especially on the precursor of the current debates, David Kaplan. It is true that his inquiry into the context-dependence of meaning focused on indexical expressions as standardly conceived. However, facing the developments in semantics and pragmatics, as well as his more recent insights into the behaviour or such pragmatics-rich items as 'oops' and 'ouch' (Kaplan 2008), it seems justified to claim that the range of Kaplan's insights is much wider than it has been acknowledged so far.[12]

Kaplan (1989a: 505) defines characters as 'functions from possible contexts to contents'. To repeat, indexicals such as 'I', 'he', 'here', 'tomorrow' have a character (linguistic meaning) that is context-sensitive, not 'fixed'. Non-indexicals, such as, to adapt Kaplan's example, 'all persons alive in 2012', have a 'fixed' character in that the same content is invoked in all contexts. Characters provide the first step in his two-dimensional analysis. In order to understand the concept 'fixed', we have to move to the second step of the theory, namely to the content and to circumstances of evaluation. To repeat, non-indexicals invoke the same content in all contexts. The way to understand it is that differences between the sets of people associated with the expression 'all persons alive in 2012' as it is used in a particular sentence have to do *not* with the context but with *different possibilities the world might have been*, or, different extensions in different circumstances of evaluation. Proper names are even

---

[12] For some proposed extensions see Predelli 2005a, b.

more complicated: they are genuinely ambiguous and have their referent established *pre-semantically*. They have a fixed character and a fixed content (see Kaplan 1989a: 562). Content (intension) is a function from such circumstances of evaluation to extensions. In other words, the decisions we make in the first step (context) enable the identification of content, while the second step (circumstances of evaluation) throws up content understood as various extensions pertaining to each of the relevant circumstances of evaluation. Character, the notion of the first dimension, is *actual*; as Chalmers (2006: 100) puts it, it 'is put forward at least in part as a way of better capturing the cognitive or rational significance of an expression' and corresponds to 'what may be the case'. It is associated with *a priori* knowledge. The second dimension is counterfactual; it reflects 'what might have been the case' (*ibid.*).

This gives us indexicals with characters that are context-dependent (not 'fixed') and contents that do not differ with circumstances of evaluation (are 'fixed'), and, on the other hand, non-indexicals that have fixed characters and not-fixed contents. But as I demonstrate in the remainder of this book, this rigid distinction is a philosophers' fiction: important as it is for a conceptual analysis of language, it is in need of substantial adjustments if we are to use it to model compositional language interaction in DS—and to use it we want, because it offers the best available insight into the two dimensions of meaning.

What is not commonly noticed is that the character/content distinction provides a significant step towards contemporary contextualism. Characters of what are commonly called indexicals and non-indexicals do not exhibit polar differences: non-indexicals do not have fixed characters, and, on the other hand, the alleged indexicals do not have fixed content. Also, as I am going to propose here, we ought to adopt a more dynamic perspective on meaning: characters can correspond to syntactically simple, monolexemic units, as well as to complex ones, assuming that some rules of meaning composition operate at that level. These two distinctions, (i) fixed vs. not fixed and (ii) syntactically simple vs. syntactically complex, make characters good candidates for an umbrella term under which our flexible inferential bases ($[\ldots]_{\text{CPI}}$ in Σ) and flexible default-generating bases ($[\ldots]_{\text{CD}}$ and $[\ldots]_{\text{SCWD}}$ in Σ) can be subsumed.

Let us first consider the length of the unit that enters into semantic composition. Geurts (1999, 2009, 2010) proposes a distinction between implicature, which is regarded as a global, post-propositional phenomenon, and 'local pragmatics' that takes care of other types of pragmatic contents. For example, in Geurts (1999) he presents presupposition as a local phenomenon, in contrast to implicature. As we will see, however, defining the latter as global may be a matter of adjusting the terminology. It has to be remembered that he takes the localism/globalism debate to apply to sentence *types*: if the sentence does not give rise to correct defaults when handled through local inferences, then it constitutes a counterexample to localism. But perhaps there is a different explanation; perhaps localism and globalism are not the only options. After all, they are both fairly radical in the attempt to subsume discourse processes under a stable pattern. A more flexible proposal would be to assess the phenomenon on a case by case basis, where 'case by case' means 'situation of discourse by situation of discourse', paying due consideration to the particular speaker's intentions and the requirements posed by the common ground. As a result, 'local' or 'global' would turn out to mean 'local' or global' *for the context*: while the enrichment of the conjunction 'and' may be local in one context, it may require the processing of the entire sentence, or even a larger chunk of discourse, in another.

Proceeding along these lines, what becomes important about 'local' is its gradability: pragmatic interference may be more, or less, local, leaving the global, post-propositional effects as a special, limiting case. Consider (17). On the neo-Gricean account, (17) generates a GCI in (18). However, intuitively, if the utterance generates a stronger implied meaning, then it is likely to be the one in (19).

(17)   Ian McEwan believes that people like some of his novels.

(18)   It is not the case that Ian McEwan believes that people like all of his novels.

(19)   Ian McEwan believes that people don't like all of his novels.

When we assume that implicatures are always global, sentence-based, we have a difficulty with explaining such intuitive meanings of belief reports. Analogously, in (20), it seems that the implicature 'sometimes but not always' has to arise locally, after 'sometimes' has been processed, because otherwise we would obtain an interpretation in (21) that couldn't have been intended by the speaker.

(20)   Being sometimes wrong is better than being always wrong.

(21)   ?Being at least sometimes and possibly always wrong is better than being always wrong.
        (examples from Jaszczolt 2012c: 213)

A globalist could respond to these in the following way. In (17), it is the relative uninformativeness of the utterance that triggers the strengthening to (19), in agreement with Gricean maxims or post-Gricean principles or heuristics pertaining to the quantity of information. In (20), it is the sheer absurdity of the suggested reading, bearing in mind the encountered contrast between 'sometimes' and 'always' in this utterance, that triggers the strengthening of 'sometimes' to 'sometimes but not always'.

Geurts (2009) lets the case rest with such common-sense explanations. But there seems to be a better one when we adopt our solution of the degrees of localism. First, (20) is likely to be uttered with the stress on SOMETIMES and ALWAYS, putting them in contrastive focus. It is possible that 'sometimes' on its own, uttered with flat intonation, would trigger an enrichment before 'always' is processed. But even when such emphasis is missing, contrastive focus is expressed via the juxtaposition of these two quantifying expressions and it becomes available to the addressee as soon as the word 'always' is uttered. What this means is that the part of the utterance up to and including 'always' constitutes a unit (albeit, clearly, not a constituent in the syntactic sense) that allows for pragmatic modification of sense.

Coming back to the attempted adaptation of Kaplan to our semantics of interaction, it appears that we can only talk about a 'character' when we encounter such an extended unit that allows us to recover the meaning of 'sometimes' that is appropriate for this occasion of use. This dynamic nature of characters, associated with the dynamic inferential bases on which they rely, will be the conclusion we will reach, step by step, in what follows.

Next, Geurts moves to a case that is potentially more problematic. (22) is supposed to produce a Gricean implicature in (23).

(22)   Kai had the broccoli or some of the peas last night.

(23)   It is not the case that Kai had the broccoli or all of the peas last night.
       (from Geurts 2009: 56, after Sauerland 2004).

Now, since $\neg(p \lor q)$ is equivalent to $\neg p \land \neg q$, (23) is arguably equivalent to (24). But this cannot possibly be what was intended by the speaker.

(24)   Kai didn't have the broccoli and neither did he have all of the peas last night.

Localist explanations mushroom in the literature: Levinson (2000) employs 'presumptive' meaning triggered by the lexical item 'some'; Chierchia (2004, 2013) traces the enrichment to the generative power of the grammar, where grammar is capable of generating both the weak and the strong meaning of 'some', choosing the stronger one by a default rule.[13] The problem is, Geurts continues, that localism has invariantly been associated with defaultism while there is no reason to do so: it is true that some words trigger local enrichment under some conditions, but is not true that it follows that they always do so. Let us pursue this argument against 'defaultist localism'. The most plausible reading of (25) requires that 'sometimes' is locally enriched to 'sometimes but not always'.

(25)   If you sometimes check the side mirror when you change lanes, that is not safe enough; you should always do so.

Geurts points out that the enrichment to 'but not always' (scalar implicature) should not arise in such contexts because scalar effects are not supposed to be present in downward entailing constructions such as antecedents of conditionals (Chierchia

---

[13]   Cf.: 'Kai had the broccoli or not all of the peas last night'.

2004, 2006). He points out that Levinson uses such examples to support his localism while, bearing the monotonicity in mind, he ought not to do so. This seems to be a striking misunderstanding of Levinson's position on localism and defaultism. By 'local' Levinson means word-based, sometimes morpheme-based or phrase-based; never does he mean 'word-in-a-suitable-grammatical-context-based'. Nowhere does he claim that there is a grammatical constraint to do with monotonicity that warrants the suspension of a potential 'default inference'. Such a grammatical constraint would not be correct. In any case, non-emphatic uses of 'some' in antecedents of conditionals are realized as the negative polarity item 'any' and this is a fact that Levinson can easily exploit.

On the other hand, it is clear that abandoning strong defaultism has its merits in explaining such uses of 'some' as that in (26).

(26)   If some people say you are arrogant, you should perhaps think about changing something in your behaviour.
        (example from Jaszczolt 2012c: 215).

In (26), 'some people' does not trigger an inference (or a default meaning for that matter) to 'some but not all people'. Instead, it seems that 'some people' stands in a strong relation to the predicate 'say', creating a standardized expression 'some people say', as exemplified again in (27).

(27)   Some people say that he killed his wife and made it look like an accident.

It is reasonable to assume that 'some' is not a unit whose standalone lexical meaning enters into the composition process; neither is it the noun phrase 'some people'. Instead, the unit on which inference is founded is likely to be 'some people say'.

To generalize, when we take the structure of any sentence, the unit on which potential inference is founded is *flexible*: sometimes inferences arise on the basis of a word, in other cases on the basis of a phrase or a morpheme, and yet in others on the basis of some other string. This string can be subsentential, can correspond to a sentence, or even go beyond the sentence boundary. In other words, different occasions of use exploit different *inferential bases*, i.e. different units on which inference (or automatic modification) is performed.

It appears that our position on localism will turn out to be close to that of Geurts, although for different reasons. Geurts observes that sentences such as (28) give rise to implicatures which are not local: localism predicts (29), while in conversational practice we also encounter (30) and (31).

(28)   Some people like Ian McEwan's novels.

(29)   Not all people like Ian McEwan's novels.

(30)   The speaker doesn't know whether all people like Ian McEwan's novels.

(31)   The speaker doesn't have a view on whether all people like Ian McEwan's novels.

Geurts produces further strong arguments in support of globalism but this is not what interests us at present; what interests us is the fact that pragmatic modifications (variously called here scalar implicatures, GCIs, enrichments, presumptive meanings) arise on the basis of units of various lengths. The length of such a unit can vary from a morpheme to the entire discourse; browsing through examples of fiction easily testifies to the importance of such extended units. It therefore appears that the correct way to look at the localism/globalism debate is by admitting that the unit that is at the heart of the debate is a flexible one and this flexibility stems out of the flexibility of the bases on which the inference (or automatic modification, depending on whether the CPI or CD/SCWD processes are at work) is based.

Let us next consider another example in which an enrichment is predicted on the localist accounts but in fact is very unlikely to arise. (32) is supposed to give rise to (32') in virtue of the salient exclusive meaning of disjunction.

(32)   I prefer to visit Tokyo or Kyoto.

(32')   I prefer not to visit both Tokyo and Kyoto.
         (adapted from Geurts 2009: 64)

But why is it that we are led to believe that the exclusive reading should arise in (32)? Surely, it only ought to arise when we assume a static view of meaning, and a view that takes an abstract unit, a sentence, as its object. Viewed dynamically, it is clear that as the utterance unfolds, the addressee hears 'I prefer to visit...', on the basis of which he/she builds up a scenario of, say, a 'wish list' and in this context interprets 'or' as an alternative for modal choices, say, 'or perhaps'. Flexible inferential bases capture this fact, and as a result so should the concept of a character. I therefore propose that *just as inferential bases are flexible, so are characters*: they correspond to units of different length, are created for the purpose of the situation at hand, and will from now on be called *fluid characters*. They are 'fluid' in that they reflect the process of the recovery of meaning as discourse unfolds: sometimes the unit that gives rise to meaning assignment is just a word; at other times the addressee has to wait longer.

Geurts does not have a good explanation for examples such as (20) and invents for them a label 'quasi-implicature' (2009: 73), classifying them as 'context-dependent meaning shifts' (p. 75). On the contrary, on my flexible-base and fluid-character account they appear to be ordinary examples for which we have to identify the unit that enters into the interaction. In other words, we have to identify the unit given via WS—a unit that then triggers such processes as SCWD, CD, or CPI.

To elaborate, the account proposed here[14] is founded on the *processing unit* of merger representations, a unit that is sufficiently flexible to reflect the incremental nature of utterance interpretation. This flexibility allows us to avoid

---

[14] This is further development of my proposal of fluid characters from Jaszczolt 2012c.

overgeneration of pragmatic enrichments and associated with it frequent but psychologically unjustified cancellation that was a weakness of Levinson's GCIs. Although DS is not a theory of processing, identifying a psychologically plausible unit is essential for explaining the merger of information in that without it we would not be able to model the construction of discourse meaning: the processes identified in DS have to operate on something and this 'something', reflected as the material between the square brackets in Σs, has to match the constituents of a compositional process on the level of conceptual structure. In other words, while the actual units are of no interest to semantic theory such as DS, the principles for the construction of such flexible units that would allow us to model Model Speaker/Model Addressee interaction are necessary in a normative semantic theory.

One aspect that has so far been mentioned only in passing and that in fact has a strong effect on fluid characters is prosody. In (33), it is the intonation that determines the granularity of the character. Stressing SOME produces a different reading from stressing SOME PEOPLE SAY, which is different again from that of (33) said with flat intonation. This is a variation on our previous example (26).

(33)   Some people say that you sound aloof.

What counts as a character on these different readings varies. To repeat: on our DS-theoretic reanalysis of Kaplan's distinction, characters are fluid: on one occasion 'some' is a character, on another 'some people', on yet another 'some people say'. Necessarily, as characters, they are still *types* rather than *tokens*: they pertain to types of functions associated with different combinations of lexical units that are available for sentence construction.[15] But how do we describe the situation in which the primary meaning is expressed indirectly and as a result the merger representation throws up the meaning as in, say, (34)?

(34)   You should change the way in which you talk to people.

WS gives us the basic, 'literal' meaning of (33) but this meaning surfaces as secondary meaning, while (34) is the main intended and communicated content. Now, when we reanalyse Kaplan's distinction and kick it up to the level of merger representations, *the unit that corresponds to the character is the unit of WS*; counterintuitive as it may seem to advocates of Kaplanian two-dimensional semantics, this is precisely the conclusion we reach. And, for a radical contextualist view and for the purpose at hand, it is a welcome one: we have a unit that corresponds to the linguistic meaning; it is dynamic, purpose-selected for the discourse at hand, and interacts with context just as elements of language should on Kaplan's standard account.

---

[15]   I owe thanks to Tadeusz Ciecierski for drawing my attention to this question.

The fact that Kaplan had intended characters for a classificatory purpose, to differentiate between fixed and non-fixed, and thereby between non-indexicals and indexicals, only testifies to the adherence to the trend dominant in the 1970s to fit natural language into the mould of formal analysis. Should natural languages possess expressions that are unquestionably and exceptionlessly used as indexicals and expressions that are unquestionably and exceptionlessly used as non-indexicals, *ça aurait pu marcher*; sadly, they do not. Just as we have to admit the flexibility of the length of the unit, so will we have to abandon the indexical/non-indexical distinction, using the clinching argument from first-person reference in Chapter 5.

Next, fluid characters allow us to restate the meaning of 'defaults' as adopted in DS in much simpler terms. Consider (35). In suitable contexts, 'Leonardo' will acquire the referent Leonardo DiCaprio automatically, through the working of the SCWD process; in others, the addressee will have to associate the name with the actor through an inferential process, having heard the title of the film *Revolutionary Road*.

(35)   Kate and Leonardo acted superbly in *Revolutionary Road*.
       (example from Jaszczolt 2012c: 221)

What is interesting here is that we have an interplay of two factors: the length of the unit on the basis of which meaning is recovered, and the process through which it is recovered. There are many combinations possible here. On one dimension, the addressee may recover the referent (i) locally after hearing 'Leonardo'; (ii) locally but on the basis of a longer unit, say, having heard 'acted' that triggered associations with possible famous actors with the name 'Leonardo'; or finally (iii) globally upon hearing the title of the film. Needless to say, if we construct the example somewhat differently and the title appears earlier in the sentence, the title may trigger local rather than global processing; the association with the global process is merely accidental. On the other dimension, the addressee may recover the referent automatically or via a conscious inferential process. Remembering that automatically obtained meanings (via CD or SCWD) are precisely what we mean by 'defaults' in DS, it follows that defaults can arise on the basis of units of different length: automatic reference assignment may 'kick in' at different stages in the processing of an utterance of this sentence. We can now restate this relation as the principle that *defaults can arise for characters of different length*. In sum, *fluid characters support default meanings understood as automatic meaning components*. There are flexible inferential bases for CPIs and there are flexible bases for defaults SCWD and CD and both of them testify to the need for dynamically understood units which we chose to call fluid characters.

4.2.2 *The facets of context*

Kaplan had to adopt a fairly formal representation of context to pursue the two-dimensional analysis, in that context has to fulfil different semantic as well as pre-semantic roles. Context, viewed as an *index*, consists of a number of parameters, of which the standard ones are the agent, time, location, and the world. At the same time, context is flexible in that additional parameters can be added when this is required by an interpretation. Context is thus open-ended as far as its parameters are concerned. For example, we can add a point of evaluation or perspective from which a sentence is to be assessed, as in Travis's (1997) example of russet leaves painted green (see Chapter 1, Section 1.3.2). In other words, 'context provides whatever parameters are needed' (Kaplan 1989b: 591). It is employed before truth and reference are established and thus belongs clearly in the domain of semantics. If so, there is nothing to stop us from posing the question concerning the types of expressions for which context can perform such an intra-semantic role. However, it is *how* it performs this role that has to be reanalysed. It does not suffice to distinguish the pre-semantic role, the role in fixing the referent, and the role in the delivery of content. The difficulty lies in the fact that indexicality creeps in potentially in the case of every word, as we argued in Section 4.1, and in addition words enter into clusters that, so to speak, behave 'like indexicals', as we argued in Section 4.2.1. And it is at this point that a more eclectic construal of context may be of use.

In Gricean approaches to meaning, context is pragmatic: it is not easily formalizable and, as post-Gricean contextualists construe it, it often affects the truth-conditional content of utterances 'top-down', in a manner that arguably cannot be captured by any well-delineated 'parameters'. Gricean contexts are also *expansive*: they increase incrementally with every processed unit of information. But context is also semantic in the sense that it affects the truth-conditional content of an utterance. In a sense, Kaplan's index is precisely what contextualism needs: it needs systematization and categorization of aspects of contextual information that would allow us to test contextualist predictions—say, concerning particular cases of quantifier domain restriction as in (36), enabling the construction of general rules or algorithms and giving the theory its normative character and thereby predictive power.

(36)   Everybody ($\rightarrow_E$ everybody in the room) was bored by the speech.

It is important to remember that constraint-free modification (such as enrichment) of sense does not yet mean that the adopted notion of context has to be vague and unwieldy. Contexts can be minimal or expansive, they can contain very few or more parameters depending on the requirements that are placed on them, but the expansiveness or the multi-parametric quality do not preclude a clear classification of these parameters and the conditions under which they are to be consulted. Going any further with this proposal is, however, difficult in that the parameters will not be dictated by grammatical or semantic categories such as pronouns, proper names or common nouns. Neither will they be dictated by the semantic function such as an indexical or a definite description. They will be dictated by what counts as context-given character, following the principle of flexible inferential bases proposed in the previous section.

Now, as I argued in Jaszczolt (2012b), Kaplan's context as presented in his 'Demonstratives' (1989a) is a metaphysical construct: it is formalized into parameters, it is quite minimal, and has a clearly specified role in securing the reference and providing circumstances of evaluation. But this metaphysical conception becomes complicated when in his 'Afterthoughts' Kaplan (1989b) introduces the so-called 'directing intention' whose role is to associate the character of a demonstrative with content. This move makes his context reinterpretable as an epistemic notion, deriving the speaker's semantic content—what Korta and Perry (2007) and Perry (2009) subsequently called *locutionary content*—to distinguish it from the content recovered by the addressee (their *what is said*).[16] It is here perhaps that the Gricean and the Kaplanesque concepts of context meet. We want them to meet. It is our metasemantic desideratum in that in a normative account such as DS context has to be formal and parametrized, but at the same time flexible enough to help explain the all-pervasive flexibility of meaning.

It has been emphasized throughout that context has an important role to play in every class of expression. Even the indexical/non-indexical distinction does not stand up to scrutiny when we look for data in the use of natural language lexicon. Just as pronouns require contextual resolution, so do, very often, common nouns, adjectives, and other elements of the uttered sentence, as example (1) discussed in Section 4.1 and repeated below as (37) demonstrates.

(37)   The country is tired of the austerity measures.

Metaphorical meanings, reference shifts (predicate transfers) as in (38), testify to this ubiquity of contextual resolutions of reference.

(38)   The steak and kidney pie at table 5 wants another drink.

Indexicality becomes reanalysed as a means to capture the degrees of context-dependence. The 'pragmaticized' Kaplanian character captures the messy reality of meaning in natural language use where, as Chapter 5 further demonstrates, there is no clear division into indexicals and non-indexicals, and therefore no clear division between 'not-fixed' and 'fixed' characters. Neither is there an interesting semantic distinction between monolexical and complex units in the cases in which the latter function as characters. The latter conclusion appears to support the idea of the lexicon/syntax continuum within construction grammar.

---

[16] To repeat, in DS this distinction need not be made in that DS, modelling the meanings construed as intended by the Model Speaker and recovered by the Model Addressee, does not attend to cases of miscommunication. This construal follows from the desideratum of normativity.

A radical contextualist of an orientation other than that of DS is likely to object here that there is no need for a notion of a fluid character: fluid characters are merely a way to turn contextualism into all-pervasive indexicalism. But if this strategy proves to work, it will bring us precisely an account of interactive compositionality that is needed for explaining natural language discourse. *Pragmaticized Kaplan's characters*, paired with an *orderly notion of context*, give us an insight into the interaction of WS, CD, SCWD, and CPI—the first two reflected in the characters and the other two ruled by the context. In addition, some recent approaches to the lexicon discussed earlier in this chapter are broadly on similar lines: Borg's (2012) emphasis on the combinatorial potential in the lexicon and Asher's (2011) emphasis on the role of context in creating (and shifting) semantic types are both more compatible with all-pervasive indexicality than with top-down free modification. What we obtain here is a two-dimensional semantics, but a *two-dimensional interactive, conceptual semantics where the characters are pragmaticized* and regulated by a functional definition.

It has to be pointed out that this pragmatization of the character does not affect the core principles of Kaplan's two-dimensionalism where content is a function from circumstances of evaluation to extensions. All we have done is make the unit dynamic and variable, dependent on the function of the speech act rather than on language system alone. It is true that fluid characters are elusive from the syntactic point of view: they need not be syntactic constituents and, given one and the same sentence, they can vary in length from one situation to another. But this is also where their adequacy lies in that they reflect the dynamic nature of the composition of meaning.

As I have demonstrated in this section, this dynamic perspective obliterates the need for the debates between localism and globalism, putting forward instead a perspective of an unfolding basis for inference (CPI) and analogously an unfolding basis for automatic meaning assignment (CD and SCWD). It also clarifies the role of automatic processes, allowing them to be envisaged as operating on fluid characters.

4.3 Referring expressions and referring agents

Our metasemantic investigation has not yet sufficiently addressed the fundamental question of reference in discourse. Formal semantics that avails itself of truth conditions, possible worlds and model theory has to adopt a reliable concept of a referent. Since a predicate gets its meaning from the generalization over extensions in possible worlds, it is important what we put in these extension sets. Having long acknowledged (at least since Russell) problems with referential semantics that relies on real objects, and having acknowledged (for even longer, at least since Husserl) problems with adopting mental objects, semantics can resort to a theoretical construct of a referent that draws both on the metaphysical and on the conceptual, such as a discourse referent of DRT. In DRT, discourse referent is a formal equivalent of an individual, understood as an atomic or non-atomic unit—the latter for groups of objects functioning for the purpose of a given utterance as a single referent. The DRS condition then contains such discourse referents in the positions of arguments of a predicate and captures the idea that the represented individual satisfies the predicate.[17] Discourse referent of DRT has been directly adopted into DS. The *x*s, *y*s, *e*s etc. in the top row of Σs stand for discourse referents. To repeat, DS is one of the 'daughter' theories of DRT, applied to pragmatic units that represent intended and recovered messages. And it is precisely this pragmatic nature of its representations that necessitates the reanalysis of the concepts of reference and discourse referents.

First, merger representations represent not agent-independent propositions but rather the intended meanings that are recovered by the Model Addressee, thereby including in them various natural possibilities of reference ascription such as the biased or partial information about the referent, or a referential mistake. In the early days of DS I presented various arguments and evidence for the default, salient status of the referential reading over the attributive one, the *de re* reading of belief reports over the *de dicto* one, making in the process claims about the strength of referring associated with the salient and less salient interpretations of a sentence (Jaszczolt 1997, 1999, 2005a). These representations also accounted for referential mistakes. For example, in the case of belief reports involving definite descriptions, the most salient reading (*modulo* evidence to the contrary from the sources of information identified in DS) is the *de re* one in that it corresponds to the strongest intentionality of the associated mental state, and thereby to the highest degree of informativeness of the act of communication. Next comes also a *de re* reading, a reading about a particular individual (*res*) but about, so to speak, a 'wrong one', containing a referential mistake—in my examples, it was usually a mistaken referent for a phrase such as 'the architect of La Sagrada Familia', 'the author of *Oscar and Lucinda*', and so forth. The fact that DS can cater for scenarios of referential mistakes in spite of adopting the perspective of a Model Speaker and Model Addressee and therefore reducing psychological considerations to the minimum required in a normative semantic theory[18] testifies to the importance of capturing the facts about referring in discourse that a minimal formal semantic theory leaves out. In agreement with the adopted orientation of Salience-Based Contextualism, DS construes merger representations in such a way that they reflect the acts of referring and the recognition of the acts of referring. Say the speaker, seeing that his friend is reading *The Chemistry of Tears* on his Kindle, and not being able to see the name of the author as one does on the cover of a paper copy, utters (39).

(39)   The author of *The Chemistry of Tears* is a good novelist. He has a new book out, *Sweet Tooth*. Have you read a lot of Ian McEwan?

---

[17]   See Kamp and Reyle (1993: 61).
[18]   See Section 3.3 on psychologism.

It is clear from (39) that the speaker is confusing Peter Carey, the author of *The Chemistry of Tears*, with Ian McEwan, the author of *Sweet Tooth*. This is not a case of conversation going wrong or a conversation breakdown that ought to be excluded from a semantic theory. This is a case of the flexibility of words. Notice that on the scenario as it is presented here, the addressee has two options: either to recover the referent as Ian McEwan but ascribe to the speaker a certain deficiency of information concerning the novels he wrote, or to recover the referent as the author of *The Chemistry of Tears* when, say, he really liked the novel and his opinion of the novel is the main reason for calling the author a 'good novelist', independently of what else he may, correctly or incorrectly, attribute to him (including the attribution of a correct or incorrect name). We cannot tell which one is the case on a particular scenario. If the addressee simply does not know, then we do indeed have a case of a conversation breakdown that is in need of repairing as in (40).

(40)   Do you mean Peter Carey, the author of *The Chemistry of Tears*?

On this scenario (39) will not correspond to a complete Σ. But if the situation makes it clear to the addressee which reading was intended, the case of this referential mistake is easy to handle in that the referent is arrived at via CPI.

I have been discussing referential mistakes at length since the early 1990s and will not pursue their DS-theoretic representations here. Instead, what will interest us are the following questions: How is reference achieved in discourse? What is the role of a linguistic expression in securing reference? More generally, what is the role of WS vis-à-vis other sources of information in securing the reference? We have already established that because DS caters for acts of communication rather than for sentences (as minimalists do) or sentences in context (as 'fixers' do), it has to capture the referential intention whenever this referential intention is indeed captured by the addressee. This desideratum stems from the Model Speaker/Model Addressee requirement: a referent was intended and although the act of referring was more, or less, clearly executed, yet the reference went through. This stance on representing reference is also in agreement with the view on propositions that has been gaining ground in recent discussions in philosophy of language, namely that propositions that are of interest are not Russellian, agent-independent entities but rather representations of mental states, or, as Soames (2014) calls them, *cognitive propositions*, or *cognitive event types*. A proposition includes information about what the agent 'aims to represent' in that this can constitute 'a *cognitive* difference encoded in the cognitive acts that provoke the structure of the event types with which propositions are identified' (p. 124). Differences between Soames' account and DS regarding the role of truth conditions notwithstanding, the concept of agent-dependent propositions is present in both.

Likewise, Hawthorne and Manley (2012) successfully dissociate reference from the language system in arguing that it belongs with the cognitive mechanism rather than with types of noun phrases: indefinite and definite noun phrases, demonstratives, and proper names all have referential and non-referential uses and there is no type of natural language expression that could be legitimately called 'a referential term'. They leave out the first-person pronoun 'I' as the only possible candidate for a truly referential term. As we will see in Chapter 5, even this concession is overly optimistic: 'I' has many different uses, not all of them indexical, just as non-indexicals can serve the purpose of expressing first-person reference. They conclude on a rather Strawsonian note as follows:

'One pessimistic option is complete eliminativism about reference: just as no substance fits the role of "phlogiston" sufficiently well to count as its meaning, there is no semantic natural kind that will serve as the meaning of "reference".

A more tolerant conclusion eschews any fundamental role for reference in compositional semantics, but brings it closer to the use of "refers" in ordinary language. On this approach, one thinks of reference as something that the speaker does on an occasion with a noun phrase, emphasizing that this can occur even if one's favored typology for formal semantics does not associate an object with that expression for the purpose of computing truth conditions compositionally.'

Hawthorne and Manley (2012: 245–6)[19]

Other options include marking reference in the logical form when the 'mental file' dictates it.[20] Similar sensibilities are expressed by Richard (2011: 276) in the context of propositional attitude ascription where the identification of ways of thinking about an individual is, again, dissociated from types of linguistic expressions used to convey them and instead is made dependent on their 'cognitive properties, properties reflected by such facts as whether (if the expressions are terms) the user accepts or is disposed to accept the relevant identity'.

In short, the association of reference with cognitive states is in vogue again: it is the discursive referring rather than the abstract concept of reference that is endowed with the necessary explanatory powers. For a linguist of a radical contextualist orientation it is not difficult to agree that reference belongs with the cognitive processes and is associated with linguistic expressions only in the course of the processing of these expressions: this is precisely the stance that DS has always taken on reference, associating it not with the grammatical type of expression but rather with the CD process when the referent is arrived at automatically and with CPI when achieved as a result of a conscious process. But DS goes beyond the sympathies expressed in such philosophical arguments as the above by allocating a place for this object of consciousness in the compositional theory of discourse meaning. The next

---

[19] See also Allan 2013.

[20] See also Elbourne (2005) who argues that pronouns and proper names are not directly referring terms but function as predicates, sharing semantic properties with definite descriptions. Elbourne's is an earlier and not as such a functional view that would cut across the categories but by disposing of direct reference it testifies to the diminishing faith in pegging the semantics of reference on expression types.

question that arises will have to concern the *contents* of these reference-securing cognitive states, and in particular the problem of commensurability of the speaker's and the addressee's mental states as far as information about the referent is concerned. Here DS gets away with a methodological assumption that a theory ought to model *model situations*: the meanings recovered by Model Addressees and at the same time intended by Model Speakers. Applied to the problem of reference, it models *representations of referents* recovered by Model Addressees and at the same time intended by Model Speakers. While we have already established that it is not the linguistic expression but the overall result of the act of referring that enters into the compositional structure, we have not inquired into the 'at the same time' qualification in that condition on representations. But perhaps we can get away without doing so. The salient reading of a definite description corresponds to the referential and strongly informative reading and is represented as a proper name encased by square brackets indexed for the CD process. For example, on a strong referential reading of 'the author of *The Chemistry of Tears*' we obtain the representation [Peter Carey]$_{CD}$. The referential reading with a referential mistake (when the mistake is recognized by the addressee) as in (39) corresponds to [Ian McEwan]$_{CPI}$.[21] The attributive reading corresponds to [the author of *The Chemistry of Tears*]$_{CPI}$—'CPI' in that the default, strong referential reading of the description results in [Peter Carey]$_{CD}$. And this is the only level of detail that matters for our semantic *qua* conceptual representations: the individual and the process of its recovery that in itself conveys information about the default reading as opposed to the non-default readings. In short, merger representations capture what any theory of word meanings tells us: that we don't have to have identical concepts in order to understand each other.

To sum up, discourse conditions associated with discourse referents combine information coming from different sources and through a variety of processes identified in DS. Any type of expression that can be used to refer has various discourse functions associated with it, so it is not plausible to build a theory of referring that would rely on the syntactic category such as a noun phrase, or even a semantic category such as a definite description.[22] Instead, DS adopts a cognitive and thereby a *functional perspective* on reference where the discourse referent corresponds to the intended and recovered *conceptual representation*, pegged on an identifiable individual where appropriate (viz. [Ian McEwan]$_{CD/CPI}$) but left as a concept where not (viz. [*The Chemistry of Tears*]$_{CPI}$). This will allow us to explain (in Chapter 5) the fact that, say, common nouns can fulfil the role of an indexical, while what looks like a natural language realization of the philosophers' concept of an indexical may fail to function as predicted.

---

[21] This representation covers both scenarios of interpreting (39) mentioned above.

[22] Note that definite noun phrases need not perform the role of a definite description: for example, a definite noun phrase can be used generically.

A disclaimer is in order at this point in that we will not be concerned here with the varieties of objects that speakers refer to. For example, one can refer to '*the coldness* of her expression', 'tiger' as a natural kind, actions (demonstrative 'thus'), situations ('that' + a proposition), among others.[23] The reason is that while from the metaphysical and epistemological perspective abstract objects of discourse are indeed a worthy topic of discussion, when we focus on sources and processes producing merger representations they are often, in a way, simpler: simple abstract objects such as 'redness' in 'the redness of his face' or 'coldness' in 'the coldness of her expression' are arrived at via lexical salience and context-driven salience, as was described in Chapter 2. There are no potential ambiguities involved, save the ones that pertain to the entire proposition in that, for example an utterance of (41) may on occasion express the primary meaning in (42) or even, in an appropriate context, the indirect (43).

(41) The excessive *weight* of my luggage caused a *delay* at the check-in.

(42) $\rightarrow_{PM}$ We were delayed at the check-in because my luggage was too heavy.

(43) $\rightarrow_{PM}$ I almost missed the plane.

While the ontological status of such referents gives rise to various interesting syntactic and semantic restrictions and as such also merits a linguistic discussion, the functional analysis clearly favours (42) and (43) as primary meanings. (41) throws up, say, [The excessive weight of x's luggage]$_{WS}$ or [The excessive weight of x's luggage]$_{WS/CPI}$, with the referent for 'my' accounted for separately in the discourse condition for x that represents 'my'. On the other hand, (42) and (43) are significantly simpler to represent in a discourse-function-driven analysis of DS.

All in all, we are left to surmise that possibly the only bastion of reference that is secured by language system is the first-person pronoun 'I'. This is the tentative conjecture in Hawthorne and Manley (2012: 245) who conclude: '... reference turns out to be less prevalent than we thought—perhaps there are only a few expressions, like "I", that are truly referential'. This is why our case study for the final chapter is precisely this putative stronghold of language-internal referentiality: the first-person singular pronoun 'I' in English (and, briefly, also in a contrastive cross-linguistic perspective) and its suitability for the role of the first-person indexical.

---

[23] For an excellent typology and analysis of types of abstract objects see Moltmann 2013.

5

The demise of indexicals: A case study

'What was *he*, stripped of all the signs he flashed? People were standing up every-where, shouting "This is me! This is me!" Every time you looked at them they stood up and told you who they were, and the truth of it was that they had no more idea of who or what they were than he had. *They* believed their flashing signs too. They ought to be standing up and shouting, "This *isn't* me! This *isn't* me!" They would if they had any decency. "This *isn't* me!" Then you might know how to proceed through the flashing bullshit of this world.'

Philip Roth, American Pastoral (1998, London, Vintage, p. 410)

5.1 Expressing the SELF: A preamble

This final chapter follows with a case study: since indexicals are often given as an example of syntactically and semantically pure cases of reference, in the sense of providing lexical and semantic prompts for searching for a referent which then exhausts their semantic role (a phenomenon known as direct reference), I ask whether this direct reference picture stands up to scrutiny when investigated in the example of the first-person indexical.

Thoughts, feelings, emotions, and attitudes can be expressed in a variety of ways. For a linguist and a philosopher of language, the main means of expressing oneself that is of interest is linguistic communication, and within this domain, the main expression type that is employed for this purpose, namely the first-person singular pronoun 'I' or some morphological equivalent of it in null-subject languages. On the other hand, *The Oxford Handbook of the Self* (Gallagher 2011) does not contain a single chapter on linguistic expression of the SELF. The closest it comes to semantic concerns is the idea of embodiment (in Cassam's (2011) argument that a perceiving, thinking and acting self has to be embodied) and Perry's (2011) discussion of the specificity of the 'self' perspective in achieving reference. Perhaps this is significant in that self-expression is a multi-faceted rather than linguistic phenomenon. As we will see by the end of this chapter, there is no simple way of covering this topic in that speakers express the SELF whatever they do in conversation, by the very choices they make: to take a conversational turn or not, to communicate a certain thought rather

Meaning in Linguistic Interaction. Kasia M. Jaszczolt.
© Kasia M. Jaszczolt 2016. Published 2016 by Oxford University Press.

than another, and to communicate it using certain form of expression rather than another. One need not use the pronoun 'I' to communicate the primary meaning concerning the SELF. Hence, for example, by uttering (1) I may intend to communicate the primary meaning in (2).

(1)   This was a mean thing to do.

(2)   →$_{PM}$ I am angry with you/I am disappointed with your behaviour.

Similarly in (3) and (4).

(3)   It is late.

(4)   →$_{PM}$ I would like to go home.

Even in explicit communication it is not necessary to use the pronoun designated for this purpose. (5) and (6) make use of a common noun and a proper name respectively, which seem to be more natural in certain contexts than the first-person pronoun.

(5)   [Mother to a crying toddler:]

Mummy will pick you up in a minute.

(6)   [A toddler to mother:]
Tommy wants milk.

This phenomenon is not restricted to child speak and 'parentese' (child-directed speech). In (7), the speaker uses a recognizable name of a fictitious character to identify himself as a DIY-expert. These forms of self-reference belong to the category of so-called 'imposters' (Collins and Postal 2012).

(7)   Don't worry, Bob the Builder will fix it.

Next, many languages offer options in-between the direct and the indirect, such as the English 'one', French 'on' or German 'man' as in (8).[1]

(8)   One can tell that he is not telling the truth.

Personal taste predicates also, arguably, present an in-between case of a statement that cannot be regarded as predicating merely about the SELF. While this is a moot point in the literature,[2] on the most common-sense level of description, the speaker would not utter (9) knowing that no one else is likely to like *Ben and Jerry* ice creams and therefore benefit from this information. In the latter scenario the speaker is more likely to utter (10).

---

[1]   Moltmann (2010) calls this phenomenon *generalizing detached self-reference*.

[2]   The literature on this topic is vast. For references and an interesting semantic analysis see Pearson 2013.

(9)   *Ben and Jerry* ice creams taste delicious.

(10)   I like *Ben and Jerry* ice creams but many people find them too sweet.

There is a wide spectrum of expressions that can be employed, within a single natural language, to serve the purpose of expressing the SELF and even more specifically referring to oneself. In a salience-based contextualist approach such as DS where the primary meaning is free from the constraints of the logical form, the description of this diversity can reach its full potential. In what follows we begin with a brief discussion of the importance of the concept of *self-awareness* for the description of *self-referring* and for the DS-theoretic representation of the *self-ascription of proper-ties* in Σs, founded on the *self-attribution of mental states*. In the process we will justify the need for all four of these terms. Next, we move to the core task of this chapter, namely the argument that the first-person indexical does not have a reliable realization in natural language; it appears to be philosophers' fiction. On the one hand, referring to oneself can be executed by using indexical and non-indexical terms. On the other, the English pronoun 'I' that is standardly given as an example of such an indexical term can also have non-indexical functions. In addition, in the case of some natural languages there is no realization of the first-person indexical even as far as the particular *use* (as opposed to lexical item) is concerned in that all words employed for this purpose also obligatorily convey other meanings. Finally, I provide DS-theoretic representations for some instances of self-referring, as well as reporting on self-referring (*de se*) which will testify to the need for a pragmatics-rich, contextualist approach to talking about oneself in preference to looking for natural language equivalents of Kaplan's indexicals.

5.2 First-person perspective

Peter Strawson in his *Individuals* (1959) argues for the priority of the concept of the person: 'person' combines conscious states and bodily characteristics; it is of a person that consciousness is predicated. As a primitive, '[t]he concept of a person is not to be analysed as that of an animated body or of an embodied anima' (Strawson 1959: 103). If so, it follows that we can only *ascribe* mental and bodily characteristics to a person, rather than *define* personhood through them. It is certainly plausible to conclude that Locke's account, as well as some more recent attempts in phenomenology at delimiting personal identity through experiences, memories, and anticipation discussed in the previous chapter, do not fully succeed in answering the question—perhaps, as Strawson would argue, because they do not fully grasp this primitiveness of the concept. But is there such a primitive concept? In what follows we will not engage in the discussions of metaphysics directly but will merely contribute a modest argument from a cross-linguistic analysis of expressions used for self-reference. This linguistic analysis will suffice to throw some doubt on the question of the unique SELF, as well as, on the level of semantics that interests us more here, call into question the construct of a first-person indexical. If the latter turns out not to stand up to a linguistic scrutiny, then the *raison d'être* for the conceptual 'I' as an 'essential indexical' is undermined; and, arguably, if it is undermined, then so may be the primitive status of the 'person' as opposed to 'aspects of the person', be it Cartesian ('I$_{body}$' vs. 'I$_{mind}$') or founded on a different distinction ('I$_{private}$' vs. 'I$_{public}$', 'I$_{individual}$' vs. 'I$_{social}$', and so forth). In what follows, linguistic evidence will shed more light on these options.

Referring to oneself presupposes a concept or concepts of the self. When we say 'I', do we mean one's conscious states, subconscious states, the body, all of them at once, or perhaps some other referent? When Locke, for example, and many after him, appeal to the ability to reflect on one's experiences, extended into the past and the future through memory and anticipation, they attempt to grasp this foundational role of the SELF:

> 'When we see, hear, smell, taste, feel, meditate, or will anything, we know that we do so. Thus it is always as to our present sensations and perceptions: and by this every one is to himself that which he calls self (. . .). For, since consciousness always accompanies thinking, and it is that which makes every one to be what he calls self, and thereby distinguishes himself from all other thinking things: in this alone consists personal identity, i.e., the sameness of a rational being; and as far as this consciousness can be extended backwards to any past action or thought, so far reaches the identity of that person . . . '
>
> Locke (1694: 39)

Memory is indeed important, and so is placing oneself in the present and the anticipation of one's future. But, as Shoemaker (1970: 276) rightly adds, memories and anticipations point out to the *importance* of personal identity, rather than help with its definition. And so do experiences and reflections on them.[3] So, how is the self to be delimited?

The self is also characterized by permanence, as Perry (2002: 212) remarks:

> 'Unlike most of the other agent-relative roles, identity is permanent. I will have many things in front of me, talk to many people, be in many places, and live through many days in the course of my life. But there is only one person I will ever be identical with, myself.'

This self-perspective is then reflected in the indexicality of beliefs: when I believe something about myself (*de se*), the proposition that captures the belief (as opposed to capturing merely the object of that belief) has to include this (essential) indexicality (Perry 1979).[4] Perry's well-known scenario of a shopper trying to catch the

---

[3] We will not be interested here in the status of experiences and their comparison with objective knowledge. But see e.g. Perry 2001a on his *antecedent physicalism*.

[4] On construing self-knowledge in terms of the self-ascription of properties see also Lewis (1979a: 521):

'. . . sometimes property objects will do and propositional objects won't. Some belief and some knowledge cannot be understood as propositional, but can be understood as self-ascription of properties.'

culprit who leaves a trail of sugar on the supermarket floor well exemplifies the importance of this self-ascription.[5]

But what does 'indexicality' mean in the case of the first-person thoughts and first-person utterances? What is this 'I' that it is pegged on? In order to answer this question, we are not going to engage in the old philosophical debates concerning propositions and properties.[6] Instead, we shall approach the concept of the self from the perspective of how it is expressed in natural language in order to demonstrate that languages do not testify to a unique notion of the SELF.[7] In order to do so, we are going to take on board the delimitation of indexicality. In a sense, saying that a belief is indexical is an easy part: one acknowledges that (11a) differs from (11b).

(11a)   I have a meeting in half an hour.

(11b)   The person who agreed to chair the Faculty Board this term has a meeting in half an hour.

The referent can be the same if I happened to agree to do it (but forgot all about it in due course) but the *de se* element is crucial for explaining behaviour: I rush to the meeting or stay put. While *de se* vis-à-vis *de re* beliefs create philosophical problems of their own, and sometimes associated problems for the semantics of belief reports, the latter to be attended to in DS in what follows,[8] the first question I want to address is that of the linguistic realization of the concept of the first-person indexical: What exactly does it mean that the 'I' is an indexical expression?

It can mean different things. First, it can entail that there is a conceptual category of indexical expressions that have their counterparts in expressions of natural languages. But it can also entail that there is a conceptual category of indexical expressions that have their counterparts in the *uses* of expressions of natural languages. Or it can entail that indexicals *are* natural language expressions. Kaplan (1989a: 491) seems to mean the latter when he says that '[a]mong the pure indexicals are "I", "now", "here" (in one sense), "tomorrow", and others'. Note that he adds in a footnote that these are 'uses of pure indexicals' by which he means uses of e.g. 'I'. But he then adds that his theory is a *semantic theory* understood as 'a theory of word meaning, not speaker's meaning. It is based on linguistic rules known, explicitly or

---

[5]   'I once followed a trail of sugar on a supermarket floor, pushing my cart down the aisle on one side of a tall counter and back the aisle on the other, seeking the shopper with the torn sack to tell him he was making a mess. With each trip around the counter, the trail became thicker. But I seemed unable to catch up. Finally it dawned on me. I was the shopper I was trying to catch.' Perry (1979: 3).
See also Perry 2012 on detached notions of a person and buffer notions (formed through perception).

[6]   For an excellent discussion of this topic and a defence of *de se* perspective using self-ascription of properties see Feit 2008.

[7]   SELF and EGO are used in this chapter metalinguistically, for the concept of the first-person. EGO is intended as a more general concept, while SELF as the first-person concept pertaining to a *de se* thought.

[8]   On *de se* attitudes in linguistics and philosophy see e.g. Feit and Capone 2013 and Feit 2008. On semantic representations of *de se* beliefs and reports in DS see also 5.4 below and Jaszczolt 2013c.

implicitly, by all competent users of the language' (*ibid.*). It appears that 'I' is *the* (or perhaps *a*?) first-person indexical in English *tout court*.

It appears at this point that *indexicality of thought* is a much less controversial aspect of the debates surrounding the self than the proposed indexicals that express it. It may have been one of the biggest mistakes of philosophy of language to take this step from metaphysics and epistemology to linguistics. As I demonstrate in what follows, the naturalness of the step is rather deceptive.

5.3 Delimiting the first-person indexical

5.3.1 A view from elsewhere

Markers of first-person reference exhibit a considerable cross-cultural diversity. South-East Asian languages tend to have multiple equivalents of the English pronoun 'I'. Japanese has been reported to have at least fifty-one forms for 'I' (Tanaka 2012), including obsolete terms, or possibly as many as a hundred and sixteen according to a different classification (Christofaki, in progress) and Thai at least twenty-seven (Siewierska 2004: 228). The main source of this variety is honorification: words and phrases for 'slave', 'royal slave', 'servant', 'Buddha's servant', or Thai 'mouse' (used by women as the, alas, group with a lower social status) and other forms of self-denigration are typically used in this role of a first-person indicator, albeit without conveying the concept associated with that noun or phrase. Their role as the first-person indicator is important for our purposes in that we want to establish the exact association of such forms with the conceptual phenomenon of the first-person indexical. Next, these languages also use spatial deixis in the function of the first-person marker, for example Thai *phŏm$_1$ nii$_2$* ('one male this'), or Vietnamese *hây* ('here').[9] Reflexives, such as Japanese *zibun* or Vietnamese *mình* are also used for this purpose. *Zibun* is an interesting marker in that it used to function as a first-person pronoun during the Heian period (ninth century AD) and in contemporary Japanese stands for the private, 'naked' SELF (Hirose 2014), as opposed to public SELVES. It is also used as a logophor and to signal the subject's viewpoint. I list some of the first-person markers in Japanese in (12) below (after Hirose 2014).

(12) *boku*   I$_{\text{male casual}}$

      atasi   I$_{\text{female casual}}$

      watakusi   I$_{\text{very formal}}$

      ore   I$_{\text{male casual/vulgar}}$

      atai   I$_{\text{female vulgar}}$

      zibun   I$_{\text{private 'naked'}}$

---

[9] See also Jaszczolt 2013b.

> otoosan   I_father
> okaasan   I_mother
> sensei   I_teacher

The indices do not sum up to a unidimensional classification in that while *zibun* stands for the private SELF, other terms are inherently permeated with public roles (Hirose, *ibid.*, fn 5). In addition, Japanese has a wide array of reflexives that capture different aspects of the anaphoric relations. For example, *karada* is used for 'self$_{body}$' in a construction 'wash oneself', while *atama* or *kokoro* for 'self$_{mind}$' as in, for example, 'trouble oneself'. While ascribing properties to onself, *zibun-zisin* signals the perspective of the agent on the agent's own self, while *kare-zisin* signals the perspective of the speaker, as in (13a)–(13b).

(13a)   Akio-*wa*   zibun-zisin-*o*   semeta.
        Akio-*Top*   self-self-*Acc*   blamed.
        Akio blamed himself.

(13b)   Akio-*wa*   kare-zisin-*o*   semeta.
        Akio-*Top*   him-self-*Acc*   blamed.
        Akio blamed himself.
        (adapted from Hirose 2014: 109)

Zibun and *kare* function here as perspective markers rather than reflexives. As can be predicted, when used for the direct object, they are not interchangeable: *kare* cannot fulfil the function of a reflexive as (14a)–(14b) demonstrate.

(14a)   Akio-*wa*   zibun-*o*   semeta.
        Akio-*Top*   self-*Acc*   blamed.
        Akio blamed himself.

(14b)   Akio-*wa*   kare-*o*   semeta.
        Akio-*Top*   him-*Acc*   blamed.
        Akio blamed him.
        (adapted from Hirose 2014: 110)

This is only the tip of the iceberg as far as self-reference in Japanese is concerned but even this brief exemplification signals that in Japanese the distinctions in first-person markers are not merely a topic for sociolinguistics: they are not confined to honorifics that signal the social status of the interlocutors but also pertain to the mind/body, social/private, and first-/third-person point of view, among others. While quite often the multiplicity of such forms in South-East Asian languages can be explained through the process of grammaticalization, the fact remains that in the current synchronic state of the language they are present, they pertain to distinctions that are compulsory, and as such they are widely used and correspond to conceptual distinctions that would be lost if we were to explain them as additions to the simple semantic role of a pure indexical.

There is nothing to signal that the mould of an indexical term should be adopted for their semantics, especially that in addition to the richness of meaning these markers are not even pronouns as we understand the term; they exhibit the characteristics of both nouns and pronouns. It has been widely argued that either (i) there is no adequate definition of a pronoun that would capture the characteristics of person-reference in all languages or (ii) some languages, such as Japanese, do not have personal pronouns but instead use for person-reference terms whose morphosyntactic characteristics resemble those of nouns. Da Milano (2014) calls them 'person terms'. For example, they allow adjectival, demonstrative and clausal modification as in Japanese 'kono watasi' ('this I'). They belong in the same group as kinship terms, titles, proper names, or age-status terms. Most of them originated from nouns or demonstratives, as for example 'boku' ('slave' >> 'I') or 'watasi' (private matters in contrast to public matters >>'I') (Da Milano 2014). These markers resemble nouns in that they do not form a closed class and they allow for morphological marking of the plural. This is also the case for many other South-East Asian languages, for example Thai, Korean, Vietnamese, Burmese, Javanese, Malay or Khmer.

Now, Heine and Song (2011: 619) remark that if it were indeed the case that these forms were personal pronouns that developed from common nouns, they would exhibit the loss of the referential function. But these 'pronouns' are in fact referential. So, either there is no grammaticalization involved here or the definition of grammaticalization would have to be broadened to account for this case. We opt for the more common-sense classification, namely that, in view of the lack of conclusive characteristics that tease them apart, pronominals and fully lexical items belong to one grammatical category.

This is a serious problem for Kaplan's characters. In fact, it is a problem for the category of indexicals itself in that if in various natural languages we cannot discern a lexical element that can be bi-uniquely associated with such a role, the role becomes a philosophical construct that has no support in natural language. There are two routes from here. First, we can surmise that the EGO associated with philosophers' first-person indexical is not universal on the level of concepts that are used in communication. South-East Asian languages would testify to the existence of a concept of a, say, EGO_{mind} vs. EGO_{body}, or $EGO_{private}$ vs. EGO_{public}. This concept is likely to be a primitive one in that lexicalization does not go any deeper into conceptual distinctions. Or perhaps one can concoct some reliable semantic decomposition that would still allow us to maintain a universal concept of EGO, possibly to be captured as the character of the first-person indexical. However, no such credible decomposition has been offered. Second, we can attempt to subsume various Japanese, Thai, etc. equivalents of *I* under a universal concept of the first-person indexical—a semantic object whose characteristic is merely to 'find the correct person' in the context and 'stand proxy for it', so to speak: no more, no less. The richness of the semantic distinctions that these terms convey would then have to be relegated to the status of an additional pragmatic overlay, or an implicature.

But this, surely, would not be correct. It cannot be correct because when we consult native speakers of these languages, they say that making a mistake in the use of such a term feels like a serious deficiency in language competence; the forms are taught to children and second-language learners with emphasis not lesser than that placed on the correctness of grammatical constructions.[10] Next, it cannot be correct because these meanings are not cancellable. In accordance with the arguments from cancell-ability advanced in Chapter 3, we have to conclude that these meanings belong with primary meanings and as such with the truth-conditional content.

A failure to acknowledge such arguments is precisely the problem with some attempts in philosophy at justifying Kaplan's distinction. I have argued here that first-person pronoun is far removed from the 'I' of Kaplanesque fiction. Here is an alternative coming from Kaplan's camp. One can attempt to dissociate various aspects of the meaning of 'I' or, better, of its various equivalents in languages with honorifics and with the 'I_{body}', 'I_{mind}', or 'I_{social}' distinctions, from the 'core' that is arguably provided by the self-referring role. This would indeed secure the indexical. Let us try for a moment to make use here of Predelli's (2013) *character-bias* distinction. He suggests that the character does not exhaust the meaning of an expression; there is also a 'bias', such as addressee-directed bias in the case of child-directed speech and denotational bias in the case of honorifics. Expressives, such as 'whore' as opposed to 'prostitute', or 'faggot' as opposed to 'homosexual', also contain denotational bias in addition to the truth-conditional content captured by their character; the pairs are, as he says, 'character-indistinguishable' (p. 97). In this way, he can claim that:

'the idea of character provides a formal representation of at least *some aspects* of the conventional meaning of an expression—that is, of some aspects of the features associated with that expression by the conventions of the language, and, in the case of natural languages, presumably mastered by competent speakers.'

Predelli (2013: 11)

But here is the problem: if one wants to keep the truth-conditional content minimal, one excludes perfectly legitimate and crucial aspects of word meaning as 'bias'. Predelli continues:

'The aspects in question have to do with *those portions of meaning*[11] that make a truth-conditional difference: the character of *e* is the sort of property that eventually impacts on the truth-conditions of sentences containing *e*.' (*ibid.*)

[10] Hye-Kung Lee, p.c.   [11] My emphasis.

On the other hand, when one opts for contextualist truth conditions, what was relegated to the 'bias' can remain within the semantic content. This latter option allows us to avoid 'portioning meaning', to use Predelli's phrase. It also allows us to avoid internal inconsistencies. Predelli (2013: 101) admits that some slurs do have truth-conditional relevance. So, for example in (15) 'Italian' and 'wop' are not 'character-indistinguishable' as the theory proposes but instead what ought to be a 'bias' looks like truth-conditionally relevant content. The slight artificial flavour of this made-up example notwithstanding, (15) captures the relevant point.

(15)   Cosimo is Italian, but he is not a wop.

Needless to say, this also messes up the minimalists' story about the associated extensions and no qualifications concerning special uses will save it. Again, we score a point or two in favour of Salience-Based Contextualism.

The interim conclusion has to be that we have plenty of evidence from natural languages that self-reference does not proceed according to the alleged properties of the characters associated with indexicals. In fact, even inflected Indo-European languages that mark the gender in sentences with first-person subject belong in the group of counterexamples: Polish (16a) and (16b) convey more than a slot for the self-referring author. Self-expression consists here of the morphological endings for tense and person/number/gender.[12] Polish is a *pro*-drop language and pronoun *ja* ('I') would be used in (16b) only for emphasis, for example for contrastive focus.

(16a)   Prze-czyta-ł-**am**   *Dumę i uprzedzenie.*
           Perf-read-*Past-1SgF*   *Pride and Prejudice.*
           I have read *Pride and Prejudice.*

(16b)   Prze-czyta-ł-**em**   *Dumę i uprzedzenie.*
           Perf-read-*Past-1SgM*   *Pride and Prejudice.*
           I have read *Pride and Prejudice.*

The gender distinction is marked only in the past tense constructions (on all associated aspectual variations), one of the two main forms for the future, but is not marked on the present tense forms. But it suffices for the sake of our argument that it is marked on some of the forms: the indexical is not discernible as an item. As we saw, in many languages, it is not discernible as a function either, so we have a real quandary.

We can return at this point to the question of the putative universal status of the first-person. If it was indeed a semantic *qua* conceptual universal, then it would have to be lexically or morphologically realized in all natural languages, at least according

---

[12] Only those grammatical distinctions that are relevant for the present argument are marked in the gloss.

to Wierzbicka's (1996) theory of semantic universals. Polish, Russian or French morphological markers seem to withstand this test in that the forms do not have to capture the concept EGO alone, and, in addition, there is a pronoun *ja/ja/je* that realizes this concept. But Wierzbicka also imposes a requirement of the existence of an unmarked variant among the different forms (allolexes). Here the justification of the universal status of EGO becomes more tricky. Gender-differentiated forms can be defended as passing Wierzbicka's test in that they merely reflect the requirements of a language system and there is no explicit I_{male}/I_{female} distinction across grammatical forms at large. On the other hand, arguably, the multiple forms in Japanese or Thai do not pass the test: I_{body} and I_{mind}, $I_{private}$ and I_{public} carry different meanings and have to fulfil the requirements of the given context, and so it is very unlikely that any default or unmarked status of any of them can be uncovered.[13]

This diversity of forms associated with the diversity of self-concepts also tentatively suggests that perhaps when Strawson (1959) advocated the primitive status of the concept of the person, he overlooked the possibility that (i) there may not be a universal concept of the person that would apply to speakers of all languages or, if there is, (ii) the concept of the person is present on the level of atomic concepts but not on the level of language-specific concepts, purpose-made for communication (variously called 'thinking for speaking' (Slobin 1996), molar level of concepts (Levinson 2003), among others). To repeat, while in this analysis we shall not advance specific arguments in favour of either stance, (ii) is tacitly assumed as a stance that appears to be more compatible with cross-linguistic evidence as well as with conceptual analyses: there are universals on the level of the language of thought, just not on the level of natural language structures compared across cultures. A bolder suggestion might be that the inculcated Cartesian dualism gains some ground when we attest the I_{body}/I_{mind} distinction across different languages, just as perhaps Chomskyan (less inculcated) I-language/E-language distinction gains some ground through the $I_{private}/I_{public}$ dichotomy (in association with the I_{body}/I_{mind}, through being itself Cartesian). But this may, at present, be too long a shot.

Now, a universal concept of the person, even if such can be uncovered on some level of human concepts, is not yet a first-person indexical: it may still be tainted by a whiff of I_{mind}, I_{body}, or some other conceptual patina—we simply don't know prior to any data-based study.[14] Let us assume however, for the sake of argument, that on the level of atomic concepts there is an EGO that conforms to the Kaplanesque first-person indexical. So, for example, Japanese *boku* ('$I_{male\ casual}$') is a molecular concept

---

[13] Hirose's (2014) analysis suggests such an outcome, and so does Srioutai's (2000) search for an unmarked allolex of 'someone' in Thai, but a more extensive, perhaps corpus-based analysis is needed here.

[14] This project is currently in progress, funded by The Leverhulme Trust, and partially supporting this research: *Expressing the Self: Cultural Diversity and Cognitive Universals*, University of Cambridge http://www.mml.cam.ac.uk/dtal/expressing-the-self.

that can be decomposed into atoms: an indexical that functions as a mere slot-holder for a person, and the semantic components 'male', 'casual' and 'public'. This is what Christofaki (in progress) calls different *facets of the self* that accompany the universal concept, where both aspects of the expression, the universal and the culture-specific, are present in the conceptualization. But this does not yet give us first-person reference as a clearly delineated component that would be relevant for the composition of meaning in the semantics of linguistic interaction such as DS. Merger representations of DS do not descend to semantic decomposition; they account for concepts on the level on which thoughts are conducted, be it in natural language or some other language of thought.[15] Just as we do not attempt a decomposition of lexical items such as 'dog', 'kill', or 'bachelor', so we abstain from delving below the level of thoughts in the case of expressing the SELF. As a result, even if there are conceptual equivalents of first-person indexicals in all languages, they would still remain outside the domain of a semantic analysis as it is construed here: a truth-conditional theory of meaning in linguistic interaction.

But are we even justified in making an assumption that there are pure first-person concepts on the atomic level in the first place? Note that there are languages that lack pronominal expressions altogether, for example Acoma (New Mexico) and Wari' (Brazil, see Heine and Song 2011, after Jeffrey Heath). Juxtaposing this with the observation that some languages have markers that do not conform to a pronominal/ nominal distinction, we seem to be on dubious grounds in attempting to extract from the practice of self-referring a pure dummy that stands for a physical person and including it in the semantic representation.[16]

Kaplan's desideratum that the value of an indexical term is determined exclusively by the context of the act of utterance, discussed in the literature as a Fixity Thesis (Schlenker 2003), does not seem to work for languages such as Amharic where 'I' in attitude contexts such as 'John says that I am a hero' can refer to John himself rather than the speaker.[17] The latter phenomenon has been well aired in the literature since Schlenker (2003), also in conjunction with the behaviour of logophoric pronouns, including arguments in favour of inadmissibility of such examples as evidence against the Fixity Thesis.[18]

The value of evidence from Amharic is at least debatable. It indeed appears that Amharic displays the phenomenon of free indirect speech in which the first-person marker can take reference from the context of current speech as well as from the

---

[15] See Section 2.2.2.

[16] This is how indexicals are normally understood in formal semantic theory. Interestingly, DRT preserves this 'dummy' role of first-person markers, explaining away gender agreement in construction rules. But that is not to say that the DRSs offered for better known Indo-European languages would have to be replicated once a new phenomenon of reference marking is encountered in another language.

[17] See also Schlenker 2011; Roberts 2014.

[18] See e.g. Predelli 2011b, 2014.

reported context. Interestingly, the context-shift can occur even within one sentence as in (17).

(17)   wändəmme   käne gar   albälamm   alä
        my-brother "with-**me** I-will-not-eat",   he-said
        My brother refused to eat with me.
        (from Leslau 1995: 778)

This construction exemplifies free indirect speech. The corresponding situation need not involve the brother's act of uttering 'I will not eat with you', or even 'I will not eat'; it has to involve some form of behaviour that amounts to an act of refusal. Notably, inanimate subjects can also enter such constructions as evidenced by (18).

(18)   mäskotu   aləkkäffät   alä
        the-window "I-will-not-be opened" it-said
        'The window wouldn't open'
        (from Leslau 1995: 782)

But the situation with Amharic may in fact be less complicated than the accounts to date suggest. On the one hand, even if we don't have here direct speech, the message has some form of a quotative feeling to it (Yoseph Mengistu, p.c.) in that it reflects the subject's thought processes as if they were speech. Note that in the case of inanimate subjects the construction is only permissible when the object interacts with the speaker's will: the window will not open, the wood will not dry, and so forth. The first-person is, so to speak, inherent in the concept conveyed by the verb (Yoseph Mengistu, p.c.) when the corresponding activity pertains to this person. And this is then reflected in the grammar as evidenced by (17). In (17), *albälamm* makes it into the report as one concept—a thought from the first-person perspective, 'I refuse to eat'. The problem then remains how to explain the fact that we also have in this sentence *käne gar* ('with me')—seemingly a first-person object juxtaposed with the first-person subject. But this is not the right way to approach this sentence. To do so would be to approach it through the perspective of the English language, transposing its way of conveying the situation onto Amharic. Instead, we ought to start with the *tertium comparationis*—the platform of comparison for contrastive studies, or an *independent concept* to be explained, and see how it is realized in Amharic and in English. Approached in this way, we are likely to reach the conclusion that Amharic follows the conceptualization on the level of thoughts rather closely. A reanalysis of (17) that best captures the conceptualization behind such utterances seems to be that in (17a)

(17a)   wändəmme   käne gar   albälamm   alä
        my-brother with-me   "I-will-not-eat",   he said

Let us take another example from Leslau (1995: 777), as in (19) below.

(19) yäsəra gʷaddäññočče   käne gar annəsäramm   alu
      my-colleagues   "with-me we-will-not work"   they-said
      'My colleagues refused to work with me'.

As Leslau (p. 778) points out, the sentence can be reinterpreted as 'with me, my friends, "we will not work" they said'. Now the only material in quotes is 'we will not work'. The verb of saying in simple imperfect form (*alä*) performs a great variety of functions in Amharic, many of which cannot be translated, or even conceived of, as 'saying'. It normally conveys intention or even, as in the case of inanimate subjects, a metaphorical rendering of intention: intention from the perspective of the speaker against whose will these objects may behave. So, coming back to (17) and (19), 'I will not eat' and 'we will not work' are indeed quotative but only in the sense of reflecting the language of thought so to speak: the agent refusing to eat or refusing to work with the speaker need not have uttered it; s/he could have simply acted in a manner that demonstrates such a refusal. A good example of this use would be the verb 'ignore': in 'he ignored me' we don't have a speech act of saying 'I am ignoring you' and yet the situation would be expressed using the verb *alä*.

Now, Schlenker (2003) uses the following argument to opt for the non-quotative status of these examples. He says that because the Amharic translation of 'I didn't hear what he told me to bring' has a construct 'what bring' in the construction 'what bring he told me I didn't hear' (see Schlenker 2003: 68), the quotation view is to be rejected: the speaker didn't say it, neither did he issue an order 'Bring what!'. As Schlenker (2003: 69) puts it, '[T]he fact that there is an indirect question shows that the embedded clause is not quoted'. But the evidence is not so robust. When we go to the original source of this example (Leslau 1995: 779), we can see a more common-sense reconstruction: 'I didn't hear what he said to me "bring what?"' 'Bring' can be construed as quoted, and because it is an echoic construction, 'what' substitutes for the requested object. In other words again, we have 'I didn't hear [he said to me: ["bring what"]]'. It is only 'what' that is not quoted; according to my source,[19] 'bring' is processed as an imperative echoing the third party's uttered command that is followed by something not heard. As such, it can be construed as quotative. So, the supporting evidence against quotation is dubious indeed.

All in all, it appears that the semantic fact that the subject imposes, so to speak, the first-person perspective that is then inseparable from the relevant verb (cf. 'window' and 'open', 'brother' and 'eat', etc.), aided by the fact that the verb *alä* seems to be used to reflect the conceptual rather than (or in addition to) the speech-act content, make these first-person constructions appear logically and conceptually straightforward

---

[19] Yoseph Mengistu, p.c.

ways of expressing thoughts. One can look at this in the following way. What is there in the grammar of Amharic, English has to render by a conceptual shift, opting for the speaker's perspective, rather than the perspective that belongs to the subject of the activity or state in question.[20] In conclusion, the quotative reading seems to be clearly present in Amharic examples and therefore we will not use them as evidence for the pragmatic variability of the first-person indexical.

5.3.2 A view from home

We will now stay closer to home and focus on English alone and the vagaries of expressing the SELF in order to gather some more support for relegating the first-person indexical to the domain of philosophers' fiction—fiction that is useful for conceptual analyses but not for natural language semantics that aspires to reasonable psychological reality. For this purpose, we may have to rehearse some observations scattered in previous discussions, adding some new ones as we proceed.

Kaplan (1989a: 491) famously insists that uttering 'I' and pointing at someone else is 'irrelevance or madness'. But it seems pertinent here that uttering 'I' and pointing at different 'temporal slices' of oneself as in (20) is not uncommon.

(20)   [*Scenario: The speaker and her friend watch a home video from a holiday*]
        Look, here the goat is about to attack me but I don't realize it is me because I think all the time that this is a window, not a mirror. So, I am trying to find out how to open the window to warn her until . . .

Examples of temporal shift on written notes as in (21) are of that ilk.

(21)   [*Scenario: A secretary pins a note to the office door*]
        I am not in. Back at 2pm.

Explanations through context as a conventional setting (Corazza 2004) or speaker intentions (Predelli 2011b) notwithstanding, this is clearly the case of a tainted 'I'.

Neither is it uncommon to use 'I' as a bound variable as in (22) discussed by Kratzer (2009) and dubbed by her a 'fake indexical' in that the second occurrence of 'I' is semantically unspecified.

(22)   Only *I* admitted what *I* did wrong.[21]

---

[20] I am leaving open the question of the grammaticalization of *alä* in that the question of the loss of semantic content is not relevant to the discussion; what matters is that the semantic content pertaining to reflecting intentions, or reflecting the object's acting against the speaker's intentions, is uniformly present in these constructions.

[21] See also Schlenker 2003, pp. 89–90 on the role of 'only' that is similar to that of a syntactic binder. Cf. also an argument from ellipsis for the bound variable use: 'Not only *I* admitted what I did wrong; Peter did too'.

Fake indexicality does not generalize well across languages though: a more common way of expressing this 'conceptual binding' is a reflexive pronoun, as in Polish (22a) or (23a), an equivalent of (23).[22]

(22a) Tylko ja jedna   przyznałam   się do (swojego)
         Only   I   sole*SgFNom* admit*1SgPastF* *Refl* to *ReflPronSingMGen*
         błędu.
         mistake*SgMGen*

(23)   I'm the only one around here who can take care of *my* children.

(23a) Tylko ja jedna   tutaj potrafię   zajmować się
         Only   I   sole*SgFNom* here can*1SgPres* care*Inf*   *Refl*
         swoimi   dziećmi.
         ReflPronPlInstr   child*PlInstr*

This variation in the employment of fake indexicality works in favour of our current argument: markers of first-person reference are messy, exhibiting language-specific patterns as well as diversity of syntactic roles that do not carry from one language to another. At the same time, in spite of the language-specificity of this construction, we can glean a general conceptual characteristic: bound-variable pronouns may not be referential but they convey self-awareness that carries through from the binder to the anaphor. And in this sense, arguably, they testify to the grammatical marking of self-awareness.[23]

This is not a place to conduct a thorough discussion of the uses the English 'I'. Suffice it to say that just as 'I' has different meanings and even different syntactic functions, so marking of self-reference in itself can be diversified. Let us return first to the examples of lexical words from Section 5.1. Child-directed speech and child speak in (5) and (6) testifies to the use of common nouns in their role of a first-person marker.[24] (7), uttered by a DIY-expert, demonstrates that the phenomenon also extends to professions—not unlike in the case of the Japanese kinship terms and terms for professions that assume the role of a marker of the 'public SELF' (Hirose 2014). Next, we have already mentioned the generalizing detached self-reference as in (8) repeated below as (24).

---

[22] From Kratzer (2009: 1888), after Partee.

[23] I discuss the grammatical foundations of self-reference in more detail in Section 3.1 of Jaszczolt 2013c.

[24] It has to be noted in this context that children's self-awareness is documented to develop as their understanding of first-person pronoun progresses (see e.g. Corazza 2004: 177). But this fact of developmental psycholinguistics does not make the observation that common and proper nouns are used for self-reference any less valid—especially that, as is exemplified below, the phenomenon is not confined to child speak and child-directed speech.

(24)   One can tell that he is not telling the truth.

Moltmann (2010: 440) explains this generalizing self-reference as the speaker's standing for individuals with whom the speaker identifies herself/himself or whom the speaker simulates. While one can no doubt find examples that would contradict the 'identification' characteristic,[25] the detachment and the generalization are certainly there—either for the purpose of sharing information of a more general interest as in (25) or for the purpose of maintaining polite rapport as in (26).

(25)   One can park there free on weekends.

(26)   One shouldn't pry into other people's affairs.

On Moltmann's account, arbitrary (non-controlled) PRO performs a similar function of generalized self-reference, although the degree of detachment from 'first-personhood' appears to be somewhat greater here, as the paraphrases in (25a) and (26a) exemplify.

(25a)   It is possible PRO to park there free on weekends.

(26a)   It is wrong PRO to pry into other people's affairs.

Next, 'if I were you', 'In your place I would . . .' also fall in the category of detachment, although when analysed from the perspective of DS, they are of a lesser importance in that their function is more restricted. They are likely to communicate speech acts of advice, recommendation and other addressee-oriented polite directives and as such be associated with indirect primary meaning without a first-person marker. In agreement with the rejection of the syntactic constraint on merger representations, the Σ will then not contain a discourse referent that stands for the speaker. For example, (27) is likely to produce the primary meaning in (28).

(27)   If I were you I wouldn't worry about it.

(28) $\rightarrow_{PM}$ Please don't worry about it.

The usual disclaimers apply, in that the flexibility with which people issue directives allows for first-person readings to occur as well.

---

[25] As I argued in Jaszczolt (2013b: 61–2), self-identification seems to be a matter of degree, as (i)–(iii) repeated here exemplify. Sentence (i) exhibits the highest degree of 'self-identification', perhaps even enhanced by irony, and (iii) the lowest in that it states an objective fact. (ii) is a middle case in that it expresses the speaker's ethical stance—or at least the fact that the speaker supports a certain norm of behaviour.

   (i)   One sometimes wonders if something called 'free time' exists at all.
   (ii)   One should not gossip behind people's backs.
   (iii)   One can take a lift to the top of the Empire State Building.

All in all, what we are left with is a simple fact that perspective (the concept that we use after Recanati 2007) is rendered differently in different languages. Sometimes, as in Amharic, the subject's perspective is so entrenched in the grammar that it withstands the addition of the perspective of the speaker, and in other cases it is implicitly there in the salient, shared knowledge that the reporting (and often also various epistemic attitude) contexts only seemingly overrides it.[26] While the Amharic solution copes well with expressing intentions through the grammar (the first-person pronoun is uniformly interpreted *de se*), English relies on pragmatic inference or default interpretations, leaving grammatical constructions potentially more prone to ambiguous interpretations. But as I have argued elsewhere (Jaszczolt 2012a), lexical, grammatical and pragmatic means are equally adequate for conveying meaning and as such are subject to the 'division of labour'—or, as I called them, the 'lexicon-grammar-pragmatics trade-offs'. In short, the perspective is conveyed in one way or another, and as such, in DS, it makes its way into the semantic representation.

Now, for Roberts (2014) this variation in the choice of perspective suggests that the so-called *doxastic centers*, such as that pertaining to the situation of reporting as opposed to the original situation, are ranked differently for different languages, and sometimes also ranked differently for different predicates within a language.[27] A doxastic center is 'an ordered pair consisting of a doxastic agent a and a time t: <a,t>' (p. 32). The doxastic centers can change as discourse progresses and these changes can be reflected in the anchoring of an indexical expression. The proposal is founded on Stalnaker's (1978) and Lewis' (1979a, b) idea of centred worlds, where the center can also be adopted on pragmatic grounds, for the purpose of the discourse at hand. In her semantics, doxastic centers are the basis for the theoretical construct of a discourse center: a pair of a DR-theoretic (Kamp and Reyle 1993) discourse referent and a time <d,t>:

'...I assume only that in discourse we track those discourse referents which are understood to be *centers* at that point in the discourse, in the sense of agents whose doxastic perspective is immediately relevant, with the corresponding discourse referents logically accessible in the DRS sense. Different languages may, and certainly do, use different mechanisms to indicate which entities are taken to be centers in this sense. I assume that when multiple doxastic agents are under discussion, their relative salience is a function of general mechanisms for tracking relevance and salience, but more importantly, that grammatical factors, like the doxastic modal semantics of certain attitude predicates, play an overarching central role in determining which centers are available, relevant and preferred.'

Roberts (2014: 61)

---

[26] See e.g. Roberts 2014 for extensive examples of languages that employ different solutions to the perspective problem. For example, in Zazaki many different indexicals can shift but only under a certain verb, while in Slave, only first-person and occasionally second-person indexicals shift, but under a variety of verbs. Some types of shifts are obligatory, while others are optional. Other discussed languages include Nez Perze, Uyghur, and Japanese.

[27] Many thanks to Minyao Huang for drawing my attention to this publication.

These centers can shift as discourse progresses, so a character of an indexical term is not allocated content once and for all: it can shift. This is captured by her proposed 'perspective shifting function'.[28] However, since the case of Amharic appears to be quotative after all, and since indexicality does not seem to be confined to a specific class of expressions but rather, as we have argued here, constitutes a function, a different kind of dynamic approach seems to be called for. Instead of making the anchoring of the indexical expression dynamic as discourse progresses (as would indeed be prudent should languages such as Amharic exemplify an unquestionably non-quotative shift), what we need is a dynamic account of the lexicon at large where the very anchoring is subjected to (i) language-systematic principles, (ii) conventional presuppositions, as well as (iii) context-specific mechanisms.

Moreover, Roberts (2014: 79) extends her perspective-shifting function to definite and indefinite descriptions—in accordance with her treatment of anaphoric use as a subcategory of indexical use. But then, if directly referential expressions share the context-shifting property with various 'occasion-indexicals', it seems to follow that shifting is a redundant concept after all; variable reference and dynamic reference assignment are features of lexical items themselves. Just as they are features of common nouns employed in the function of indexicality, so are they features of items on Kaplan's list. Put in a broader perspective, indexicality is a function of an expression and this expression can belong to various grammatical classes. So, while it is true that when processing 'I', 'you', or 'here' we conventionally presuppose that there is a contextually salient individual or place that is referred to, in the case of common nouns we may infer such an anchoring in the context. The definition of indexicality needs broadening and pragmaticizing.

In other words, it is not merely the case that '[f]ixed context and Character are empirically inadequate because changes in context in the course of interpreting an utterance can bear on the interpretation of an indexical' (Roberts 2014: 83) but rather what counts as an indexical is itself context-dependent. This dependency cuts into both camps: the expressions traditionally listed as indexicals (since their non-indexical uses, including 'reference-to-a-character uses', i.e. reference to the linguistic meaning of the word alone, are not uncommon) and the traditional non-indexicals that can adopt the indexical function with various degrees of ease, ranging from expressions such as 'muggins' (Manning 2013), or 'mummy' all the way to those that have to be coerced in an unusual way in an unusual context. There is more at stake here than merely tracking discourse referents.

---

[28] 'A perspective shifting function $\mathscr{P}$ takes as argument a context, a center and a familiar discourse referent d. In the context given, the center is the agent-at-a-time whose doxastic perspective is brought to bear, and the discourse referent will be coindexed with the NP whose interpretation is being shifted.' Roberts (2014: 79).

Now, Stalnaker (2014: 121) refers to a scenario on which John Perry says the following: 'I was talking with Bob Stalnaker, but he didn't realize that it was me that he was talking with. He thought I might be Fred Dretske.' and analyses it as follows:

'There is a shift here: consider the world that John correctly takes to be compatible with my beliefs in which the person I was talking with was Fred Dretske. The "me" in John's remark picks out Perry in that world, while the "I" picks out Dretske.'

But one may reasonably argue that what is 'picked out' is merely a description. And this is precisely what pragmaticizing indexicality is all about: 'I' can behave like a description, just as descriptions can perform the 'indexical function'. All in all, Stalnaker (2014: 2) is definitely correct in saying that '...a language-independent account of attitudes and their contents is (...) important for an adequate understanding of discourse'. Merger representations of DS presented in Section 5.4 are one way of capturing such conceptual structures.

5.3.3 Mode of self-presentation

Let us next consider the self-attribution of properties. *De se* thoughts can be *de se* through necessity, so to speak, and *de se* accidentally. The first contain self-ascription that cannot be mistaken for ascription to other individuals; in other words, they are immune to error through misidentification. Immunity to error through misidentification (IEM, Shoemaker 1968) characterizes some first-person thoughts, namely those that cannot possibly be ascribed to the self by mistake. For example, when I think that I have a headache, the headache cannot belong to someone other than me. On the other hand, when I look through a glass pane believing it to be a mirror and think that I am wearing a red scarf, on an appropriate scenario I could be wrong: the person who is standing at some distance on the other side of the glass pane and who looks a lot like me is wearing a red scarf.[29] Recanati (2007, 2012d) calls the first *implicit de se* in that they are *de se* in virtue of incorporating self-ascription rather than ascription of properties that is identified as ascription to oneself. In other words, they are 'inherently *de se*'. In terms of Recanati's (2012e: 57–67; 2013) mental files, the SELF-file contains both kinds of information: immune to error (inherently *de se*) as well as conceptual information that is not immune (externally *de se*), for example that I was born in 1963.

In English, sentences with controlled PRO seem to convey such an immunity to error. For example, (26) can only be uttered truthfully when the speaker directly self-ascribes the property of writing the article rather than, say, identifies herself with the author while reading the name at the top of the paper.[30]

---

[29] Note that IEM is not specific to *de se* thoughts but, arguably, affects singular thoughts at large (Wright 2012). For recent discussions of IEM see Prosser and Recanati 2012 and Cappelen and Dever 2013.

[30] See e.g. Recanati 2007; Stanley 2011; Folescu and Higginbotham 2012.

(29)   I remember PRO writing this article.

But then, as Higginbotham (2003) points out, IEM can be easily destroyed by tweaking this construction as in (29a) or (29b).

(29a)   I remember my writing this article.
(29b)   I remember (that) I wrote this article.

I called this phenomenon elsewhere (Jaszczolt 2013b: 63) 'attenuated *de se*' or 'degrees of remembrance' in that while (29) is an expression based on a memory of an event, the tweaked versions may merely report on a fact that is somewhat misremembered: it may have been my project partner who wrote the article, or I may have taken notes but haven't actually written the final draft. Needless to say, further periphrastic methods of attenuation and hedging are ample.

Now, Jason Stanley (2011: 87) remarks that while first-person controlled PRO conveys self-attribution of mental states (and, in our semantic jargon, also self-ascription of properties), third-person-controlled PRO does not. It is indeed true (*pace* Corazza forthcoming) that (30) does not guarantee that a five-year-old Lidia is actively thinking of herself as a future scientist; she may merely show a particular interest in scientific experiments.

(30)   Lidia wants PRO to be a scientist.[31,32]

So, neither indexicality itself nor even PRO are good guarantees of immunity. The reason is simpler than it appears to be: just as there are *degrees* to which a natural language expression functions as an indexical, in that even standard first-person pronouns in many languages (and contexts) contain an admixture of other conceptual content, so there are *degrees* to which one is committed to a first-person statement. One cannot be mistaken about whose pain one is experiencing in thinking 'I have a headache', but in the case of 'My legs are crossed' (an example often quoted

---

[31] See also Manson 2012 on different kinds of attitudinal knowledge, including unconscious wishes: these can also be reported as 'I want *x*' in the sense that 'Apparently (so I am told) I want *x*'. While Manson leaves these cases out of his particular topic of inquiry, it seems that they provide an important example of a diversity of uses of 'I' (cf. 'It is not me that wants *x*; it is this other person inside me.').

[32] Corazza (2004: 348) puts forward a claim that one only masters indexicals when one also masters quasi-indexicals. In other words, I only understand (i) if I am able to understand (ii) where 'she' is coreferential with 'Lidia', that is, acts as a quasi-indicator (Castañeda 1967).

(i)   I am happy.
(ii)   Lidia believes she is happy.

This is so because to fully understand the concept of the self, one has to be able to understand it *of others*, so to speak.

Clearly, this discussion suffers from the common oversight discussed here: while the only role of 'she' in (ii) is to pick up coreference, 'I' in (i) has different roles to play—and arguably these roles are semantically significant when our semantics is to represent the intended and conveyed content as DS does.

in the literature), IEM characterizes only those thoughts that are arrived through proprioception; if one looks through a glass pane believing it to be a mirror, IEM is not guaranteed. Next, progressing towards the no-IEM cases, these, surely, come with a greater or smaller degree of certainty. Hence a cline. And, for our current purpose, hence the cline in the reliability of 'I' as a peg on which expressing the SELF can be hung. And hence the cline in the reliability of the controlled PRO construction.

Next, we use factive and non-factive verbs to report on our attitudes. Factives come with a strong commitment, non-factives with a degree of detachment from the described state of affairs, as in (31) and (32).[33]

(31)   I know Ian McEwan wrote *Black Dogs*.

(32)   I believe Philip Roth wrote *Indignation*.

'I believe' used as a hedge of illocutionary force for reasons of politeness is a related phenomenon.[34]

All in all, while formal semanticists often attempt to associate self-reference with a particular role, function, cognitive status, looking for clear-cut bi-unique correspondence, talking about oneself, even when assessed in English alone, is full of rather messy uses and as yet unexplained phenomena such as the degree of commitment of the EGO_{mind} or the degree of 'stepping outside', as from $EGO_{private}$ to EGO_{public}. We seem to have sufficient evidence to ascertain that, for example, Chierchia's (1989: 28) attempted generalization to the effect that the 'cognitive access to oneself' which we would here dub *self-reference* (accompanied by *self-awareness* and *self-attribution* of properties and *self-ascription* of mental states) is 'systematically excluded from the interpretation of (non-pronominal) referential expressions' does not stand up to scrutiny; we have seen that there are categories of nouns such as kinship terms or terms for professions that give rise to a fairly systematic employment in the role of self-reference—not only in English or Japanese but presumably as a fairly widespread pattern. Neither is the cognitive access to oneself 'systematically and unambiguously associated with the interpretation of PRO the null subject of infinitives and gerunds' (*ibid.*): there are examples with third-person subjects, where this access is absent altogether, and there are examples in which it is present to different degrees. Next, self-reference is indeed, as Chierchia says, 'systematically present in the interpretation of overt pronouns' (*ibid.*), but these pronouns also allow for other functions, as well as for admixing other concepts that co-exist with their function as an indexical.

The good reputation enjoyed by the concept of the first-person indexical receives support from various strands of externalism. There is no doubt that 'uncontaminated'

---

[33]   Note that 'factives' is a label that I attach to verbs, not to mental states in that knowledge and certainty are not connected in a simple way—see ample literature on high- vs. low-stakes scenarios and discussions form the relativist perspective, e.g. Blome-Tillmann 2013.

[34]   See Kauppinen 2010.

indexicals make Truth-Conditional Semantics simple by differentiating between fixed and non-fixed characters and systematizing the roles context can play in the theory. Here Stalnaker (2008: 130) advances an externalist argument that self-knowledge means viewing the self as if from the outside:

'...mental sentences, individuated by their content, have essential properties that are extrinsic to the mind, and so are not accessible to the person who is thinking the thought.'

It is true in the specific domain of inquiry pursued here that the most successful way to carry out semantic analysis is to include what in DRT is called 'external anchors': individuals on which we can peg the discourse referents. Indeed, to do otherwise means risking a subjectivist semantics, a conceptual analysis that does not go beyond mental objects to reality. But this reliance on objective reference even for first-person statements takes the edge off the contrast between the first-person and the third-person perspectives and ends up assimilating the first to the latter as far as the truth-conditional content is concerned. This seems to be the case in all minimalist and contextualist accounts save for DS. DS, which unites the speech-act perspective with a truth-conditional method, allows for accommodating the conceptual 'contamination' exemplified in this chapter. To repeat, in view of the evidence and the arguments against splitting what effectively cannot be split up, these aspects of meaning are not seen as implicit or external to the content but as part of the truth-conditional content itself. In the following section we will demonstrate how this analysis is conducted in practice in the example of a few merger representations.

Another reductionist argument comes from the public availability of individual experiences. Chalmers (2010) argues that there is an important sense in which first-person experience is not special in that first-person experience can be replicated by others; it cannot be directly shared but it can be compared and juxtaposed with experiences of other people, viz. '...it is usually straightforward to cross-validate observations with reports from many subjects' (Chalmers 2010: 53). Further arguments against the special status of first-person thought are ample in philosophy and cognitive science (see e.g. Wright 2012; Carruthers 2011) but it would be difficult to use them in connection with our argument from natural language: first-person experience has a special status and even if this status is reducible to a common perspective with other-experience, this does not mean that it is less special on the level of self-concepts an insight into which is given to us by the ways natural languages allow us to refer to the SELF.

All in all, we can see that there is no direct evidence from morphosyntax that the indexical is the most adequate way of representing self-reference for the purpose of semantic theory. Perhaps Cappelen and Dever are right in their *Inessential Indexical* (2013) when they argue that indexicality is not necessary for explaining the EGO. Perhaps indexicality and the introduction of the perspectival viewpoint are merely 'predictable consequences of imperfect agents going about their task of trying to represent the world as it objectively and impersonally is' (Cappelen and Dever 2013: 182). If so, one either leaves the imperfections of the perspective outside the semantics or incorporates them by adjusting the content. Salience-Based Contextualism of DS adjusts it but retains a functional view on indexicality: words of natural language are never exact correlates of philosophers' indexicals; the latter are idealized concepts without support from cross-linguistic studies. Indexicality is at best a transient property of natural language expressions, realized as default self-awareness.

Perhaps what we need instead is a more finely-grained semantic representation like we do for Frege cases of belief reports. For Frege cases, a contextualist semantics requires some equivalents of senses or mode of presentation. I would suggest that to capture self-reference we need a semantic representation that captures the way of thinking about oneself, or, say, *mode of self-presentation*. Referring to oneself is achieved in discourse by means of the lexicon, grammar, or pragmatics and not only does it exhibit cross-linguistic differences but also affords considerable choices within one single language system. These differences pertain not only to honorification or the mind/body distinction but also to the degrees of emphasis placed on the self as opposed to the degrees to which the statement is generalized, predicated of, or valid about, other individuals. Impersonal 'one' constructions or impersonal evidentials 'it seems that' are good examples of this gradation. This attenuated commitment does not even correlate with the type of expression: first-person pronoun can also be used for this purpose, for example in hedges 'I think' or 'I believe'. Further, the pronoun itself can occasionally serve functions other than straightforward self-referring, such as referring to a 'temporal slice' of oneself or bound-variable use as in the so-called 'fake indexicals'. Next, even PRO constructions, commonly associated with the strong access to oneself and often also IEM, do not always correlate with this cognitive status. With this evidence in front of us it appears that the most adequate way to represent self-reference and self-ascription is a pragmatics-rich contextualist account that is able to capture these trade-offs between the lexicon, grammar, and pragmatics on the one hand, and the types and degrees of talking about the self on the other. In the next section I demonstrate how merger representations of DS put this idea into practice.

5.4 *De se* thoughts and *de se* reports in Default Semantics

There are ample advantages of including the *de se* perspective in the semantic content, the most important of which is the ability to represent conceptual differences between self-ascription and other-ascription of properties and thereby also the self-attribution and other-attribution of mental states. Rich, contextualist content is also more accurate in representing the practice of self-referring: we talk about ourselves having assumed an adequate concept of the self, be it public, private, physical, mental, or undifferentiated, not to mention more finely-grained distinctions pertaining to, say, social deference or the hierarchy of power in some in-group discourse, to give just one example. In what follows we will assume that since merger representations of DS are going to be used to capture this rich content, then the *de se* perspective has to be included in a proposition-based account rather than relegated to 'relations to oneself' as early discussions on the subject suggested.[35] We will construe differences between *de se* and *de re* about oneself as truth-conditionally significant but pertaining to a proposition that stands for the intended and recovered thought, represented as a conceptual (merger) representation.

Let us recall the scenario from Section 5.2. Knowing (11b) does not make me act in a way that knowing (11a) does although on our scenario I am the person who agreed to chair the Faculty Board this term. The difference is that in (11b), on our scenario, I don't know what I know knowing (11a): say, I forgot that I had agreed to act as chair and entertain merely a third-person belief. In referential semantics, however, there is no difference on the level of content: both (11a) and (11b) are represented as (33), where 'h' stands for 'has a meeting in half an hour'.[36]

(33) $\lambda x \, [h(x)]$ (kasia jaszczolt)

As Perry (2001b) puts it, there is no difference on the level of 'official', referential content—also called by him the 'default' content. It is 'official' because it captures the meaning as it is given by the language system—its synchronically fairly stable lexicon and rules of functional application. But it is only so given if we assume an indexical account of personal pronouns and a referential account of definite descriptions: it is the Kaplanesque content associated with the Kaplanesque character in this context that enters semantic composition. The essential component of self-awareness becomes relegated at best to a different kind of content (there is no shortage of those in Perry, e.g. 2001b, 2009) and as such to pragmatics rather than semantics. Moreover, on this semantics, the three possible types of reading of (11b) that we owe to the behaviour of the definite description also become obliterated: we lose insight into the pure attributive reading as well as into a reading on which the speaker is referentially mistaken—say, on our scenario, I am convinced that the person who agreed to chair the Faculty Board this term is my colleague David Willis (on this scenario, of course, the analogous puzzle would have to involve a case of my misidentification of the person). In short, when we assume Kaplanesque context (which I called in Section 4.2.2 *metaphysical* context), the character gives us a referent that enters the possible-world truth-conditional evaluation; as such, the indexical analysis of 'I' suffices. It also suffices in Stalnaker's (1978, 2011) construal of two-

---

[35] See Lewis 1979a.

[36] Needless to say, 'in half an hour' is a temporal adverbial that invokes analogous problems: 'I have a meeting at 2pm' thought by me at 1.30pm need not result in the same action on my part as 'I have a meeting in half an hour' when I am unaware of the correct current time. I discussed temporal reference in many different places (see e.g. Jaszczolt 2009a) and will not present the details of a DS-theoretic representation here; suffice it to say that the problem with indexicality is analogous there.

dimensional semantics where 'I' leads to a propositional concept that takes into account differences in the interlocutors' resolution of the indexical and the differences in their worlds. The context proposed there is an epistemic one: it is a common background, a *context-set*, founded on the interlocutors' presuppositions. But it does not yet extend to what we want context to do: to give us the relevant concept of the self. For the latter, Kaplanesque character is not sufficiently finely-grained.

All in all, rich semantic content is once again preferred as more explanatorily adequate, on the proviso that one is willing to relinquish the Holy Grail of a system-based formal theory of meaning. It will have to include the *fact* that the belief is indexical[37] but also what we called above the mode of self-presentation.

But is it necessary to resort to contextualism to capture self-awareness? It seems that it is necessary to abandon referentialist semantics but this is not to say that one cannot construe a minimalist account in such a way that self-awareness is represented. I have already suggested that although bound-variable uses of first-person pronouns may not be referential, they convey self-awareness. The point I am making now is that just as grammar can be regarded as a vehicle of self-awareness there, so, in general, grammar can be endowed with the role of the vehicle of the *de se* meaning in the case of intended and recovered self-referring.

This can be done in two different ways. Within minimalism, the character 'I' can be taken for what it is: a marker for first-person reference, *tout court*. Let us envisage a version of minimalism on which the character becomes, so to speak, 'its own content'. (34a) enters the representation as (34b).

(34a)   I am late for a meeting.

(34b)   The speaker is late for a meeting.

This version of minimalism would be even more minimal, so to speak, than Bach's (2001) minimalism on which pure indexicals (indexicals with stable semantic roles) acquire reference via an automatic procedure that is guaranteed by the grammar. Such token-based minimalism has a whiff of some vintage discussions ('I' refers to the speaker of *this token*). It clearly suffers when juxtaposed with the truth-conditional method and with the requirement of informativeness of semantic theory, but apart from these vices, it is workable. So, when the question is: *Is grammar the carrier of self-awareness?*, the answer, even within our 'most minimalist of minimalisms', is 'yes'. There is no need here for a multidimensional account. But, on the other hand, there is a need for more informativeness.

Moving now to the 'most contextualist of contextualisms', the answer to this question will depend on how we want to construe our grammar. In DS, it is a grammar of conceptual structures (Σs) and as such it makes use of context in all its

---

[37] Cf. 'The indexical fact may have to be taken as primitive.' Chalmers (1996: 85).

guises in that it makes use of all sources of information identified (and, if any, to be identified in the future) in DS. Grammar so construed will capture self-awareness associated with self-reference that is conveyed in a normal, predictable manner, i.e. a manner in which intentions coincide with decoding (WS), inferences (CPI) and defaults (SCWD, CD). It will capture readings that *need not* be associated with a given structure but which, considering the context, *are, pace* misunderstandings, associated with it. If this is what we agree that grammar ought to do, then self-reference and self-awareness are indeed attributable to the power of grammar.

Let us now move to the representations proper, beginning with expressions of *de se* thoughts, and progressing to reports *de se*—the latter subdivided into self-reports *de se* and other-reports *de se*. Using our previous example, we focus on the following structures in (35)–(36):

(35) I have a meeting at 2 o'clock.

(36) I believe I have a meeting at 2 o'clock.

(37) Kasia believes she has a meeting at 2 o'clock.

Sentence (35) can only represent a situation on which I self-attribute a mental state of believing I have a meeting at 2 o'clock. To repeat, since we are concerned here with representing first-person reference rather than temporal reference, we will not discuss the scenario on which the speaker is not aware of the current temporal location—say, that 'at 2 o'clock' and 'in half an hour' refer to the same moment in time. The merger representation of (35) will be as in Figure 5.1 below.

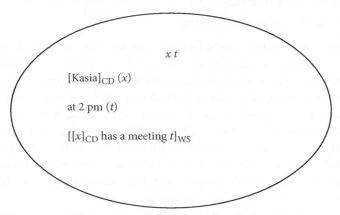

$x\ t$

$[\text{Kasia}]_{CD}\ (x)$

at 2 pm (t)

$[[x]_{CD}$ has a meeting $t]_{WS}$

Figure 5.1 Σ for example (35): 'I have a meeting at 2 o'clock.'[38]

---

[38] For the sake of simplicity, the full representation of temporal reference in terms of the ACC operator is omitted where it is not directly relevant for the case at hand. Likewise, a detailed structural analysis is omitted where not relevant. For example, in Figure 5.1, 'has a meeting' is treated as a simple predicate and

Entertaining other possibilities would take us into the domain of Lewisian (1979a) philosophical debates concerning self-knowledge and 'two gods' scenarios that would allegedly justify a report as in (35a), where 'this person' stands for the referent in the speaker's thought. In an exposition of the semantics of linguistic interaction this would take us too far into the area of disputable identity crises.[39]

(35a)   I have a meeting at 2 o'clock but only if this person is really me.

In any case, any detachment from certainty as to one's identity—say, caused by perception or knowledge that fails to discriminate individuals, or by referring to 'temporal slices' of oneself—would trigger a report with a marker of detachment such as 'I think' or 'I believe', which takes us to example (36).

Let us thus consider a self-report in (36), remembering that the superficially innocuous structure can also be used with the lack of self-awareness as in (38)— albeit stretching somewhat the natural manner of reporting on beliefs as well as the credibility of the scenario.

(38)   Look, I did believe yesterday morning, in a sense, that I had a meeting at 2 o'clock. The Chair of the Faculty had a meeting and I had been appointed Chair—the fact that I temporarily failed to remember!

What I am saying here is that although self-reports *de re* are in principle possible and can be expressed unambiguously, they have to be expressed periphrastically in that the natural *de se* reading is very hard to avoid. On the other hand, since this reading is generated by the general (perhaps universal) conceptual distinction between *de se* and *de re* about oneself rather than by sentence structures, it generalizes easily to other languages as the free translation into Polish in (38a) demonstrates.

(38a)

Wiesz co,	właściwie	to	ja	wiedziałam	wczoraj	rano,
you know	actually	*DemPart*	I	know-*Past1SgF*	yesterday	morning
że	będę miała	zebranie	o	drugiej.	Dziekan wydziału	
that	have-*Fut1SgF*	meeting-*Acc*	at	two.	Dean of the Faculty	
miał		zebranie,	a		to	przecież ja
have-*Past3SgM*	meeting-*Acc*	and-*Contr*	*DemPart*	actually	I	
jestem	dziekanem –	tyle tylko,	że	chwilowo	nie	
be-*Pres1SgM*	dean-*Instr*	only	that	momentarily	*Neg*	

---

is not fully analysed into 'meeting (*y*)' and '*x* has *y* at *t*'. Where this is the case, merger representations are *partial representations*.

[39] See also Cappelen and Dever 2013—to quote the title, 'on the philosophical insignificance of perspective and the first person'.

> pamiętałam,   że   podjęłam   się   tej
> remember-*Past1SgF* that undertake-*Past1SgF* *Refl DemPron-SgFGen*
> funkcji.
> role-*Gen*

Self-referring and self-attribution of mental states become dissociated, so to speak: while I can refer to my *enduring* EGO, I attribute mental states to my *perduring* temporal parts. Omitting the endurance/perdurance distinction from a merger representation would be like an omission of conceptual content from a conceptual representation. So, the passage from Kaplan (1989a: 491) we quoted in Section 5.3.2 that uttering 'I' and pointing at someone else is 'irrelevance or madness or what?' has to be qualified: the semantics may have to be able to represent these different 'kinds of *Is*', without creating a 'monster' context.[40]

Merger representations capture these readings in the following way. Sentence (36) has the standard *de se* reading as in Figure 5.2.

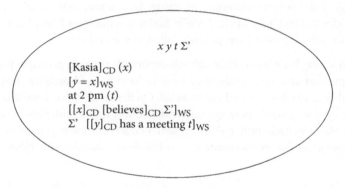

$$x\,y\,t\,\Sigma'$$

$[Kasia]_{CD}\,(x)$
$[y = x]_{WS}$
at 2 pm (t)
$[[x]_{CD}\,[believes]_{CD}\,\Sigma']_{WS}$
$\Sigma'\;[[y]_{CD}\,\text{has a meeting}\,t]_{WS}$

Figure 5.2 Σ for the default *de se* self-ascribing reading of sentence (36): 'I believe I have a meeting at 2 o'clock.'

The belief operator corresponds here to the strongest intentionality of the underlying mental state and hence to the CD-driven interpretation about the *res*, which, in combination with the information from binding in $[y = x]_{ws}$, results in the default *de se* reading. It is important to notice that we achieve this *de se* reading without the intervention of a general or underspecified *de re* interpretation proposed on Maier's (2009) or Percus and

---

[40] 'Monsters' is Kaplan's (1989a) term for putative operators that shift the context of evaluation of indexical expressions. On Kaplan's theory, the reference of an indexical term is fixed by the context of utterance and therefore monster operators cannot exist. But, arguably, there are such operators: in Amharic, the belief operator 'shifts' the reference of 'I' from the speaker to the subject of the main clause as in 'John₍ᵢ₎ believes that I₍ᵢ₎ am late' (see Schlenker 2003; Predelli 2014).

Sauerland's (2003) accounts. The coreference on the conceptual level $[y = x]_{ws}$ gives us *de se*, which then combines with the type of attitude: $[\text{believes}]_{CD} \Sigma'$.[41]

Next, the non-default *de re* self-report would be represented in Figure 5.3, remembering that this reading only occurs on very restricted scenarios and as such requires hedging, as for example in (38). The represented sentence is that in (39).

(39)   I did believe yesterday morning, in a sense, that I had a meeting at 2 o'clock.

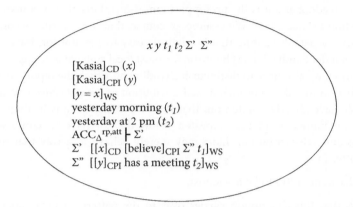

$$x\, y\, t_1\, t_2\, \Sigma'\, \Sigma''$$

$[\text{Kasia}]_{CD}\ (x)$
$[\text{Kasia}]_{CPI}\ (y)$
$[y = x]_{WS}$
yesterday morning (t_1)
yesterday at 2 pm (t_2)
$ACC_\Delta{}^{rp,att} \vdash \Sigma'$
$\Sigma'\ [[x]_{CD}\ [\text{believe}]_{CPI}\ \Sigma''\ t_1]_{WS}$
$\Sigma''\ [[y]_{CPI}\ \text{has a meeting}\ t_2]_{WS}$

Figure 5.3 Σ for the non-default *de re* self-ascribing reading of sentence (39): 'I did believe yesterday morning, in a sense, that I had a meeting at 2 o'clock.'

The lack of self-ascription and self-awareness are signalled by the introduction of the conceptual referent $[\text{Kasia}]_{CPI}$ (y), retaining the coreference through $[y = x]_{WS}$. The temporal location of the belief state in the past is signalled by the superscript 'rp' on delta in ACC, standing for the regular past. This is accompanied by another index marking the attenuated acceptability ACC, pertaining to the context-specific mode of presentation of the content of the belief, abbreviated as 'att', producing $ACC_\Delta{}^{rp,att}$ $\vdash \Sigma'$.[42] The 'att' index captures the hedging device 'in a sense' used in the report. Next, the non-default status of the belief is signalled by the CPI index in $[\text{believe}]_{CPI}$. The belief operator stands for a mental state that corresponds to what I call in my earlier writings on propositional attitudes (e.g. Jaszczolt 1997, 1999, 2005a) 'scattered' intentionality: intentionality that is weakened in that it does not quite reach the real object. All in all, through the combination of the indexing on the referent and the indexing on the belief operator that signal the context-driven, inferential process, we are able to represent this uncommon, marked reading.

---

[41]   For a different but also DRT-based way of incorporating *de se* reference into semantic representations see Wechsler 2010.
[42]   For details of the modality-based account of temporal reference see Section 2.2.2 and in particular Jaszczolt 2009a.

Moving now to the structure in (37), we have to distinguish the standard, default *de se* reading from the rare but possible reading *de re about oneself*—such as, say, on our earlier scenario on which I believe that the Chair of the Faculty has a meeting at 2 o'clock but I don't remember I agreed to step in to take on this role. There have been various solutions to this ambiguity of reading, including type-shifting that alters the proposition-based reading (*de re*) to property-based one (*de se*; Percus and Sauerland 2003), or the DR-theoretic solution where the DRSs are originally underspecified as to the kind of reading and it is the presupposition-as-anaphora that produces the *de se* interpretation (Maier 2009). We assume, of course, that in (37) 'she' is coreferential with 'Kasia'—a default reading that is relatively easy to account for, for example by adopting van der Sandt's (1992) heuristic for most local suitable binding.

In addition, we also have to distinguish a reading on which the report corresponds to the situation that does not include self-attribution of mental states relevant to the report. We have already pointed out that the PRO constructions in English with a third-person binder as in (30) repeated below do not have to come with self-awareness and self-attribution: Lidia may merely behave in a way that makes the speaker utter (30).

(30)   Lidia wants PRO to be a scientist.

It appears that this description carries over to the pattern in (37), albeit only to carefully delimited scenarios. These are the scenarios on which the meaning of the verb of epistemic attitude such as 'believe' or 'doubt' can be extended to go beyond the cases of self-ascription, leaving nevertheless the *mental state—attitude verb* default connection intact. In (40), imagine Lidia walking out of the house taking her umbrella with her.

(40)   Lidia thinks it is going to rain.

The report is perfectly acceptable even if Lidia habitually takes an umbrella, without consciously considering the weather forecast. We could at a stretch extend this to (41).

(41)   Lidia thinks she might get wet.

However, to repeat, these reports only work when we extend the meaning of attitude verbs—just as we can extend 'say' to mean the implied content in (42) or 'think' to report on the behaviour of a pet dog in (43) whose thought processes are unknown to us and normally not penetrable.

(42)   In refusing to come to my party, Susan is basically saying that she doesn't like me.

(43)   Look, Fifi thinks that nobody can see her steal that roast.

Now, to repeat, in semantics it has often been proposed that the *de se* reading is to be represented via *de re*. This solution, however, reverses the psychological plausibility of the interpretations. As we could see, the *de re* about oneself is a very unusual interpretation, limited to rather contrived scenarios. So, we would be deriving the natural, default reading via the marked, restricted one. Fortunately, this convoluted semantics is not called for in DS. We do not need to embellish the logical form of the sentence; we need not represent what we called earlier modes of self-presentation by adding a conceptual component to the logical form. Instead, as in the case of all other language constructions, we annotate the conceptual structure with information concerning the processes that are responsible for its component parts. These processes identify the type of interpretation. For example, CD corresponds to the default *de se*, while CPI corresponds to the unusual and highly context-driven *de re* about oneself. *De se* without self-awareness will rely on the reported eventuality being constructed in the CPI manner by the speaker.

The merger representations for these cases are given in Figures 5.4–5.6. Figure 5.4 corresponds to the default scenario of *de se* other-ascription in (37).

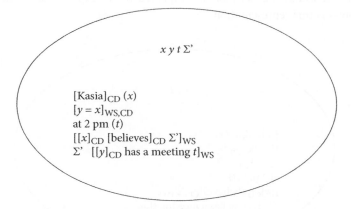

Figure 5.4 Σ for the default *de se* reading of sentence (37): 'Kasia believes she has a meeting at 2 o'clock.'

The coreference between x and y is guaranteed by the strongest anaphoric reading and therefore is marked as being processed via WS. Next, like in the case of the default *de se* self-ascription in (36), the belief operator captures the reading of the report that corresponds to the strongest intentionality of the underlying mental state, which means a reading about an individual *res*, rather than *dictum* (*de dicto*). The general *res*, combined with the information from $[y = x]_{\mathrm{WS}}$, produces the default *de se* reading—to repeat, this is achieved without going through the step of adjusting the *de re* interpretation as proposed on Maier's (2009) or Percus and Sauerland's (2003) account.

The representation of the default *de se* other-report is almost identical as the default *de se* self-report in Figure 5.2 above. The only difference is the addition of the

CD index in the condition $[y = x]_{ws,CD}$ to signal that the non-coreferential reading is also possible but would correspond to attenuated intentionality and therefore a lesser degree of informativeness: it would have to rely on an antecedent arrived at through cross-sentential (discourse) binding or accommodation in terms of van der Sandt's (1992) presupposition as anaphora (and, anaphora as presupposition) in DRT. This virtual identity of the two merger representations shows that these conceptual representations do not differentiate between the EGO concept and the ordinary discourse referents x or y that stand for an individual. In contexts where the 'take on oneself' is semantically significant, this first-personhood would be represented by a separate discourse condition—say, EGO_{publ} (x) for the public image of the self. I return to this aspect of problematic indexicality of the first-person pronoun in the concluding part.

Next, Figure 5.5 represents the *de re* about oneself reading of other-report. To repeat, this reading is unlikely to arise for (37) in that this interpretation is heavily restricted and would normally be accompanied by an explanation. When it does arise, it obtains this representation.

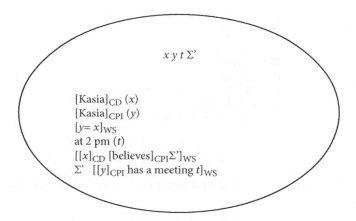

Figure 5.5 Σ for the *de re* about oneself reading of sentence (37): 'Kasia believes she has a meeting at 2 o'clock.'

The referent of the embedded clause is opaque: although there is coreference marked by $[y = x]_{ws}$, the anaphor pertains to a concept that is not identical with $[Kasia]_{CD}$ (x) in its informative content, hence it is marked as $[Kasia]_{CPI}$ (y). Likewise, the belief operator stands for a mental state that corresponds to 'scattered', attenuated intentionality—analogous to that described for Figure 5.3. Hence, we have a context-driven reading of 'believe' indexed as CPI. However, in natural conversation it is more likely that the *de re* about oneself reading of other-report can be found in cases of referring to 'temporal slices' of the person as in the third-person equivalent of our earlier (39) in (44).

(44)   Kasia did believe yesterday morning, in a sense, that she had a meeting at 2 o'clock.

The merger representation will then be constructed analogously as in Figure 5.3 above, allowing for $ACC_\Delta^{\text{rp,att}} \vdash \Sigma'$.

Finally, Figure 5.6 represents the *de se* reading without self-ascription or self-awareness, as in example (41).

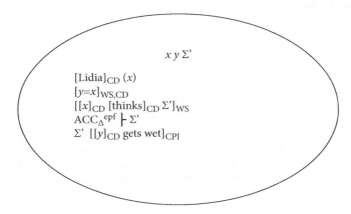

$$x\,y\,\Sigma'$$

$$[\text{Lidia}]_{CD}\,(x)$$
$$[y{=}x]_{WS,CD}$$
$$[[x]_{CD}\,[\text{thinks}]_{CD}\,\Sigma']_{WS}$$
$$ACC_\Delta^{\text{epf}} \vdash \Sigma'$$
$$\Sigma'\ [[y]_{CD}\ \text{gets wet}]_{CPI}$$

Figure 5.6 Σ for the non-default *de se* reading of (41): 'Lidia thinks she might get wet.'

'Thinks' corresponds to strong intentionality of the underlying mental state, the coreference is also provided via the strong, WS-driven process, but the content of the thought is inferred from the situation by the speaker—hence $[[y]_{CD}$ gets wet$]_{CPI}$. The index 'epf' on ACC stands for 'epistemic possibility future'.

In all these merger representations we were able to capture the concept of self-referring that allows for differences with respect to the associated self-awareness and self-attribution of mental states. In this respect we have already departed from the neat indexicality assumed in Kaplan's two-dimensional semantics. But we haven't yet had a need to represent the differences in the very concept of the self that gave rise to our revision of the indexicalist account discussed in Section 5.3.1. This is so because these differences are not normally explicitly communicated in English—the fact that led Kaplan to such a neat and simple account of first-person reference for the semantics of English. But if we want our semantics to apply to linguistic interaction at large, in different natural languages, what was a natural thing to do for Kaplan and for English begins to look like an oversight. Take Thai example (45).

(45) $d_1 iaw_3^{IV}$ $n_2 u$: $'_1$ aw $ch_3 a$: $m_3 a$: $h_2 ay_3^{II}$
      soon   I   bring   tea   come   give
'I will bring you tea.'[43]

In DS, the representation will have to reflect the social status conveyed by the form '$n_2 u$:', as in Figure 5.7. The condition '$[n_2 u: (x)]_{WS}$' signals that the lexical form used for self-reference is processed as part of the primary meaning. The word '$n_2 u$:', meaning 'mouse' when used as a common noun, also serves as a first-person pronoun in Thai. As a pronoun, it is a fully grammaticalized honorific that is used mostly by women in conversation with interlocutors of either sex but normally superior in the hierarchy of power.[44]

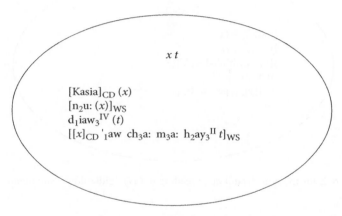

$x\,t$

$[Kasia]_{CD} (x)$
$[n_2 u: (x)]_{WS}$
$d_1 iaw_3^{IV} (t)$
$[[x]_{CD} '_1 aw\ ch_3 a:\ m_3 a:\ h_2 ay_3^{II}\ t]_{WS}$

Figure 5.7 Σ for example (45): '$d_1 iaw_3^{IV}$ $n_2 u$: $'_1 aw\ ch_3 a$: $m_3 a$: $h_2 ay_3^{II}$'

The fifty-one or so forms for first-person reference in Japanese, as well as variations on the degree of generalization of self-reference in English, will also have to be represented using analogous methods.

---

[43] From Jiranthara Srioutai, p.c. I follow the transliteration system from Diller 1996. Vowel phonemes are transliterated as (high) *i*, *u'*, *u*, (mid) *e*, *oe*, *o*, and (low) *ae*, *a*, *o'*. There are three diphthongs transliterated as *ia*, *u'a*, and *ua*. A colon stands for a long vowel. Next, the subscripts 1, 2, and 3 stand for the tone class of each syllable-initial consonant and superscripts I and II are tone markers. For an example of an extensive use of this system see also Srioutai 2006.

[44] There are occasions when it can also be used by men under analogous conditions: talking to an interlocutor of either sex, where the latter is superior on the power hierarchy, for example as a family member or a teacher. Conversely, $n_2 u$: can be used as a second-person pronoun when the addressee is lower on the hierarchy of power. I am indebted to Jiranthara Srioutai for information, discussion of the phenomenon, and the example.

5.5 Disclaimers, conclusions, and further prospects

The test case for radical contextualism presented in this chapter is a rather robust one in that, unlike various previous applications that pertained to the well-trodden areas of semantic ambiguity such as referential vs. attributive reading of definite descriptions, logical vs. pragmatic readings of sentential connectives, *de re* vs. *de dicto* readings of belief reports or time/tense mismatches, here we have the last bastion of direct reference: the first-person pronoun, whose function is standardly seen as that of a slot-holder, a 'dummy' in place of which we 'insert', so to speak, the referent itself. Its function is supposed to begin and end there. And yet, there is much more to self-reference, and in addition there is much more that a semantics with an ambition to provide conceptual representations needs to capture. In this case study I barely scratched the surface of the phenomenon, pointing out (i) the cross-linguistic differences in self-referring; (ii) the differences within self-referring in English alone; (iii) the possible universal underpinnings of these differences; as well as (iv) how one might account for all these in merger representations of DS. It is clear that the conceptual category of self-reference is needed in order to do so—captured on the dimension of the 'degree of self-awareness' either as a default *de se* thought, *de se* report, *de re* report about oneself, and, inside these quantitative differences, as qualitatively different EGOs. Just as there is no single indexical expression, be it in English or in other discussed languages, that is responsible for referring to oneself, so there is no one single reading that expressions used in this role can be pinned to once and for all. Instead, we have a diversity of forms and the diversity of their uses—a situation that clearly calls for an interactive construal of the composition of utterance meaning, where different processes account for different outcomes, as the merger representations presented in this chapter demonstrated.

Now, while on the one hand formal semantic accounts reduce first-person indexicality to the 'official' content alone, many also emphasize the irreducibility of the first-person perspective, the *perspectival concept* of EGO, captured on a different level of content (Perry 2001b).[45] In a way, this is a common-sense picture: as I have tentatively suggested here, the indexical perspective is given by the grammar, albeit the grammar of conceptual structures that has to be construed in such a way that it allows for different readings associated with structures in context. But this does not yet mean that the indexicality of thought is *always* represented in the semantic representation: in situations where it does not contribute to the overall meaning, it is not; in the situations where it does, it is accounted for. In this way the DS-theoretic account follows the same principle as the one I had adopted earlier for propositional attitude reports:[46] mode of presentation is only present when it does make a difference to the reading. Accordingly, the adicity of the belief predicate differs depending on the semantic significance (or its lack) of the mode of

---

[45] See also Chalmers 1996, 2006 for the irreducibility of the 'indexical fact'.
[46] In Jaszczolt 2007b.

presentation. Although we are not talking here about the representation on the level of logical form (WS), the principle is the same: the contributors to Σ vary depending on the intended and recovered meaning that they capture.

DS is not alone in proposing a novel, cognitive-representation-driven outlook on indexicals. In cognitive linguistics, Gärdenfors (2014b) defends the view that there is no qualitative distinction between common nouns and pronouns; instead, some words change their meaning 'slowly', while others change it 'rapidly':

'For example, in spite of all scientific advances, the meaning of *horse* has presumably not changed much since the Stone Age. On the other hand, there are several components of language, for example pronouns, that only receive meaning during the fast process. For example, the meaning of the word *this* changes almost every time it is used. Consequently, I do not draw any sharp border between semantics and pragmatics.'

Gärdenfors (2014b: 5)

Gärdenfors's argument is different from the one propounded here in that it is built around the idea of levels of communication. If interaction without using intentional communication does not suffice, humans proceed, step by step, to higher levels of interaction: instruction through speech acts, increasing the information in the common ground, and, finally, negotiation of meanings.[47] And the latter three levels permeate the use of all classes of words, be it for example nouns, verbs, adjectives or pronouns. The distinction between levels is orthogonal to the grammatical class distinction and replaces it as a more informatively adequate one in that all classes participate in the levels, just they do so with different degrees of malleability—viz. slow or rapid acquisition of meaning by a word in context.

In a sense, DS goes further in obliterating the grammatical distinctions because it views word classes on the level of their *functions* in discourse interaction. In spite of his professed dedication to the interactive outlook, Gärdenfors's grammatical categories are static; it is the levels that are supposed to endow them with the interactive meaning. On the contrary, in DS, indexicals and nouns themselves are conceived of as dynamic categories. On the analysis put forward in this section, what is in the static system a noun (say, 'mother', 'servant') may function as a (static) indexical term ('I') and this is a sufficient reason to replace the traditional, static distinction with a new dynamic one, according to which if there are indexicals, they do not engender Kaplan's list but rather they pertain to functions that lexical items adopt—in the true spirit of a semantics of linguistics interaction.

All in all, perspectival thought is a fact, and so is indexicality. But first-person indexicals turn out to be philosophers' fiction—fiction that serves some theoretical purposes in analysing the corresponding conceptual construct of indexicality but also misses many important language-specific as well as universal facts about self-reference. Only by conceiving of indexicality as a phenomenon that applies to *functions* of various word classes and only by envisaging characters as *dynamic*, 'fluid' concepts can we get it right.

---

[47] See Chapter 2, fn 44.

Conclusion: Dispelling semantic myths

The semantics of linguistic interaction dispels some myths about meaning in language. One of the ways to be 'wrong about meaning' is to see it as analysable within the constraints of a language system. Even when one attempts to analyse only context-free aspects of meaning, one falls back on some form of minimal context-dependence which we called Cognitive Minimalism. Meaning is not static and does not stem from static words and their static composition rules; it is co-constructed in discourse and it stems from the intention to express and negotiate one's views and attitudes. This dynamic foundation of meaning has to be well reflected in semantic representations and the best way to do so is to make the unit of meaning dynamic, as it was proposed here in the form of fluid characters, flexible bases for inference, and flexible bases for default interpretations.

Another way to be wrong about meaning is to insist that the grammar and the lexicon are responsible for giving the foundation of the semantic representation. This is what we called a syntactic constraint: the primary message intended by the speaker and recovered by the addressee would have to fit within the mould of the logical form of the sentence, allowing only for some limited 'filling in' and 'fleshing out', to use Kent Bach's apt expressions. We have rejected the syntactic constraint and provided arguments in favour of modelling the main meaning intended and recovered in discourse within what we called Salience-Based Contextualism. We have also provided representations of such primary meanings, arguing in favour of merging this primary-speech-act perspective with a truth-conditional method.

The third way to be wrong about meaning is to insist on compositionality of sentence-based meaning. Instead, in the semantics of linguistic interaction, compositionality is a property of conceptual structures that combine information conveyed through different linguistic as well as non-linguistic means of communication. Just as 'there can be a kind of semantics independent of language' (Hurford 2007: 49), there can be a semantics that allocates to language the role of one of many vehicles of meaning.

Meaning in Linguistic Interaction. Kasia M. Jaszczolt.

Yet another way to be wrong about meaning is to approach it via instances of miscommunication and conversation breakdown. When the objective is to offer a normative theory that enjoys predictive power, it is necessary to curtail psychologism and focus on a Model Speaker and a Model Addressee and the processes of meaning construction such as those recognized in the radical contextualist theory of Default Semantics, in that their interaction brings about replicable, formalizable interpretations.

Finally, 'wrong about meaning' can also affect research methods. The foundation for a semantics of linguistic interaction has to be a conceptual analysis, when necessary aided by data from linguistic interaction obtained through extant corpora or purpose-made databases. 'Wrong about methods' pertains to mistaking conceptual methods for 'intuition' or, even worse, 'introspection'.[1] Theoretical arguments use inferential and experiential methods, which are diametrically different from intuition-based analyses. In this context, Default Semantics begins with the defence of a radical contextualist stance through a conceptual analysis and proceeds to developing a model of the composition of meaning, testing it on varieties of language constructions. Types of language constructions provide the empirical basis. Descending to tokens in databases is only justified when the conceptual analysis indicates that there is a need for it—as in the example of the disparity of uses of sentential connectives. A leap to the level of tokens, without first improving through a conceptual analysis on what we should count as types (as in our case study of first-person reference) is precisely being wrong about methods of inquiry.

Next, the case study of first-person reference brought about a striking conclusion that even what is standardly considered to be the last bastion of regular, pure indexicality turned out to be heavily irregular and even context-driven: languages use a variety of means to express reference to oneself and, on the other hand, these means convey more than just direct reference. In addition, expressions that are used for self-referring are also put to other uses. The philosopher's construct of a first-person indexical, with its fixed content but free character, proved to be a philosophers' fiction, not supported by any natural language realizations: not even the English 'I'. Further, the cross-linguistically well attested use of common nouns in the role of self-referring made us opt for functional distinctions rather than grammatical categories.

In this way, the sensibilities that have been more and more often expressed in recent papers that 'the scope of semantic research should be extended to wider areas than one normally encounters within linguistics and philosophy' (Gärdenfors 2014b: 19) have been taken here, on the level of semantic as well as metasemantic investigations, as a springboard for providing a new way of building a conceptual structure.

---

[1] See here Cappelen's (2012) *Philosophy without Intuitions*.

References[1]

Allan, K. 2011. 'Graded salience: Probabilistic meaning in the lexicon'. In: K. M. Jaszczolt and K. Allan (eds). *Salience and Defaults in Utterance Processing*. Berlin: De Gruyter Mouton. 165–87.

Allan, K. 2013. 'Referring to "what counts as a referent": A view from linguistics'. In: A. Capone, F. Lo Piparo and M. Carapezza (eds). *Perspectives on Linguistic Pragmatics*. Dordrecht: Springer. 263–84.

Allan, K. and K. M. Jaszczolt. 2011. 'Introduction' to K. M. Jaszczolt and K. Allan (eds). *Salience and Defaults in Utterance Processing*. Berlin: De Gruyter Mouton. 1–10.

Ariel, M. 2010. *Defining Pragmatics*. Cambridge: Cambridge University Press.

Asher, N. 2011. *Lexical Meaning in Context: A Web of Words*. Cambridge: Cambridge University Press.

Asher, N. and A. Lascarides. 1995. 'Lexical disambiguation in a discourse context'. *Journal of Semantics* 12. 69–108.

Asher, N. and A. Lascarides. 2003. *Logics of Conversation*. Cambridge: Cambridge University Press.

Asher, N. and A. Lascarides. 2013. 'Strategic conversation'. *Semantics and Philosophy* 6. 1–62.

Atlas, J. D. 1977. 'Negation, ambiguity, and presupposition'. *Linguistics and Philosophy* 1. 321–36.

Atlas, J. D. 2011. 'Whatever happened to meaning? Remarks on contextualisms and propositionalisms'. In: K. Turner (ed.) *Making Semantics Pragmatic*. London: Emerald. 19–47.

Austin, J. L. 1962a. *Sense and Sensibilia*. Oxford: Oxford University Press.

Austin, J. L. 1962b. *How to Do Things with Words*. Oxford: Clarendon Press.

Bach, K. 1984. 'Default reasoning: Jumping to conclusions and knowing when to think twice'. *Pacific Philosophical Quarterly* 65. 37–58.

Bach, K. 1994. 'Semantic slack: What is said and more'. In: S. L. Tsohatzidis (ed.). *Foundations of Speech Act Theory: Philosophical and Linguistic Perspectives*. London: Routledge. 267–91.

Bach, K. 2001. 'You don't say?' *Synthese* 128. 15–44.

Bach, K. 2004. 'Minding the gap'. In: C. Bianchi (ed.). *The Semantics/Pragmatics Distinction*. Stanford: CSLI Publications, 27–43.

Bach, K. 2005. 'Context *ex Machina*'. In: Z. G. Szabó (ed.). *Semantics versus Pragmatics*. Oxford: Clarendon Press. 15–44.

Bach, K. 2006. 'The excluded middle: Semantic minimalism without minimal propositions'. *Philosophy and Phenomenological Research* 73. 435–42.

Baker, G. P. and P. M. S. Hacker. 2003. 'Functions in *Begriffsschrift*'. *Synthese* 135. 273–97.

---

[1] Where two editions are specified, page references in the text are made to the later edition. For example, Grice (1975: 39) refers to page 39 of the 1989 edition.

Barker, C. 2012. 'Quantificational binding does not require c-command'. *Linguistic Inquiry* 43. 614–33.

Benferhat, S., J. F. Bonnefon and R. da Silva Neves. 2005. 'An overview of possibilistic handling of default reasoning, with experimental studies'. *Synthese* 146. 53–70.

Berlin, B. and P. Kay. 1969. *Basic Color Terms: Their Universality and Evolution.* Berkeley: University of California Press.

Blome-Tillmann, M. 2008. 'Conversational implicature and the cancellability test.' *Analysis* 68. 156–60.

Blome-Tillmann, M. 2013. 'Knowledge and implicatures'. *Synthese* 190. 4293–319.

Blutner, R. 2000. 'Some aspects of optimality in natural language interpretation'. *Journal of Semantics* 17. 189–216.

Blutner, R. and H. Zeevat. 2004. 'Editors' introduction: Pragmatics in Optimality Theory'. In: R. Blutner and H. Zeevat (eds). *Optimality Theory and Pragmatics.* Basingstoke: Palgrave Macmillan. 1–24.

Boole, G. 1847. *The Mathematical Analysis of Logic: Being an Essay towards a Calculus of Deductive Reasoning.* Cambridge: Macmillan, Barclay, and Macmillan. Reprinted in 1998 by Bristol: Thoemmes Press.

Borg, E. 2004. *Minimal Semantics.* Oxford: Clarendon Press.

Borg, E. 2007. 'Minimalism versus contextualism in semantics'. In: G. Preyer and G. Peter (eds). *Context-Sensitivity and Semantic Minimalism: New Essays on Semantics and Pragmatics.* Oxford: Oxford University Press. 339–59.

Borg, E. 2010. 'Minimalism and the content of the lexicon'. In: L. Baptista and E. Rast (eds). *Meaning and Context.* Bern: Peter Lang. 51–77.

Borg, E. 2012. *Pursuing Meaning.* Oxford: Oxford University Press.

Brogaard, B. 2012. 'Context and content: Pragmatics in two-dimensional semantics'. In: K. Allan and K. M. Jaszczolt (eds). *The Cambridge Handbook of Pragmatics.* Cambridge: Cambridge University Press. 113–33.

Burton-Roberts, N. 2006. 'Cancellation and intention'. *Newcastle Working Papers in Linguistics* 12–13, 1–12.

Byatt, A. S. 1991. *Possession.* London: Vintage.

Capone, A. 2009. 'Are explicatures cancellable? Towards a theory of the speaker's intentionality'. *Intercultural Pragmatics* 6. 55–84.

Capone, A. 2011. 'Default Semantics and the architecture of the mind'. *Journal of Pragmatics* 43. 1741–54.

Cappelen, H. 2012. *Philosophy without Intuitions.* Oxford: Oxford University Press.

Cappelen, H. and J. Dever. 2013. *The Inessential Indexical: On the Philosophical Insignificance of Perspective and the First Person.* Oxford: Oxford University Press.

Cappelen, H. and J. Hawthorne. 2009. *Relativism and Monadic Truth.* Oxford: Oxford University Press.

Cappelen, H. and E. Lepore. 2005a. *Insensitive Semantics: A Defense of Semantic Minimalism and Speech Act Pluralism.* Oxford: Blackwell.

Cappelen, H. and E. Lepore. 2005b. 'A tall tale: In defense of semantic minimalism and speech act pluralism'. In: G. Preyer and G. Peter (eds). *Contextualism in Philosophy: Knowledge, Meaning, and Truth.* Oxford: Clarendon Press. 197–219.

Carey, P. 2010. *Parrot and Olivier in America*. London: Faber and Faber.

Carnap, R. 1952. 'Meaning postulates'. *Philosophical Studies* 3. 65–73. Reprinted in: R. Carnap. 1956. *Meaning and Necessity*. 2nd edition. Chicago: Chicago University Press. 222–9.

Carruthers, P. 1996. *Language, Thought and Consciousness: An Essay in Philosophical Psychology*. Cambridge: Cambridge University Press.

Carruthers, P. 2006. *The Architecture of the Mind: Massive Modularity and the Flexibility of Thought*. Oxford: Clarendon Press.

Carruthers, P. 2011. *Opacity of Mind: An Integrative Theory of Self-Knowledge*. Oxford: Oxford University Press.

Carston, R. 1988. 'Implicature, explicature, and truth-theoretic semantics'. In: R. M. Kempson (ed.). *Mental Representations: The Interface Between Language and Reality*. Cambridge: Cambridge University Press. 155–81.

Carston, R. 1998. 'Postscript (1995)' to Carston 1988. In: A. Kasher (ed.). *Pragmatics: Critical Concepts*. Vol. 4. London: Routledge. 464–79.

Carston, R. 2002. *Thoughts and Utterances: The Pragmatics of Explicit Communication*. Oxford: Blackwell.

Carston, R. 2007. 'How many pragmatic systems are there?' In: M. J. Frápolli (ed.). *Saying, Meaning and Referring: Essays on François Recanati's Philosophy of Language*. Basingstoke: Palgrave Macmillan. 18–48.

Carston, R. 2012. 'Metaphor and the literal/non-literal distinction'. In: K. Allan and K. M. Jaszczolt (eds). *The Cambridge Handbook of Pragmatics*. Cambridge: Cambridge University Press. 469–92.

Cassam, Q. 2011. 'The embodied self'. In: S. Gallagher (ed.). *The Oxford Handbook of the Self*. Oxford: Oxford University Press. 139–56.

Castañeda, H.-N. 1967. 'Indicators and quasi-indicators'. *American Philosophical Quarterly* 4. 85–100.

Chalmers, D. J. 1996. *The Conscious Mind: In Search of a Fundamental Theory*. New York: Oxford University Press.

Chalmers, D. J. 2006. 'The foundations of two-dimensional semantics'. In: M. García-Carpintero and J. Macià (eds). *Two-Dimensional Semantics*. Oxford: Clarendon Press. 55–140.

Chalmers, D. J. 2010. *The Character of Consciousness*. Oxford: Oxford University Press.

Chierchia, G. 1989. 'Anaphora and attitudes *de se*'. In: R. Bartsch, J. van Benthem, and B. van Emde Boas (eds). *Semantics and Contextual Expression*. Dordrecht: Foris. 1–31.

Chierchia, G. 2004. 'Scalar implicatures, polarity phenomena, and the syntax/pragmatics interface'. In: A. Belletti (ed.). *Structures and Beyond: The Cartography of Syntactic Structures*, vol. 3. Oxford: Oxford University Press. 39–103.

Chierchia, G. 2006. 'Broaden your views: Implicatures of domain widening and the "logicality" of language'. *Linguistic Inquiry* 37. 535–90.

Chierchia, G. 2013. *Logic in Grammar: Polarity, Free Choice, and Intervention*. Oxford: Oxford University Press.

Chierchia, G. *et al.* 2004. 'Semantic and pragmatic competence in children's and adults' comprehension of *or*'. In: I. A. Noveck and D. Sperber (eds). *Experimental Pragmatics*. Houndmills: Palgrave Macmillan. 283–300.

Christofaki, R. In progress. *Expressing the Self in Japanese*. PhD dissertation, University of Cambridge.

Clapp, L. 2012. 'Three challenges for indexicalism'. *Mind and Language* 27. 435–65.

Clark, B. 2013. *Relevance Theory*. Cambridge: Cambridge University Press.

Clark, H. H. 1996. *Using Language*. Cambridge: Cambridge University Press.

Collins, C. and P. M. Postal. 2012. *Imposters: A Study of Pronominal Agreement*. Cambridge, MA: MIT Press.

Corazza, E. 2004. *Reflecting the Mind: Indexicality and Quasi-Indexicality*. Oxford: Clarendon Press.

Corazza, E. 2011. 'Unenriched subsentential illocutions'. *Philosophy and Phenomenological Research* 83. 560–82.

Corazza, E. 2012. 'Same-saying, pluri-propositionalism, and implicatures'. *Mind and Language* 27. 546–69.

Corazza, E. 2016. 'She and herself'. In: A. Capone, F. Kiefer and F. Lo Piparo (eds). *Indirect Reports and Pragmatics*. Dordrecht: Springer. 507–519.

Crimmins, M. and J. Perry. 1989. 'The prince and the phone booth: Reporting puzzling beliefs'. *Journal of Philosophy* 86. 685–711.

Croft, W. 2001. *Radical Construction Grammar: Syntactic Theory in Typological Perspective*. Oxford: Oxford University Press.

Culicover, P. W. and R. Jackendoff. 2005. *Simpler Syntax*. Oxford: Oxford University Press.

Da Milano, F. 2014. 'Referential ambiguity of personal pronouns in Japanese (and other East Asian languages)'. Unpublished paper.

Davidson, D. 1984. *Inquiries into Truth and Interpretation*. Oxford: Clarendon Press.

Davis, W. A. 1998. *Implicature: Intention, Convention, and Principle in the Failure of Gricean Theory*. Cambridge: Cambridge University Press.

Davis, W. A. 2007. 'How normative is implicature?' *Journal of Pragmatics* 39. 1655–72.

Davis, W. A. 2013. 'Dyadic contextualism and content relativism'. *Intercultural Pragmatics* 10. 1–39.

DeRose, K. 1992. 'Contextualism and knowledge attributions'. *Philosophy and Phenomenological Research* 52. 913–29.

DeRose, K. 2009. *The Case for Contextualism: Knowledge, Skepticism, and Context, Vol. 1*. Oxford: Clarendon Press.

Devitt, M. 2006. *Ignorance of Language*. Oxford: Clarendon Press.

Devitt, M. 2010. 'What "intuitions" are linguistic evidence?'. *Erkenntnis* 73. 251–64.

Diller, A. 1996. 'Thai and Lao writing'. In: P. T. Daniels and W. Bright (eds). *The World's Writing Systems*. New York: Oxford University Press. 457–66.

Donnellan, K. 1966. 'Reference and definite descriptions'. *Philosophical Review* 66. 281–304. Reprinted in: P. Ludlow (ed.). 1997. *Readings in the Philosophy of Language*. Cambridge, MA: MIT Press. 361–81.

Doran, R., G. Ward, M. Larson, Y. McNabb, and R. E. Baker. 2012. 'A novel experimental paradigm for distinguishing between what is said and what is implicated'. *Language* 88. 124–54.

Dummett, M. 1973. *Frege: Philosophy of Language*. London: Duckworth.

Dummett, M. 1981. *The Interpretation of Frege's Philosophy*. Cambridge, MA: Harvard University Press.

van Eijck, J. and H. Kamp. 1997. 'Representing discourse in context'. In: J. van Benthem and A. ter Meulen (eds). 1997. *Handbook of Logic and Language*. Amsterdam: Elsevier Science. 179–237.

Elbourne, P. D. 2005. *Situations and Individuals*. Cambridge, MA: MIT Press.

Elbourne, P. 2011. *Meaning: A Slim Guide to Semantics*. Oxford: Oxford University Press.

Elder, C.-H. 2014. *On the Forms of Conditionals and the Functions of 'If'*. PhD dissertation, University of Cambridge.

Elder, C.-H. and K. M. Jaszczolt. 2013. 'Conditional utterances and conditional thoughts: Towards a pragmatic category of conditionals'. Unpublished paper.

Evans, N. and S. C. Levinson. 2009. 'The myth of language universals: Language diversity and its importance for cognitive science'. *Behavioral and Brain Sciences* 32. 429–92.

Everett, D. 2012. 'The social instinct'. *New Scientist*, 10 March 2012. 32–5.

Feit, N. 2008. *Belief about the Self: A Defense of the Property Theory of Content*. Oxford: Oxford University Press.

Feit, N. and A. Capone (eds). 2013. *Attitudes De Se: Linguistics, Epistemology, Metaphysics*. Stanford, CA: CSLI Publications.

Feldman, J. 2010. 'Embodied language, best-fit analysis, and formal compositionality'. *Physics of Life Reviews* 7. 385–410.

von Fintel, K. and L. Matthewson. 2008. 'Universals in semantics'. *The Linguistic Review* 25. 139–201.

Fleck, D. W. 2007. 'Evidentiality and double tense in Matses'. *Language* 83. 589–614.

Fodor, J. A. 1975. *Language of Thought*. New York: Thomas Y. Crowell. Reprinted in 1976 by Hassocks: Harvester Press.

Fodor, J. A. 1998. *Concepts: Where Cognitive Science Went Wrong*. Oxford: Clarendon Press.

Fodor, J. A. 2008. *LOT 2: The Language of Thought Revisited*. Oxford: Clarendon Press.

Folescu, M. and J. Higginbotham. 2012. 'Two takes on the *de se*'. In: S. Prosser and F. Recanati (eds). *Immunity to Error through Misidentification: New Essays*. Cambridge: Cambridge University Press. 46–61.

Frege, G. 1879a. 'Begriffsschrift, eine der arithmetischen nachgebildete Formelsprache des reinen Denkens'. Halle: L. Nebert. Transl. as 'Conceptual notation: A formula language of pure thought modelled upon the formula language of arithmetic' by T. W. Bynum in: *Conceptual Notation and Related Articles*. 1972. Oxford: Oxford University Press. 101–203.

Frege, G. 1879b. 'Begriffsschrift, eine der arithmetischen nachgebildete Formelsprache des reinen Denkens'. Halle: L. Nebert. Part 1, §§1–12 transl. as '*Begriffsschrift*: a formula language of pure thought modelled on that of arithmetic' by M. Beaney in: M. Beaney (ed.). 1997. *The Frege Reader*. Oxford: Blackwell. 47–78.

Frege, G. 1884a. *Die Grundlagen der Arithmetik, eine logisch mathematische Untersuchung über den Begriff der Zahl*. Breslau: W. Koebner. Transl. as *The Foundations of Arithmetic: A Logico-Mathematical Enquiry into the Concept of Number* by J. L. Austin. 1953. Oxford: B. Blackwell. Second edition.

Frege, G. 1884b. *Die Grundlagen der Arithmetik, eine logisch mathematische Untersuchung über den Begriff der Zahl*. Introduction. Breslau: W. Koebner. Transl. by M. Beaney in: M. Beaney (ed.). 1997. *The Frege Reader*. Oxford: Blackwell. 84–91.

Frege, G. 1892. 'Über Sinn und Bedeutung'. *Zeitschrift f. Philosophie und Philosophische Kritik* 100. 25–50. Transl. as 'On sense and reference' in P. T. Geach and M. Black (eds). 1952. *Translations from the Philosophical Writings of Gottlob Frege.* Oxford: B. Blackwell. Reprinted in 1960. Second edition. 56–78.

Frege, G. 1893. *Grundgesetze der Arithmetik.* Vol. 1. Preface. Jena: H. Pohle. Transl. by M. Beaney in: M. Beaney (ed.). 1997. *The Frege Reader.* Oxford: Blackwell. 194–208.

Frege, G. 1894. Review of E. G. Husserl, *Philosophie der Arithmetik I (Philosophy of Arithmetic I).* *Zeitschrift für Philosophie und philosophische Kritik* 103. Transl. by H. Kaal in: G. Frege. 1984. *Collected Papers on Mathematics, Logic, and Philosophy* ed. by B. McGuinness. Oxford: Blackwell. 195–209.

Frege, G. 1897/1969. *Logic.* In: 1969. *Nachgelassene Schriften.* Hamburg: Felix. Meiner. Transl. by P. Long and R. White in: 1979. *Posthumous Writings.* Oxford: Blackwell. Sections 1 ('Introduction') and 2 ('Separating a thought from its trappings') reprinted in: M. Beaney (ed.). 1997. *The Frege Reader.* Oxford: Blackwell. 227–50.

Frege, G. 1918–19. 'Der Gedanke'. *Beiträge zur Philosophie des deutschen Idealismus* I. Transl. as 'Thoughts' (Part I of *Logical Investigations*) by P. Geach and R. H. Stoothoff in: G. Frege. 1984. *Collected Papers on Mathematics, Logic, and Philosophy* ed. by B. McGuinness. Oxford: Blackwell. Reprinted in: M. Beaney (ed.). 1997. *The Frege Reader.* Oxford: Blackwell. 325–45.

Gallagher, S. (ed.). 2011. *The Oxford Handbook of the Self.* Oxford: Oxford University Press.

Gärdenfors, P. 2014a. *Geometry of Meaning: Semantics Based on Conceptual Spaces.* Cambridge, MA: MIT Press.

Gärdenfors, P. 2014b. 'Levels of communication and lexical semantics', *Synthese* online publication, 12 June 2014, DOI 10.1007/s11229-014-0493-3.

Gauker, C. 2011. *Words and Images: An Essay on the Origin of Ideas.* Oxford: Oxford University Press.

Geurts, B. 1999. *Presuppositions and Pronouns.* Oxford: Elsevier.

Geurts, B. 2009. 'Scalar implicature and local pragmatics'. *Mind and Language* 24. 51–79.

Geurts, B. 2010. *Quantity Implicatures.* Cambridge: Cambridge University Press.

Geurts, B. and E. Maier. 2003. 'Layered DRT'. Unpublished paper, University of Nijmegen.

Gibbs, Jr. R. W. and G. C. van Orden. 2010. 'Adaptive cognition without massive modularity'. *Language and Cognition* 2. 149–76.

Gigerenzer, G. 2000. *Adaptive Thinking: Rationality in the Real World.* Oxford: Oxford University Press.

Gigerenzer, G. 2008. *Rationality for Mortals: How People Cope with Uncertainty.* Oxford: Oxford University Press.

Gigerenzer, G., P. M. Todd, and the ABC Research Group. 1999. *Simple Heuristics That Make Us Smart.* New York: Oxford University Press.

Ginzburg, J. 2012. *The Interactive Stance: Meaning for Conversation.* Oxford: Oxford University Press.

Giora, R. 2003. *On Our Mind: Salience, Context, and Figurative Language.* Oxford: Oxford University Press.

Giora, R. 2012. 'The psychology of utterance processing: Context vs salience'. In: K. Allan and K. M. Jaszczolt (eds). *The Cambridge Handbook of Pragmatics.* Cambridge: Cambridge University Press. 151–67.

Green, K. 2006. 'A pinch of salt for Frege'. *Synthese* 150. 209–28.

Grice, H. P. 1957. 'Meaning'. *Philosophical Review* 66. Reprinted in: H. P. Grice. 1989. *Studies in the Way of Words*. Cambridge, MA: Harvard University Press. 213–23.

Grice, H. P. 1975. 'Logic and conversation'. In: P. Cole and J. L. Morgan (eds). *Syntax and Semantics*. Vol. 3. New York: Academic Press. Reprinted in: H. P. Grice. 1989. *Studies in the Way of Words*. Cambridge, MA: Harvard University Press. 22–40.

Grice, H. P. 1978. 'Further notes on logic and conversation'. In: P. Cole (ed.). *Syntax and Semantics*. Vol. 9. New York: Academic Press. Reprinted in: H. P. Grice. 1989. *Studies in the Way of Words*. Cambridge, MA: Harvard University Press. 41–57.

Grice, H. P. 1989. *Studies in the Way of Words*. Cambridge, MA: Harvard University Press.

Groenendijk, J. and M. Stokhof. 1991. 'Dynamic Predicate Logic'. *Linguistics and Philosophy* 14. 39–100.

Groenendijk, J. and M. Stokhof. 2000. 'Meaning in motion'. In: K. von Heusinger and U. Egli (eds). *Reference and Anaphoric Relations*. Dordrecht: Kluwer. 47–76.

Hansen, N. and E. Chemla. 2013. 'Experimenting on contextualism'. *Mind and Language* 28. 286–321.

Harnish, R. M. 2009. 'The problem of fragments'. *Pragmatics and Cognition* 17. 251–82.

Haugh, M. 2008. 'The place of intention in the interactional achievement of implicature'. In: I. Kecskes and J. Mey (eds). *Intention, Common Ground and the Egocentric Speaker-Hearer*. Berlin: Mouton de Gruyter. 45–85.

Haugh, M. 2010. 'Co-constructing what is said in interaction'. In: T. E. Németh and K. Bibok (eds). *The Role of Data at the Semantics/Pragmatics Interface*. Berlin: Mouton de Gruyter. 349–80.

Haugh, M. 2011. 'Practices and defaults in interpreting disjunction'. In: K. M. Jaszczolt and K. Allan (eds). *Salience and Defaults in Utterance Processing*. Berlin: De Gruyter Mouton. 189–225.

Haugh, M. and K. M. Jaszczolt. 2012. 'Speaker intentions and intentionality'. In: K. Allan and K. M. Jaszczolt (eds). *The Cambridge Handbook of Pragmatics*. Cambridge: Cambridge University Press. 87–112.

Hawthorne, J. and D. Manley. 2012. *The Reference Book*. Oxford: Oxford University Press.

Heine, B. and K.-A. Song. 2011. 'On the grammaticalisation of personal pronouns'. *Journal of Linguistics* 47. 587–630.

Higginbotham, J. 1988. 'Contexts, models, and meanings: A note on the data of semantics'. In: R. M. Kempson (ed.). *Mental Representations: The Interface between Language and Reality*. Cambridge: Cambridge University Press. 29–48.

Higginbotham, J. 2003. 'Remembering, imagining, and the first person'. In: A. Barber (ed.). *Epistemology of Language*. Oxford: Oxford University Press. 496–533.

Hinzen, W. and M. Sheehan. 2013. *The Philosophy of Universal Grammar*. Oxford: Oxford University Press.

Hirose, Y. 2014. 'The conceptual basis for reflexive constructions in Japanese'. *Journal of Pragmatics* 68. 99–116.

Horn, L. R. 1984. 'Toward a new taxonomy for pragmatic inference: Q-based and R-based implicature'. In: *Georgetown University Round Table on Languages and Linguistics 1984*. Ed. by D. Schffrin. Washington, D.C.: Georgetown University Press. 11–42.

Horn, L. R. 1988. 'Pragmatic theory'. In: F. J. Newmeyer (ed.). *Linguistics: The Cambridge Survey.* Vol. 1. Cambridge: Cambridge University Press. 113–45.

Horn, L. R. 2004. 'Implicature'. In: L. R. Horn and G. Ward (eds.). *The Handbook of Pragmatics.* Oxford: Blackwell. 3–28.

Horn, L. R. 2006. 'The border wars: A neo-Gricean perspective'. In: K. von Heusinger and K. Turner (eds). *Where Semantics Meets Pragmatics.* Amsterdam: Elsevier. 21–48.

Horn, L. R. 2012. 'Implying and inferring'. In: K. Allan and K. M. Jaszczolt (eds). *The Cambridge Handbook of Pragmatics.* Cambridge: Cambridge University Press. 69–86.

Hurford, J. R. 2007. *The Origins of Meaning.* Oxford: Oxford University Press.

Husserl, E. 1900–1901. *Logische Untersuchungen.* Vol. 2. Halle: Max Niemeyer. Reprinted in 1984 after the second edition (1913–21). The Hague: Martinus Nijhoff. *Husserliana* 19/1. Transl. by J. N. Findlay as *Logical Investigations.* 1970. London: Routledge and Kegan Paul.

Jackendoff, R. 1983. *Semantics and Cognition.* Cambridge, MA: MIT Press.

Jackendoff, R. 2002. *Foundations of Language: Brain, Meaning, Grammar, Evolution.* Oxford: Oxford University Press.

Jackendoff, R. 2011. 'What is the human language faculty? Two views'. *Language* 87. 586–624.

Jackendoff, R. 2012. *A User's Guide to Thought and Meaning.* Oxford: Oxford University Press.

Janssen, T. M. V. 1997. 'Compositionality'. In: J. van Benthem and A. ter Meulen (eds). *Handbook of Logic and Language.* Amsterdam: Elsevier. 417–73.

Jaszczolt, K. M. 1992. *Belief Sentences and the Semantics of Propositional Attitudes.* D.Phil. thesis, University of Oxford.

Jaszczolt, K. M. 1997. 'The Default *De Re* Principle for the interpretation of belief utterances'. *Journal of Pragmatics* 28. 315–36.

Jaszczolt, K. M. 1999. *Discourse, Beliefs, and Intentions: Semantic Defaults and Propositional Attitude Ascription.* Oxford: Elsevier Science.

Jaszczolt, K. M. 2002a. *Semantics and Pragmatics: Meaning in Language and Discourse.* London: Longman.

Jaszczolt, K. M. 2002b. 'Against ambiguity and underspecification: Evidence from presupposition as anaphora'. *Journal of Pragmatics* 34. 829–49.

Jaszczolt, K. M. 2005a. *Default Semantics: Foundations of a Compositional Theory of Acts of Communication.* Oxford: Oxford University Press.

Jaszczolt, K. M. 2005b. Review of E. Borg, *Minimal Semantics. Journal of Linguistics* 41. 637–42.

Jaszczolt, K. M. 2006a. 'Defaults in semantics and pragmatics'. In: E. N. Zalta (ed.). *Stanford Encyclopedia of Philosophy.* http://plato.stanford.edu/contents.html. Revised edition 2010.

Jaszczolt, K. M. 2006b. 'Meaning merger: Pragmatic inference, defaults, and compositionality'. *Intercultural Pragmatics* 3. 195–212.

Jaszczolt, K. M. 2007a. 'Variadic function and pragmatics-rich representations of belief reports'. *Journal of Pragmatics* 39. 934–59.

Jaszczolt, K. M. 2007b. 'On being post-Gricean'. In: R. A. Nilsen, N. A. A. Amfo, and K. Borthen (eds). *Interpreting Utterances: Pragmatics and Its Interfaces. Essays in Honour of Thorstein Fretheim.* Oslo: Novus. 21–38.

Jaszczolt, K. M. 2008. 'Psychological explanations in Gricean pragmatics: An argument from cultural *common ground*'. In: I. Kecskes and J. Mey (eds). *Intentions, Common Ground, and Egocentric Speaker-Hearer.* Berlin: Mouton de Gruyter. 9–44.

Jaszczolt, K. M. 2009a. *Representing Time: An Essay on Temporality as Modality*. Oxford: Oxford University Press.

Jaszczolt, K. M. 2009b. 'Cancellability and the primary/secondary meaning distinction'. *Intercultural Pragmatics* 6. 259–89.

Jaszczolt, K. M. 2009c. 'Defaults in utterance interpretation'. In: L. Cummings (ed.). *The Routledge Pragmatics Encyclopedia*. London: Routledge. 123–4.

Jaszczolt, K. M. 2010. 'Default Semantics'. In: B. Heine and H. Narrog (eds.) *The Oxford Handbook of Linguistic Analysis*. Oxford: Oxford University Press. 215–46.

Jaszczolt, K. M. 2011. 'Default meanings, salient meanings, and automatic processing'. In: K. M. Jaszczolt and K. Allan (eds). *Salience and Defaults in Utterance Processing*. Berlin: De Gruyter Mouton. 11–33.

Jaszczolt, K. M. 2012a. 'Cross-linguistic differences in expressing time and universal principles of utterance interpretation'. In: L. Filipović and K. M. Jaszczolt (eds). *Space and Time in Languages and Cultures: Linguistic Diversity*. Amsterdam: J. Benjamins. 95–121.

Jaszczolt, K. M. 2012b. 'Context: Gricean intentions vs. two-dimensional semantics'. In: R. Finkbeiner, J. Meibauer, and P. Schumacher (eds). *What is Context? Linguistic Approaches and Challenges*. Amsterdam: John Benjamins. 81–103.

Jaszczolt, K. M. 2012c. '"Pragmaticising" Kaplan: Flexible inferential bases and fluid characters'. *Australian Journal of Linguistics* 32. 209–37.

Jaszczolt, K. M. 2012d. 'Delimitation of pragmatics: Paradigms, myths and fashions. A response to Bara'. *Intercultural Pragmatics* 9. 103–12.

Jaszczolt, K. M. 2012e. 'Semantics/pragmatics boundary disputes'. In: C. Maienborn, K. von Heusinger, and P. Portner (eds). *Semantics: An International Handbook of Natural Language Meaning*. Vol. 3. Berlin: Mouton de Gruyter. 2333–60.

Jaszczolt, K. M. 2012f. 'Propositional attitude reports: Pragmatic aspects'. In: K. Allan and K. M. Jaszczolt (eds). *The Cambridge Handbook of Pragmatics*. Cambridge: Cambridge University Press. 305–27.

Jaszczolt, K. M. 2013a. 'Temporality and epistemic commitment: An unresolved question'. In: K. Jaszczolt and L. de Saussure (eds). *Time: Language, Cognition, and Reality*. Oxford: Oxford University Press. 193–209.

Jaszczolt, K. M. 2013b. 'First-person reference in discourse: Aims and strategies'. *Journal of Pragmatics* 48. 57–70.

Jaszczolt, K. M. 2013c. 'Contextualism and minimalism on *de se* belief ascription'. In: N. Feit and A. Capone (eds). *Attitudes De Se: Linguistics, Epistemology, Metaphysics*. Stanford: CSLI Publications. 69–103.

Jaszczolt, K. M. and K. Allan (eds). 2011. *Salience and Defaults in Utterance Processing*. Berlin: De Gruyter Mouton.

Jaszczolt, K. M., E. Savva, and M. Haugh. 2016. 'The individual and the social path of interpretation: The case of incomplete disjunctive questions'. In: A. Capone and J. L. Mey (eds). *Interdisciplinary Studies in Pragmatics, Culture and Society*. Dordrecht: Springer. 254–83.

Jaszczolt, K. M. and J. Srioutai. 2011. 'Communicating about the past through modality in English and Thai'. In: A. Patard and F. Brisard (eds). *Cognitive Approaches to Tense, Aspect and Epistemic Modality*. Amsterdam: J. Benjamins. 249–78.

Johnson, M. 1987. *The Body and the Mind: The Bodily Basis of Meaning, Imagination, and Reason*. Chicago, IL: University of Chicago Press.

Kamp, H. 1981. 'A theory of truth and semantic representation'. In: J. Groenendijk, T. M. V. Janssen, and M. Stokhof (eds). *Formal Methods in the Study of Language*, Mathematical Centre Tract 135, Amsterdam, 277–322. Reprinted in: J. Groenendijk, T. M. V. Janssen, and M. Stokhof (eds). *Truth, Interpretation and Information. Selected Papers from the Third Amsterdam Colloquium*. Dordrecht: FORIS. 1–41.

Kamp, H. and B. Partee. 1995. 'Prototype theory and compositionality'. *Cognition* 57. 129–91.

Kamp, H. and U. Reyle. 1993. *From Discourse to Logic: Introduction to Modeltheoretic Semantics of Natural Language, Formal Logic and Discourse Representation Theory*. Dordrecht: Kluwer.

Kaplan, D. 1978. 'Dthat'. In: P. Cole (ed.). *Syntax and Semantics* vol. 9. *Pragmatics*. New York: Academic Press. Reprinted in: P. Ludlow (ed.). 1997. *Readings in the Philosophy of Language*. Cambridge, MA: MIT Press. 669–92.

Kaplan, D. 1989a. 'Demonstratives: An essay on the semantics, logic, metaphysics, and epistemology of demonstratives and other indexicals'. In J. Almog, J. Perry, and H. Wettstein (eds). *Themes from Kaplan*. New York: Oxford University Press. 481–563.

Kaplan, D. 1989b. 'Afterthoughts'. In: J. Almog, J. Perry, and H. Wettstein (eds). *Themes from Kaplan*. New York: Oxford University Press. 565–614.

Kaplan, D. 2008. 'The meaning of *ouch* and *oops*'. Howison Lecture in Philosophy, University of California at Berkeley, 25 April 2008. http://www.uctv.tv/shows/The-Meaning-of-Ouch-and-Oops-with-David-Kaplan-8593.

Kapogianni, E. 2013. *Irony and the Literal versus Nonliteral Distinction: A Typological Approach with Focus on Ironic Implicature Strength*. PhD dissertation, University of Cambridge.

Kauppinen, A. 2010. 'The pragmatics of transparent belief reports'. *Analysis* 70. 438–46.

Kempson, R., W. Meyer-Viol, and D. Gabbay. 2001. *Dynamic Syntax: The Flow of Language Understanding*. Oxford: Blackwell.

Kissine, M. 2013. *From Utterances to Speech Acts*. Cambridge: Cambridge University Press.

Korta, K. and J. Perry. 2007. 'Radical minimalism, moderate contextualism'. In: G. Preyer and G. Peter (eds). *Context-Sensitivity and Semantic Minimalism: New Essays on Semantics and Pragmatics*. Oxford; Oxford University Press. 94–111.

Korta, K. and J. Perry. 2011. *Critical Pragmatics: An Inquiry into Reference and Communication*. Cambridge: Cambridge University Press.

Kratzer, A. 2009. 'Making a pronoun: Fake indexicals and windows into the properties of pronouns'. *Linguistic Inquiry* 40. 187–237.

Lakoff, G. and M. Johnson. 1980. *Metaphors We Live By*. Chicago: University of Chicago Press.

Lakoff, G. and M. Johnson. 1999. *Philosophy in the Flesh: The Embodied Mind and Its Challenge to Western Thought*. New York: Basic Books.

Larson, M. *et al.* 2009. 'Distinguishing the *said* from the *implicated* using a novel experimental paradigm'. In: U. Sauerland and K. Yatsushiro (eds). *Semantics and Pragmatics: From Experiment to Theory*. Houndmills: Palgrave Macmillan. 74–93.

Larson, R. K. and P. Ludlow. 1993. 'Interpreted Logical Forms'. *Synthese* 95. 305–55.

Lascarides, A. and A. Copestake. 1998. 'Pragmatics and word meaning'. *Journal of Linguistics* 34. 387–414.

Lasersohn, P. 2012. 'Contextualism and compositionality'. *Linguistics and Philosophy* 35. 171–89.

Lee, H.-K. 2002. *The Semantics and Pragmatics of Connectives with Reference to English and Korean*. PhD dissertation, University of Cambridge.

Lepore, E. 1983. 'What model-theoretic semantics cannot do'. *Synthese* 54. 167–87. Reprinted in: E. Lepore and B. Loewer. *Meaning, Mind, and Matter: Philosophical Essays*. Oxford: Oxford University Press. 31–46.

Leslau, W. 1995. *Reference Grammar of Amharic*. Wiesbaden: Harrassowitz.

Levinson, S. C. 1987. 'Minimization and conversational inference'. In: J. Verschueren and M. Bertuccelli-Papi (eds). *The Pragmatic Perspective. Selected Papers from the 1985 International Pragmatics Conference*. Amsterdam: J. Benjamins. 61–129.

Levinson, S. C. 1995. 'Three levels of meaning'. In: F. R. Palmer (ed.). *Grammar and Meaning. Essays in Honour of Sir John Lyons*. Cambridge: Cambridge University Press. 90–115.

Levinson, S. C. 2000. *Presumptive Meanings: The Theory of Generalized Conversational Implicature*. Cambridge, MA: MIT Press.

Levinson, S. C. 2003. *Space in Language and Cognition: Explorations in Cognitive Diversity*. Cambridge: Cambridge University Press.

Lewis, D. 1979a. 'Attitudes *de dicto* and *de se*'. *Philosophical Review* 88. 513–43.

Lewis, D. 1979b. 'Scorekeeping in a language game'. *Journal of Philosophical Logic* 8: 339–59.

Locke, J. 1694. *Essay Concerning Human Understanding*. Second edition. Section of chapter 27 reprinted as 'Of identity and diversity' in: J. Perry (ed.). 2008. *Personal Identity*. Second edition. Berkeley: University of California Press. 33–52.

Ludlow, P. 2011. *The Philosophy of Generative Linguistics*. Oxford: Oxford University Press.

Ludlow, P. 2014. *Living Words: Meaning Underdetermination and the Dynamic Lexicon*. Oxford: Oxford University Press.

Lutz, M. 2014. 'The pragmatics of pragmatic encroachment'. *Synthese* 191. 1717–40.

McEwan, I. 2013. *Sweet Tooth*. London: Vintage.

MacFarlane, J. 2005. 'Making sense of relative truth'. *Proceedings of the Aristotelian Society* 105. 321–39.

MacFarlane, J. 2011. 'Relativism and knowledge attributions'. In: S. Bernecker and D. Pritchard (eds). *Routledge Companion to Epistemology*. London: Routledge. 536–44.

MacFarlane, J. 2014. *Assessment Sensitivity: Relative Truth and Its Applications*. Oxford: Oxford University Press.

Maier, E. 2009. 'Presupposing acquaintance: A unified semantics for *de dicto*, *de re* and *de se* belief reports'. *Linguistics and Philosophy* 32. 429–74.

Manning, E. 2013. 'Guess who they got to write this blog post? Muggins!' http://www.macmillandictionaryblog.com/muggins.

Manson, N. C. 2012. 'First-person authority: An epistemic-pragmatic account'. *Mind and Language* 27. 181–99.

Matthews, P. H. 2014. *The Concise Oxford Dictionary of Linguistics*. Oxford: Oxford University Press. Third edition.

Mauri, C. and J. van der Auwera. 2012. 'Connectives'. In: K. Allan and K. M. Jaszczolt (eds). *The Cambridge Handbook of Pragmatics*. Cambridge: Cambridge University Press. 377–401.

Merchant, J. 2004. 'Fragments and ellipsis'. *Linguistics and Philosophy* 27. 661–738.

Mey, J. L. 2001. *Pragmatics: An Introduction*. Oxford: Blackwell. Second edition.

Mey, J. L. 2007. 'Developing pragmatics intrculturally'. In: I. Kecskes and L. R. Horn (eds). *Explorations in Pragmatics*. Berlin: Mouton de Gruyter. 165–89.

Moltmann, F. 2010. 'Generalizing detached self-reference and the semantics of generic *one*'. *Mind and Language* 25. 440–73.

Moltmann, F. 2013. *Abstract Objects and the Semantics of Natural Language*. Oxford: Oxford University Press.

Montague, R. 1973. 'The proper treatment of quantification in ordinary English'. In: J. Hintikka, J. M. E. Moravcsik, and P. Suppes (eds). *Approaches to Natural Language. Proceedings of the 1970 Stanford Workshop on Grammar and Semantics*. Dordrecht: D. Reidel. 221–42.

Montague, R. 1974. *Formal Philosophy: Selected Papers of Richard Montague*. Ed. by R. H. Thomason. New Haven: Yale University Press.

Montminy, M. 2010. 'Two contextualist fallacies'. *Synthese* 173. 317–33.

Nicolle, S. and B. Clark. 1999. 'Experimental pragmatics and what is said: A response to Gibbs and Moise'. *Cognition* 69. 337–54.

Noveck, I. A. 2001. 'When children are more logical than adults: Experimental investigations of scalar implicature'. *Cognition* 78. 165–88.

Noveck, I. A. 2004. 'Pragmatic inferences related to logical terms'. In: I. A. Noveck and D. Sperber (eds). *Experimental Pragmatics*. Houndmills: Palgrave Macmillan. 301–21.

Noveck, I. A. and D. Sperber (eds). 2004. *Experimental Pragmatics*. Houndmills: Palgrave Macmillan.

Papafragou, A. and J. Musolino. 2003. 'Scalar implicatures: Experiments at the semantics-pragmatics interface'. *Cognition* 86. 253–82.

Partee, B. H. 2004. *Compositionality in Formal Semantics: Selected Papers by Barbara H. Partee*. Oxford: Blackwell.

Pearson, H. 2013. 'A judge-free semantics for predicates of personal taste'. *Journal of Semantics* 30. 103–54.

Peleg, O. and R. Giora. 2011. 'Salient meanings: The whens and wheres'. In: K. M. Jaszczolt and K. Allan (eds). *Salience and Defaults in Utterance Processing*. Berlin: De Gruyter Mouton. 35–51.

Percus, O. and U. Sauerland. 2003. 'On the LFs of attitude reports'. In: M. Weisgerber (ed.). *Proceedings of Sinn und Bedeutung 7*. Konstanz: Universität Konstanz. 228–42.

Perry, J. 1979. 'The problem of the essential indexical'. *Noûs* 13. 3–21.

Perry, J. 1986. 'Thought without representation'. *Proceedings of the Aristotelian Society Supplementary Volumes* 60. 137–51.

Perry, J. 2001a. *Knowledge, Possibility, and Consciousness. The 1999 Jean Nicod Lectures*. Cambridge, MA: MIT Press.

Perry, J. 2001b. *Reference and Reflexivity*. Stanford: CSLI Publications.

Perry, J. 2002. 'The self, self-knowledge, and self-notions'. In: J. Perry. *Identity, Personal Identity, and the Self*. Indianapolis: Hackett. 189–213.

Perry, J. 2009. 'Directing intentions'. In: J. Almog and P. Leonardi (eds). *The Philosophy of David Kaplan*. Oxford: Oxford University Press. 187–201.

Perry, J. 2011. 'On knowing one's self'. In: S. Gallagher (ed.). *The Oxford Handbook of the Self.* Oxford: Oxford University Press. 372–93.

Perry, J. 2012. 'Thinking about the self'. In: J. Liu and J. Perry (eds). *Consciousness and the Self: New Essays.* Cambridge: Cambridge University Press. 76–100.

Pitts, A. 2005. 'Assessing the evidence for intuitions about *what is said'*. Ms, University of Cambridge.

Portner, P. and B. H. Partee (eds). 2002. *Formal Semantics: The Essential Readings.* Oxford: Blackwell.

Predelli, S. 2005a. *Contexts: Meaning, Truth, and the Use of Language.* Oxford: Clarendon Press.

Predelli, S. 2005b. 'Painted leaves, context, and semantic analysis'. *Linguistics and Philosophy* 28. 351–74.

Predelli, S. 2011a. 'Sub-sentential speech and the traditional view'. *Linguistics and Philosophy* 34. 571–88.

Predelli, S. 2011b. I am still not here now. *Erkenntnis* 74. 289–303.

Predelli, S. 2013. *Meaning without Truth.* Oxford: Oxford University Press.

Predeli, S. 2014. 'Kaplan's three monsters'. *Analysis* 74. 389–93.

Prosser, S. and F. Recanati (eds). 2012. *Immunity to Error through Misidentification: New Essays.* Cambridge: Cambridge University Press.

Pulvermüller, F. 2010. 'Brain-language research: Where is the progress?' *Biolinguistics* 4. 255–88.

Pulvermüller, F. 2012. 'Meaning and the brain: The neurosemantics of referential, interactive, and combinatorial knowledge'. *Journal of Neurolinguistics* 25. 423–59.

Pustejovsky, J. 1995. *The Generative Lexicon.* Cambridge, MA: MIT Press.

Recanati, F.1989. 'The pragmatics of what is said'. *Mind and Language* 4. Reprinted in: S. Davis (ed.). 1991. *Pragmatics: A Reader.* Oxford: Oxford University Press. 97–120.

Recanati, F. 2002. 'Unarticulated constituents'. *Linguistics and Philosophy* 25. 299–345.

Recanati, F. 2004. *Literal Meaning.* Cambridge: Cambridge University Press.

Recanati, F. 2005. 'Literalism and contextualism: Some varieties'. In: G. Preyer and G. Peter (eds). *Contextualism in Philosophy: Knowledge, Meaning, and Truth.* Oxford: Clarendon Press. 171–96.

Recanati, F. 2007. *Perspectival Thought: A Plea for (Moderate) Relativism.* Oxford: Oxford University Press.

Recanati, F. 2010. *Truth-Conditional Pragmatics.* Oxford: Clarendon Press.

Recanati, F. 2012a. 'Contextualism: Some varieties'. In: K. Allan and K. M. Jaszczolt (eds). *The Cambridge Handbook of Pragmatics.* Cambridge: Cambridge University Press. 135–49.

Recanati, F. 2012b. 'Compositionality, flexibility, and context dependence'. In: M. Werning, W. Hinzen and E. Machery (eds). *The Oxford Handbook of Compositionality.* Oxford: Oxford University Press. 175–91.

Recanati, F. 2012c. 'Pragmatic enrichment'. In: G. Russell and D. Graff Fara (eds). *The Routledge Companion to Philosophy of Language.* New York: Routledge. 67–78.

Recanati, F. 2012d. 'Immunity to error through misidentification: What it is and where it comes from'. In: S. Prosser and F. Recanati (eds). *Immunity to Error through Misidentification: New Essays.* Cambridge: Cambridge University Press. 180–201.

Recanati, F. 2012e. *Mental Files.* Oxford: Oxford University Press.

Recanati, F. 2013. 'Perceptual concepts: In defence of the indexical model'. *Synthese* 190. 1841–55.

Reese, B. and N. Asher. 2010. 'Biased questions, intonation, and discourse'. In: M. Zimmermann and C. Féry (eds). *Information Structure: Theoretical, Typological, and Experimental Perspectives*. Oxford: Oxford University Press. 139–73.

Reiter, R. 1980. 'A logic for default reasoning'. *Artificial Intelligence* 13. 81–132.

Richard, M. 2011. 'Kripke's puzzle about belief'. In: A. Berger (ed.). *Saul Kripke*. Cambridge: Cambridge University Press. 211–34. Reprinted as 'Kripke's puzzle.' In: M. Richard. *Context and the Attitudes: Meaning in Context. Vol. 1*. Oxford: Oxford University Press. 263–85.

Roberts, C. 2014. 'Indexicality: *de se* semantics and pragmatics'. Ms, Ohio State University. Draft of April 2015.

Roth, P. 1998. *American Pastoral*. London: Vintage. First published in 1997 by Jonathan Cape.

Sauerland, U. 2004. 'Scalar implicatures in complex sentences'. *Linguistics and Philosophy* 27. 367–91.

Saul, J. M. 2002. 'What is said and psychological reality; Grice's project and relevance theorists' criticisms'. *Linguistics and Philosophy* 25. 347–72.

Saul, J. M. 2012. *Lying, Misleading, and What is Said: An Exploration in Philosophy of Language and in Ethics*. Oxford: Oxford University Press.

Savva, E. 2017. *Subsentential Speech from a Contextualist Perspective*. PhD dissertation, University of Cambridge.

Sbordone, L. 2016. *The Contextual Adjective: On Indexicality, Gradability, and Vagueness in the Adjectival Domain*. PhD Dissertation, University of Cambridge.

Schiffer, S. 1977. 'Naming and knowing'. *Midwest Studies in Philosophy* 2. Reprinted in: P. A. French, T. E. Uehling, and H. K. Wettstein (eds). 1979. *Contemporary Perspectives in the Philosophy of Language*. Minneapolis: University of Minnesota Press. 61–74.

Schiffer, S. 1992. 'Belief ascription'. *Journal of Philosophy* 89. 499–521.

Schlenker, P. 2003. 'A plea for monsters'. *Linguistics and Philosophy* 26. 29–120.

Schlenker, P. 2011. 'Indexicality and *de se* reports'. In: K. von Heusinger, C. Maienborn, and P. Portner (eds). *Semantics: An International Handbook of Natural Language Meaning*. Vol. 2. Berlin: Mouton de Gruyter. 1561–604.

Schneider, A. 2009. *Understanding Primary Meaning: A Study with Reference to Requests in Russian and British English*. PhD dissertation, University of Cambridge.

Schroeder, M. 2008. *Being For: Evaluating the Semantic Program for Expressivism*. Oxford: Clarendon Press.

Searle, J. R. 1969. *Speech Acts*. Cambridge: Cambridge University Press.

Searle, J. R. and D. Vanderveken. 1985. *Foundations of Illocutionary Logic*. Cambridge: Cambridge University Press.

Sennet, A. 2011. 'Unarticulated constituents and propositional structure'. *Mind and Language* 26. 412–35.

Shoemaker, S. 1968. 'Self-reference and self-awareness'. *Journal of Philosophy* 65. 555–67.

Shoemaker, S. 1970. 'Persons and their pasts'. *American Philosophical Quarterly* 7. 269–85. Reprinted in: J. Perry (ed.). 2008. *Personal Identity*. Second edition. Berkeley: University of California Press. 249–82.

Siewierska, A. 2004. *Person*. Cambridge: Cambridge University Press.

Sileo, R. 2016. *The Semantics and Pragmatics of Racial and Ethnic Slurring Language: Towards a Comprehensive Radical Contextualist Account.* PhD Dissertation, University of Cambridge.

Simon, H. A. 1982. *Models of Bounded Rationality. Vol. 1: Economic Analysis and Public Policy.* Cambridge, MA: MIT Press.

Slobin, D. 1996. 'From "thought and language" to "thinking for speaking"'. In: J. J. Gumperz and S. C. Levinson (eds). *Rethinking Linguistic Relativity.* Cambridge: Cambridge University Press. 97–114.

Soames, S. 2014. 'Cognitive propositions'. In: J. C. King, S. Soames, and J. Speaks. *New Thinking about Propositions.* Oxford: Oxford University Press. 91–124.

Sperber, D. and D. Wilson. 1995. *Relevance: Communication and Cognition.* Oxford: Blackwell. Second edition.

Sperber, D. and D. Wilson. 2002. 'Pragmatics, modularity and mindreading'. *Mind and Language* 17. 3–23.

Sperber, D. and D. Wilson (eds). 2012. *Meaning and Relevance.* Cambridge: Cambridge University Press.

Srioutai, J. 2000. 'An application of semantic primes to dictionary definitions: SOMEONE and SOMETHING in Thai'. *Thoughts* 2000. 84–103. Bangkok: Chulalongkorn University publication.

Srioutai, J. 2004. 'The Thai c_1a: A marker of tense or modality?' In: E. Daskalaki *et al.* (eds). *Second CamLing Proceedings.* University of Cambridge. 273–80.

Srioutai, J. 2006. *Time Conceptualization in Thai with Special Reference to $d_1ay_1{}^{II}$, $kh_3oe{:}y$, k_1aml_3ang, $y_3u{:}^1$ and c_1a.* PhD dissertation, University of Cambridge.

Stainton, R. 2006. *Words and Thoughts: Subsentences, Ellipsis, and the Philosophy of Language.* Oxford: Clarendon Press.

Stalmaszczyk, P. 2006. 'Fregean predication: Between logic and linguistics'. *Research in Language* 4. 77–90.

Stalnaker, R. C. 1978. 'Assertion'. *Syntax and Semantics* 9. New York: Academic Press. Reprinted in R. C. Stalnaker, 1999, *Context and Content: Essays on Intentionality in Speech and Thought.* Oxford: Oxford University Press. 78–95.

Stalnaker, R. C. 2008. *Our Knowledge of the Internal World.* Oxford: Clarendon Press.

Stalnaker, R. C. 2011. 'The essential contextual'. In: J. Brown and H. Cappelen (eds). *Assertion: New Philosophical Essays.* Oxford: Oxford University Press. 137–50.

Stalnaker, R. 2014. *Context.* Oxford: Oxford University Press.

Stanley, J. 2000. 'Context and logical form'. *Linguistics and Philosophy* 23. 391–434.

Stanley, J. 2002. 'Making it articulated'. *Mind and Language* 17. 149–68.

Stanley, J. 2005. *Knowledge and Practical Interests.* Oxford: Oxford University Press.

Stanley, J. 2007. *Language in Context: Selected Essays.* Oxford: Clarendon Press.

Stanley, J. 2011. *Know How.* Oxford: Oxford University Press.

Stanley, J. and Z. G. Szabó. 2000. 'On quantifier domain restriction'. *Mind and Language* 15. 219–61.

Stern, J. 2000. *Metaphor in Context.* Cambridge, MA: MIT Press.

Strawson, P. F. 1959. *Individuals: An Essay in Descriptive Metaphysics.* London: Methuen.

Tanaka, H. 2012. 'Scalar implicature in Japanese: Contrastive *wa* and intersubjectivity'. Paper presented at the First International Conference of the American Pragmatics Association (AMPRA 1), Charlotte, North Carolina.

Thomason, R. H. 1997. 'Nonmonotonicity in linguistics'. In: J. van Benthem and A. ter Meulen (eds). *Handbook of Logic and Language*. Oxford: Elsevier Science. 777–831.

Tomasello, M. 2008. *Origins of Human Communication*. Cambridge, MA: MIT Press.

Tomasello, M. 2009. *Why We Cooperate*. Cambridge, MA: MIT Press.

Travis, C. 1997. 'Pragmatics'. In: B. Hale and C. Wright (eds). *A Companion to the Philosophy of Language*. Oxford: B. Blackwell, 87–107. Reprinted in: C. Travis, 2008, *Occasion-Sensitivity: Selected Essays*. Oxford: Oxford University Press, 109–29.

Travis, C. 2006a. 'Insensitive semantics: Critical notice of H. Cappelen and E. Lepore, *Insensitive Semantics*' (Oxford: Basil Blackwell), 2005. *Mind and Language* 21. 39–49. Reprinted in: C. Travis, 2008, I. Oxford: Oxford University Press. 150–60.

Travis, C. 2006b. 'Psychologism'. In: E. Lepore and B. C. Smith (eds). *The Oxford Handbook of Philosophy of Language*. Oxford: Clarendon Press. 103–26.

Travis, C. 2008. *Occasion-Sensitivity: Selected Essays*. Oxford: Oxford University Press.

Ungerer, F. and H.-J. Schmid. 1996. *An Introduction to Cognitive Linguistics*. London: Longman.

van der Sandt, R. 1992. 'Presupposition projection as anaphora resolution'. *Journal of Semantics* 9. 333–77.

van der Sandt, R. 2012. 'Presupposition and accommodation in discourse'. In: K. Allan and K. M . Jaszczolt (eds). *The Cambridge Handbook of Pragmatics*. Cambridge: Cambridge University Press. 329–50.

Veltman, F. 1996. 'Defaults in update semantics'. *Journal of Philosophical Logic* 25. 221–61.

Vicente, A. 2012. 'On Travis cases'. *Linguistics and Philosophy* 35. 3–19.

Vicente, B. and M. Groefsema. 2013. 'Something out of nothing? Rethinking unarticulated constituents'. *Journal of Pragmatics* 47. 108–27.

Wechsler, S. 2010. 'What "you" and "I" mean to each other: Person indexicals, self-ascription, and theory of mind'. *Language* 86. 332–65.

Weiner, M. 2006. 'Are all conversational implicatures cancellable?'. *Analysis* 66. 127–30.

Wierzbicka, A. 1996. *Semantics: Primes and Universals*. Oxford: Oxford University Press.

Wilson, D. 2005. 'New directions for research on pragmatics and modularity'. *Lingua* 115. 1129–46.

Wilson, D. and R. Carston. 2007. 'A unitary approach to lexical pragmatics: Relevance, inference and ad hoc concepts'. In: N. Burton-Roberts (ed.). *Pragmatics*. Houndmills: Palgrave Macmillan. 230–59.

Wittgenstein, L. 1953. *Philosophische Untersuchungen/Philosophical Investigations*. Oxford: Blackwell. Reprinted in 1958. Second edition.

Wright, C. 2012. 'Reflections on François Recanati's "Immunity to error through misidentification: What it is and where it comes from"'. In: S. Prosser and F. Recanati (eds). *Immunity to Error through Misidentification: New Essays*. Cambridge: Cambridge University Press. 247–80.

Zeevat, H. 2012. 'Pragmatics in update semantics'. In: K. Allan and K. M. Jaszczolt (eds). *The Cambridge Handbook of Pragmatics*. Cambridge: Cambridge University Press. 191–208.

Index

Note: Page numbers follwed by "n" denote mentions in the footnotes.

Printed and bound by CPI Group (UK) Ltd, Croydon, CR0 4YY